1995

Critique of Everyday Life

VOLUME I

Critique of Everyday Life

VOLUME I

Introduction

HENRI LEFEBVRE

Translated by John Moore

With a Preface by Michel Trebitsch

V

VERSO

London · New York

First published as *Critique de la vie quotidienne I: Introduction*
by Grasset, Paris 1947; second edition with new foreword by
L'Arche, Paris 1958
This translation first published by Verso 1991
Paperback edition published 1992
© Grasset 1947, L'Arche 1958
Translation © John Moore 1991
Preface © Michel Trebitsch 1991

Verso
UK: 6 Meard Street, London W1V 3HR
USA: 29 West 35th Street, New York, NY 10001-2291

Verso is the imprint of New Left Books

British Library Cataloguing in Publication Data

Lefebvre, Henri
Critique of everyday life.
Vol. 1: Introduction.
I. Title [Critique de la vie quotidienne]. *English*
302

ISBN 0-86091-587-5

Library of Congress Cataloging-in-Publication Data

Lefebvre, Henri, 1905–
[Critique de la vie quotidienne. English]
Critique of everyday life / Henri Lefebvre : translated by John
Moore : with a preface by Michel Trebitsch.
p.   cm.
Translation of the 2nd ed. of: Critique de la vie quotidienne.
Includes index.
Contents: v. 1. Introduction
ISBN 0-86091-587-5
1. Life. 2. Philosophy, Marxist. I. Title.
BD431.L36513   1991
194—dc20

Typeset by Leaper & Gard Ltd, Bristol
Printed in Finland by Werner Söderström Oy

Contents

I In Retrospect · II What Has Changed in the Last Ten
Years? · III On Chaplin, Bertolt Brecht and Some
Others · IV Work and Leisure in Everyday Life ·
V Some Overviews on the 'Modern World' · VI Once
Again, the Theory of Alienation ... · VII Alienated
Labour · VIII Philosophy and the Critique of Everyday
Life · IX Plans and Programme for the Future

CRITIQUE OF EVERYDAY LIFE

Translator's Note

Except when prefixed (*Trans.*), footnotes are from the original. Translations of quotations in the text are mine, except when the source title is given in English. Bibliographical details are presented in the original in a partial and unsystematic way, and wherever possible I have endeavoured to complete and standardize this information, a frequently difficult task, since the author uses his own translations of Marx. I wish to thank my colleagues Robert Gray, John Oakley and Adrian Rifkin for the advice and encouragement they have given me during the preparation of this project.

Preface

by Michel Trebitsch

What a strange status this book has, and how strange its destiny has been. If Henri Lefebvre can be placed alongside Adorno, Bloch, Lukács or Marcuse as one of the main theoreticians of 'Critical Marxism', it is largely thanks to his *Critique of Everyday Life* (*Critique de la vie quotidienne*), a work which, though well known, is little appreciated. Perhaps this is because Lefebvre has something of the brilliant amateur craftsman about him, unable to cash in on his own inventions; something capricious, like a sower who casts his seeds to the wind without worrying about whether they will germinate. Or is it because of Lefebvre's style, between flexibility and vagueness, where thinking is like strolling, where thinking is *rhapsodic*, as opposed to more permanent constructions, with their monolithic, reinforced, reassuring arguments, painstakingly built upon structures and models? His thought processes are like a limestone landscape with underground rivers which only become visible when they burst forth on the surface. *Critique of Everyday Life* is one such resurgence. One could even call it a triple resurgence, in that the 1947 volume was to be followed in 1962 by a second, *Fondements d'une sociologie de la quotidienneté*, and in 1981 by a third, *De la modernité au modernisme (Pour une métaphilosophie du quotidien)*. At the chronological and theoretical intersection of his thinking about alienation and modernity, *Critique of Everyday Life* is a seminal text, drawn from the deepest levels of his intellectual roots, but also looking ahead to the main preoccupation of his post-war period. If we are to relocate it in Lefebvre's thought as a whole, we will need to go upstream as far as *La Conscience mystifiée* (1936) and then back downstream as far as *Introduction à la modernité* (1962).

'Henri Lefebvre or Living Philosophy'

The year 1947 was a splendid one for Henri Lefebvre: as well as *Critique of Everyday Life,* he published *Logique formelle, logique dialectique, Marx et la liberté* and *Descartes* in quick succession. This broadside was commented upon in the review *La Pensée* by one of the Communist Party's rising young intellectuals, Jean Kanapa, who drew particular attention to the original and creative aspects of *Critique of Everyday Life.* With this book, wrote Kanapa, 'philosophy no longer scorns the concrete and the everyday'. By making alienation 'the key concept in the analysis of human situations since Marx', Lefebvre was opening philosophy to action: taken in its Kantian sense, critique was not simply knowledge of everyday life, but knowledge of the means to transform it. Thus in Lefebvre Kanapa could celebrate 'the most lucid proponent of living philosophy today'.[1] Marginal before the war, heretical after the 1950s, in 1947 Lefebvre's recognition by the Communist Party seems to have been at its peak, and it is tempting to see his prolific output in a political light. If we add *L'Existentialisme,* which appeared in 1946, and *Pour connaître la pensée de Marx* and his best-seller *Le Marxisme* in the 'Que sais-je?' edition, both of which appeared in 1948, not to mention several articles, such as his 'Introduction à l'esthétique' which was a dry run for his 1953 *Contribution à l'esthétique,* then indeed, apart from the late 1960s, this was the most productive period in his career.[2]

Critique of Everyday Life thus appears to be a book with a precise date, and this date is both significant and equivocal. Drafted between August and December 1945, published in February 1947, according to the official publisher's date, it reflected the optimism and new-found freedom of the Liberation, but appeared only a few weeks before the big freeze of the Cold War set in. 'In the enthusiasm of the Liberation, it was hoped that soon life would be changed and the world transformed', as Henri Lefebvre recalled in 1958 in his Foreword to the Second Edition. The year 1947 was pivotal, Janus-faced. It began in a mood of post-war euphoria, then, from March to September, with Truman's policy of containment and Zhdanov's theory of the division of the world into two camps, with the eviction of the Communist ministers in France and the launching of the Marshall Plan, in only a few months everything had been thrown in the balance, including the fate of the book itself. The impact was all the more brutal in that this hope for a radical break, for the beginning of a new life, had become combined with the myth of the Resistance, taking on an eschatological dimension of which the Communist Party (which also drew strength from the Soviet aura), was the principal beneficiary. With its talk of a 'French Renaissance' and a new cult of martyrs (Danielle Casanova, Gabriel Péri, Jacques Decour) orchestrated by Aragon its high priest, this 'parti des 75,000 fusillés' momentarily embodied both revolutionary promise and continuity with a national tradition stretching back from the Popular Front to 1798. Between 1945 and 1947 the PCF's dominance was both political and ideological. Polling more than 28 per cent of the votes in the November 1946 general election, it appeared to have confirmed its place as the 'first party of France', without which no government coalition seemed possible. Its ideological hegemony, strengthened by the membership or active sympathy of numerous writers, artists and thinkers – Picasso, Joliot-Curie, Roger Vailland, Pierre Hervé – put Marxism at the centre of intellectual debate. Presenting itself as a 'modern rationalism' to challenge the 'irrationalism' and 'obscurantism' brought into disrepute by collaboration, its only rival was existentialism, which made its appearance in the intellectual arena in 1945. But existentialism also located itself with reference to Marxism, as we can see from the controversy which raged for so long in the pages of *Les Temps Modernes* and *L'Esprit,* and which began in that same year with Jean Beaufret's articles in *Confluences* and above all with the argument between Sartre and Lefebvre in *Action.*[3]

In a way both were after the same quarry: Lefebvre's pre-war themes of 'the total man' and his dialectic of the conceived and the lived were echoed by Sartre's definition of existence as the reconciliation between thinking and living. At that time Lefebvre was certainly not unknown: from the beginning of the 1930s the books he wrote single-handedly or in collaboration with Norbert Guterman had established him as an original Marxist thinker. But his pre-war readership had remained limited, since philosophers were suspicious of Marxism and Marxists were suspicious of philosophy. Conversely, after 1945, he emerged as the most important expert on and vulgarizer of Marxism, as an entire generation of young intellectuals rushed to buy his 'Que sais-je?' on Marxism and the new printing of his little *Dialectical Materialism* of 1939; when he brought out *L'Existentialisme,* the Party saw him as the only Communist philosopher capable of stemming the influence of Sartre. With his experience as an elder member linking the pre-war and the post-war years and his image as a popularizer of Marxism, Henri Lefebvre could be slotted conveniently into a strategy by which the Party would exploit its political legitimacy to the full in order to impose the philosophical legitimacy of Marxism. He introduced Marxism to the Sorbonne, where he gave a series of lectures, on such topics as 'the future of capitalism' (March 1947) and 'the contribution of Marxism to the teaching of philosophy' (November). The latter was reported in *La Pensée*, 'the review of modern rationalism', in glowing terms:

> Our friend Henri Lefebvre gave a brilliant demonstration of how dialectical materialism can and should rejuvenate and bring new life to the way philosophy is traditionally taught at university. We were expecting his lecture to be a success; the extent of that success took us by surprise. We had scheduled his lecture for the Amphithéâtre Richelieu, but in the event we had to use the Sorbonne's Grand Amphitheatre, which was flooded with an expectant crowd of almost 2000 people, made up mostly of university staff, students and *lycéens*, who followed Henri Lefebvre's brilliant talk with passionate attention and frequent applause.[4]

But if we take a closer look, things were less simple. The idyllic relationship between Henri Lefebvre and orthodoxy in 1947 was to be little more than a brief encounter, an illusory and ephemeral marriage of convenience that was not without its share of opportunism, and which was soon to be shattered by the watershed of Zhdanovism. And in any event, at the precise moment when, as he himself admitted, he had been 'recognized as the best "philosopher" and French "theoretician" of the day', Lefebvre's material situation had become 'appalling', as he put it bluntly in September 1947 in a letter to his friend Norbert Guterman, whom he had just contacted again for the first time since the war.[5] His poor health made the future look rather bleak, and for a while he was even out of work – a compounding difficulty as he already had numerous offspring to support, scattered over several different homes. He had been working for Radio-Toulouse, where Tristan Tzara, in charge of cultural broadcasts, had found him a job in 1945, but the change in the political climate forced him to step down, and also to give up the classes at the Ecole de guerre which General Gambier, whom he had met during his military service, had managed to secure for him. In fact when the war ended he had the grade of officer in the Forces françaises de l'intérieur in recognition for his Resistance work in the Toulouse region, but the Vichy administration had dismissed him from the teaching profession, and he was wary of asking to be reinstated for fear of being packed off to some provincial backwater. His frenzied rush to print, some of which was purely commissioned material, can be explained in part by his financial worries, though he was finally reinstated as a teacher and appointed in Toulouse in October 1947, and then seconded to the Centre National de la Recherche Scientifique (CNRS) in 1948. Of the seven works he brought out between 1946 and 1948, six were with commercial publishers or beyond the purview of Communist publications. We should nevertheless note that although *Critique of Everyday Life* was published by Grasset, this was for distinctly political reasons. (The 'Grasset affair' was then at its height. Prosecuted for suspected collaboration, Grasset had just been acquitted by the investigative committee, but was still under attack from the Communist Party. After an unsuccessful attempt to bring in a compulsory purchase order in 1945, the Party backed a formula for control of Grasset dreamt up by René Jouglet and Francis Crémieux, who was in charge of the 'Témoins' collection, in which Lefebvre's book appeared; the aim was to take over the house on a very broad basis, 'with very "old school" Communists such as Pierre Hervé, leader writer with *L'Humanité*, but also independent personalities like Druon, Martin-Chauffier, Cassou'.)[6]

Though himself a Communist 'of the old school', Henri Lefebvre had not been integrated into the network of intellectuals 'in the service of' the Party who, with Aragon and several others as their focal point, were now dominating the stage. Indeed, according to his letters to Norbert Guterman, had this been proposed to him, he would have refused. Not that now and again he did not offer evidence of his allegiances, as for example when he took advantage of the campaign that had been mounted against 'the traitor' Nizan, his old associate of the 1920s, to settle some old scores *post mortem* in *L'Existentialisme*.[7] It is also true that he joined the editorial committee of *Nouvelle Critique*, the 'review of militant Marxism' that was founded in 1948, but, in the words of Pierre Hervé, his presence at the journal was just 'icing on the cake', an intellectual gesture rather than a genuine creative force. His contributions were few, his main articles being responses to accusations of 'Neo-Hegelianism': in March 1949 he wrote an 'Autocritique' in which he denied having used his so-warmly received lecture of 1947 to present Marxism simply as a 'contribution' to philosophy.[8] Behind all the circumlocutions, however, Henri Lefebvre held firm on three essential issues: the relations between Marxism and philosophy, those between Marxism and sociology, and the central role of the theory of alienation. Predictably, therefore, he very quickly began to fall out of favour. Between 1948 and 1957 he did not publish a single work of Marxist theory, unless one takes the view that his 'literary' studies on Diderot, Pascal, Musset and Rabelais were in fact indirect reflections on the dialectic of nature, alienation and the individual. In any case, from 1948 onwards, the Party put a stop to most of his projects.[9] *Logique formelle, logique dialectique*, which Kanapa acclaimed in 1947 as a fundamental work, was to have been the first volume in a vast general treatise on Marxist philosophy, in a consciously academic format, to be called *A la lumière du matérialisme dialectique*. The second volume, *Méthodologie des sciences*, was not only drafted, but in March 1948 it was actually printed, only to be blocked by order of the Party directorate, which was then involved in defending Lysenkoism and 'proletarian science'. Similarly, Lefebvre would not publish his *Contribution à l'esthétique*, drafted in 1949 from articles he had written in 1948, until 1953, and then it was only thanks to the subterfuge of a false quotation from Marx which was intended to reassure the Party censors.[10] As for *Critique of Everyday Life*, it was to be followed by *La Conscience privée*, but this never saw the light of day. This final failure leads us back, however, to a much earlier moment in Lefebvre's life; a moment which in turn will lead us by a series of regressions to the earliest moments of Lefebvre's life as a philosopher.

Mystification: notes for a critique of everyday life

As we have attempted to demonstrate elsewhere, Henri Lefebvre's originality, not to say marginality, lies in an unshakeable determination not only to reconcile Marxism and philosophy and to endow Marxism with philosophical status, but also to establish Marxism as critical theory, i.e. as both philosophy and supercession of philosophy.[11] We should not be fooled by the expedient eulogies of a Kanapa: *Critique of Everyday Life* is an essential document on the construction of a *critical* Marxism of this kind, and completely out of line with official arguments. If we are to believe the note in which Henri Lefebvre links the book explicitly with the ones which preceded it, it would seem to belong to a vast master plan, one whose purpose was to 'rediscover authentic Marxism', defined as 'the critical knowledge of everyday life'. He notes that the *Morceaux choisis* of Marx had drawn attention to economic fetishism, that *La Conscience mystifiée* had presented 'the entire scope' of modern man's alienation, and that *Dialectical Material-ism* had developed the notion of 'the total man', liberated from alienation and economic fetishism.[12] Far from being an a posteriori reconstruction, this note allows us to rediscover the genesis of *Critique of Everyday Life*, and even to date its birth. Although it appeared after the war, it seems to be the result of a train of thought – perhaps to call it a lengthy and determined meditation would be more accurate – which began at the start of the 1930s with the discovery in Hegel and Marx's early writings of the concept of *alienation*, and which was mapped out by the publication of several works written in collaboration with Norbert Guterman.

The plan to write a *Critique of Everyday Life* began at least as early as *La Conscience mystifiée*. The title appears among the 'Cinq essais de philos-ophie matérialiste' which are mentioned there as being 'in progress' – few of which were ever to appear.[13] But to date the birth of the *concept* of a critique of everyday life, we must go back even farther. Published in 1936, but drafted in 1933/4, *La Conscience mystifiée* reworks, sometimes verbatim, themes that had appeared as early as 1933 in the small review *Avant-Poste*. The brief history of this review, which lasted for only three numbers, is quite remarkable in its own right.[14] Pasted together in an attic room, supported by Malraux, who at that time was presiding over the *Nouvelle Revue Française*, it came out independently of Communist Party control, edited by a Communist, Henri Lefebvre, with two excluded members, Pierre Morhange and Norbert Guterman, as his assistants. A 'review of literature and criticism', it took as its main aim the analysis of Fascism as an ideological corpus – a quite daring project in view of the positions taken officially by the Party at that time. Fascism was defined less as a metamorphosis of capitalism than as a *mystification* of the revolution. Using this philosophical reading of politics as a starting point, and working closely together, Norbert Guterman and Henri Lefebvre now proceeded to develop the concept of alienation, notably in two profoundly innovative texts which were the matrices of their later contributions: 'Individu et classe' and, more particularly, 'La mystification: notes pour une critique de la vie quotidienne'.[15] Even more than *La Conscience mystifiée*, it is these texts from *Avant-Poste* to which we should return if we want to understand the confused processes by which the concept of a critique of everyday life came into being, and the extent to which it is intimately linked in Henri Lefebvre's thought with the concepts of alienation and mystification.

When Fascism calls itself revolution, 'its unreality disguises itself as the supreme reality, and tries to make true reality definitively unreal'. Starting from this extreme case of political mystification, Lefebvre and Guterman say that they intend to contribute to a 'theory of materialist knowledge by analysing, under the general heading of "Mystification", certain forms of bourgeois thinking – and even to identify a kind of general law of this thinking'. The first article attacks individualism as a mystification, and concludes with the idea that the individual consciousness cannot be explained by itself, that there is no consciousness in itself. In bourgeois society, the individual thinks he 'knows who he is', and perceives his self as 'his goods and his property'; when this illusion is shattered, the individual sinks into the anguish of 'unhappy consciousness' as he discovers the chasm which separates him from his self. Just as the subject (the individual) is *separated* from its self, the object, by becoming a commodity, becomes detached, so to speak, from itself, and the relations between men are masked by relations between objects. The second text, inspired by the Marxist theory of fetishism, leads to the idea of 'the progressive distancing of the object': alienation is not only economic, it is the inability in all areas of life to grasp and to think the *other*. It renders bourgeois thinking 'incapable of grasping the world as a totality, and distances it from the real'. The *values* it dreams up for itself make this distancing worse: 'It is when a reality has been devoured by bourgeois life that it becomes a "value".' Bourgeois life is thus alienated because it is not only *fragmented*, but *artificial*, and it is this artificiality which makes mystification possible. In *La Conscience mystifiée* Lefebvre and Guterman rework and broaden this problematic of mystification, defining the conditions for a Marxist critique of bourgeois ideology. 'How are we to proceed in order to effect a necessary rehabilitation of the mystified consciousness?' they ask. The answer is, 'by starting with the portrait of the most prosaic of men in his everyday life'.[16] The construction of the concept of mystification as a generalized process of disguise and inversion of reality derives, then, from a global reading of alienation as man's falsified relationship to the world. The sources here are well known: above all Hegel and his 'unhappy consciousness', but also Marx's early writings, in particular his 'Critique of the Hegelian Dialectic',[17] which was first published in France by *Avant-Poste*. How this led to the actual formulation of the concept of a critique of everyday life, which was only present by implication, is a more complex question.

In February 1936, a few days after their book had appeared, Lefebvre wrote to Guterman: 'Is it true what a chap who has looked through *La Conscience mystifiée* tells me: that the book just repeats what has already been said in Germany by Lukács?'[18] Indeed, how can we avoid thinking of Lukács here? It was, after all, the young pre-Marxist Lukács who first formulated the concept of *Alltäglichkeit* in 1911, in a frequently-quoted passage of *Metaphysik der Tragödie* which every Lukácsian, from Lucien Goldmann to the members of the 'Budapest School', led by Agnes Heller, would still be invoking many years later.[19] *Alltäglichkeit* designates the 'trivial life' of the human being, indistinguishable from the world of objects – the dreary, mechanical and repetitive unfolding of the everyday, which Lukács contrasts with an 'authentic life' thanks to which this being accedes to himself through the work of art, or even better, turns himself into a work of art. In 1923, as we know, *History and Class Consciousness*[20] made a radical break with this ontology of consciousness by relocating consciousness in historicity on the basis of the Marxist theory of alienation. The reversal thus effected by Lukács consisted in the transfer of the antagonism between authentic and inauthentic life to the history of class society: alienation is not simply inauthentic life, but rather that 'reification of consciousness' produced by the fetishism of commodities, which only proletarian class consciousness will be able to overcome. Here is a second sign of the curious affinity between Lefebvre and Lukács. Like *History and Class Consciousness*, *La Conscience mystifiée* offered a Marxist theory of consciousness breaking with the theory of transparency of being which had informed the philosophical tradition. Built around the theory of alienation, their Marxism is drawn from the same Hegelian source, although the concept of 'reification of consciousness', central to Lukács, is missing in Lefebvre, while the Lukács of 1923 was unaware of Marx's early writings. Moreover we must stress that when Lefebvre insisted that all consciousness is mystified, even proletarian class consciousness, he seems to be refuting aspects of the holist dream that are still present in Lukács. In this sense, his *critique* of everyday life is more of a prefigurement of Adorno's *Negative Dialectics*,[21] which, by building its critical theory on the way the negative is at work in present reality, acknowledges that this negativity embodies another 'colour' – a difference in what is possible which will allow us to stand back from the greyness of the 'already there' in order, precisely, to criticize it.

If anyone is tempted to infer from this similarity that Lukács may have influenced Lefebvre, then the letter to Guterman is material proof to the contrary, all the more so because Lefebvre, who in any case did not meet Lukács until after the war, has always insisted that he had no knowledge of *History and Class Consciousness* until after *La Conscience mystifiée* was completed. On the other hand, returning to these similarities in volume three of *Critique of Everyday Life*, he admits his debt to Heidegger, whom he mentions several times and takes to task in *La Conscience mystifiée*.[22] In *Being and Time*,[23] Heidegger also calls upon the concept of *Alltäglichkeit*, using it to characterize the inauthentic existence of *Dasein*. In so much as it is Being-with-one-another, *Dasein* stops being itself and the ascendancy of others rids it of its Being, all the more so because the other is *They*, the indeterminate, neuter *Man*:[24] in Heidegger, *Alltäglichkeit* opens the way to a loss of direction, to dereliction and disquiet. Was it then on the basis of his acquaintanceship with Heidegger – who knew Lukács's early writings, and whose *Being and Time* owes so much, as Lucien Goldmann was the first to show, to *History and Class Consciousness* and the concept of reification – that Lefebvre developed a problematic of the concept of everyday life that was unwittingly every close to Lukács'[25] If so, we must pause to examine the conditions under which, very early on, Lefebvre became acquainted with *Being and Time* via Jean Wahl, and probably even as early as 1928 via Nizan, who in 1931 published an extract from *Introduction to Metaphysics*,[26] the first Heidegger text to be translated into French, in *Bifur*. It is less a matter of attributing some kind of precedence to Henri Lefebvre in the development of the concept of a critique of everyday life, than of grasping the conditions which brought this concept forth from the heart of 'Western Marxism' in the overall context of the philosophical investigations of the 1930s.[27]

The full significance of the relationship between Lukács and Lefebvre emerges quite clearly if we think not in terms of influence but rather in terms of two parallel but chronologically separated intellectual journeys, both leading from ontology to Marxism. In *La Somme et le reste* Lefebvre recalls that his discovery of the theory of alienation was like a 'flash of inspiration': to arrive at his own concepts of mystification, of the total man and of the critique of everyday life, he had to work a reversal of the same kind as Lukács while he passed from the concept of inauthentic life to the concept of the reification of consciousness.[28] For Lefebvre, the 'path towards Marx' would lead 'from the cult of "spirit" to dialectical materialism', as he explained as early as December 1932 in a reply to Denis de Rougemont's survey of young intellectuals in the *Nouvelle Revue Française*. He writes that there had been a few young people, himself included, who believed they could refuse 'a life in which the sole act is: buying and selling, selling oneself' by following 'a call to the life of the spirit, of poetry, of eternity'. But with the onset of the economic crisis, with all its attendant perils, 'the problem was reduced to its most basic elements': 'for many people it's a question of staying alive, purely and simply of staying alive'. Thus one must 'attack the base, come to grips with the conditions of the diabolical universe of *capitalism*', and only political revolution would be capable of changing life.[29] To justify joining the Communist Party, Lefebvre challenged the very idea that Rougemont had proposed – that 'spiritual revolution' could be 'the common cause of young intellectuals' – by describing his own experiences in the 1920s. His call to revolution was both the culmination and the supersession of that romantic rejection of the world which he had espoused, in common with the avant-gardes, as a member of the *Philosophies* group.

Life is unique

'Man must be everyday, or he will not be at all': in the first pages of *Critique of Everyday Life*[30] Lefebvre uses this aphorism to show that from its starting point in everyday life the *critique* of everyday life can lead to the *revolution* of everyday life. 'Everyday man' is the man of praxis, and praxis alone will enable him to free himself from alienation and attain the concrete totality of the 'total man', at one and the same time the subject and the object of his becoming, a theme which was to become central to Lefebvre from *Dialectical Materialism* onwards (1939). In other words, the only means of acceding to totality is via revolution. This quest for totality, which was to lead Lefebvre from 'philosophical revolution' to Marxism, is none other than the quest for a theoretical method capable of reconciling thought and life, of changing life completely, of producing one's life as one creates a *work.* So, when Lefebvre defines his critique of everyday life as the 'revolutionary' way, as opposed both to the 'poetic' way embodied by the Surrealists and to the Heideggerian-style 'metaphysical' way, he is merely describing the various ups and downs within the *Philosophies* group which led him to effect his own 'reversal' of ontology and Marxism.

The first stage of this reversal was via the avant-garde. When Lefebvre accused the Surrealists of not having followed their radical ideas through to their logical conclusion, of having offered a merely 'magical' critique of the everyday, he was distancing himself from his own experiences as an avant-gardist. When in 1924, in the review *Philosophies*, Henri Lefebvre took his first steps as a philosopher alongside Pierre Morhange, Norbert Guterman and Georges Politzer, it was in the name of 'philosophical revolution'. This is not the place to give a detailed account of the history of the *Philosophies* group, of its call for a 'new mysticism' and its subsequent progressive radicalization which was to end in its fleeting rapprochement with the Surrealists, sealed in the summer of 1925 by the joint manifesto *La Révolution d'abord et toujours.*[31] For a brief moment the avant-gardes thought it would be possible to reconcile their 'revolt of the spirit' – a total revolt against the logos, the world, existing reality – with the political revolt embodied by the Communist Party. We all know Breton's famous formula: 'Marx said "Change the world", Rimbaud said "Change life": for us these two watchwords are one.' In the Surrealist experience, in the revolt of the poetic against 'the prose of the world', there is the idea that subverting the everyday will open the way to what, on its very first page, the *Manifesto of Surrealism* called *real* life. But at the same time, the modern *merveilleux*, automatic writing, the call on the unconscious and on objective chance, were being reduced to mere literary techniques. It is in this light that we must see the virulent exordium in *Critique of Everyday Life*:

> The attack on life led by poetry is just one episode, and literature is only the active-service unit of a much larger army. Like the poets, philosophers are wavering between the familiar, the trivial, the 'inauthentic', and the anguishing, the mysterious – between bourgeois reality and mystical unreality – and are pushing human reality to one side.[32]

Concord between the avant-gardes was short-lived and the choice between Marx and Rimbaud had to be made. But, stung by the initial politicization of 1925, the young *philosophes* went in the opposite direction to that of the Surrealists, who placed themselves 'in the service of the revolution' before breaking completely with the Communist Party. Between 1926 and 1927 *Philosophies* was replaced by the review *L'Esprit*, and this marked a phase of political withdrawal and sidetracking into philosophical stances that Lefebvre himself was to refer to as 'pre-existentialist'. Total revolt was replaced by the 'return to the concrete'. Only the 'return to the concrete' could reconcile thought and life, because life itself must be defined as the unity of thought and action. 'Life is unique', proclaimed the young *philosophes*, using a watchword conjured up by Pierre Morhange. They found father-figures in Spinoza, Schelling and Kierkegaard, and their guru in Jean Wahl, who published extracts from his *Malheur de la conscience dans la philosophie de Hegel* in *L'Esprit*.[33] As we have already mentioned, when Lefebvre read Hegel and discovered the theory of alienation as interpreted by Heidegger (rather than discovering Heidegger as such), it was thanks to Jean Wahl. In the 'Hegel debate' which flared up during the 1930s in France the stakes were considerable, for it was in opposition to the successful Kierkegaardian and Heideggerian Hegel introduced by the phenomenological reading of Kojève and Jean Wahl that Lefebvre vainly launched his logical and dialectical Hegel. We should note that the same refusal of both a purely phenomenological attitude towards consciousness and of Heideggerian pessimism was to power Lefebvre's post-war challenge to existentialism. In any event the 'pre-existentialist' sidetrack was curiously decisive in the encounter with Marxism, which was to culminate in Lefebvre and several members of the *Philosophies* group joining the Communist Party in 1928. Although the phase of ideological Stalinization was in full spate, the group was still impregnated with the paradoxical illusion that an autonomous theoretical development was feasible, and their final experiment was *La Revue marxiste*, which was launched in 1929, only to be immediately crushed in grotesque circumstances by the brutal intervention of the Party.[34]

In a sense it might be said that Lefebvre's plan for a critique of everyday life is the Marxianization of the slogan 'Life is unique'. It was only in 1928–29, after a long but vain search in the *philosophy of consciousness*, that Lefebvre felt that through the theory of alienation and in dialectical *method* he had discovered how to link the categories of unity, totality and reality. 'We intend to return primacy in consciousness to the object as such. The first article of our thought completely and deliberately reintegrates the external world, the concrete world, present, perceived as itself, into our consciousness.' From a text on the 'new mysticism', which in 1925 was taken as the group's first philosophical manifesto, to the affirmation in an article written in 1926 that 'to represent being to oneself is to cease to be', all the articles Lefebvre published in *Philosophies* and *L'Esprit* were – to use the title of the first of them – just so many 'Fragments of a philosophy of consciousness'.[35] In these texts, the stated aim of which was to tackle the aporias of traditional philosophy – being and representation, subject and object – when Lefebvre defined consciousness as an 'act' and as a 'relation' to the other qua other, he was in effect saying that consciousness was consciousness of the other. By recognizing the other as a mixture of presence and absence, the relation between 'the same and the other' as identity in difference and difference in identity, consciousness becomes the means of acceding to totality, i.e. to Spirit, which 'reunites and concentrates the diversity spread out through space'.[36] Lefebvre's quest for the totality, which took him as far as Schelling, had in fact begun well before he joined the *Philosophies* group, and the fragments he published were from a lengthy early manuscript, 'Esquisse d'une philosophie de la conscience', which constitutes not so much the matrix as the prehistory of his critique of everyday life. We must go back to this prehistory, which even predates the impact which the Blondelian philosophy of action was to make on him, in order to witness the emergence, from the very depths of his initial Christian experience, of the themes of unity and totality. In the beginning was his quest for *origins*: right from the start he saw the mysterious and the holy as something deeply human, and it was only after arduously searching for this original unity, forever lost, in religion and in philosophy that Lefebvre realized that it could be found in Marxist *supersession*. In the theme of 'philosophical revolution' of 1925, in the idea he took from Schelling that the philosopher lives 'not by observing his life but by producing it', we can already see the underpinnings of the 'realization' of philosophy as promised by Marxism. It was because he failed in his quest for a lost totality that Lefebvre was able to turn his attention to 'the total man'; but this failure also explains why his very definition of alienation has antecedents in the Christian thematic of the Fall and of original sin (profoundly transformed, needless to say).

'O Church, O Holy Church, when I finally managed to escape from your control I asked myself where your power came from.'[37] This is the moment to take a long look at what is certainly the most spellbinding chapter in *Critique of Everyday Life*, the enigmatic 'Notes Written One Sunday in the French Countryside', where Lefebvre describes in such detail and with such emotion the little church near Navarrenx (his 'native village'), in which the fundamental gestures of the Christian mystery are performed. The chapter closes, however, with the assertion that only Marxist method will enable us to understand these 'secrets' – these obscure aspects of the 'social mystery' and of history. He says that we can travel back in our minds to the origins of our civilization by studying the communal traditions which have persisted up to the present day in rural life. In his analysis of peasant festivals, he emphasizes that 'festivals contrasted violently with everyday life, *but they were not separate from it*'.[38] In this chapter, which is very similar to a long passage in *La Conscience mystifiée* about *lack of differentiation* in primitive societies, he defines traditional everyday life in a general way as based on non-separation, on the absence of differentiation in the cosmic order which formerly bound man and nature together. Thus *alienation* appears as a *historical* process of down-grading, of loss of this ancient 'human plenitude', by virtue of a dual movement of separation and abstraction: on the one hand, a separation of the social and the human, culminating in the division of labour and specialization of spheres of human activity; on the other hand, an increasing abstraction of human actions stripped of their living substance in favour of signs and symbols. Alienation thus leads to the impoverishment, to the 'despoliation' of everyday life; and yet for Lefebvre everyday life is not reduced to the inauthenticity of *Alltäglichkeit*, as in Heidegger or Lukács. It is not simply a residuum, or rather, its residual aspect bespeaks one or several strata of deeper meanings; it is both a parody of lost plenitude and the last remaining vestige of that plenitude. Even if Lefebvre's distinction between 'everyday life' and 'the everyday' only appears later, and is never fully developed, his critique of everyday life is a dual reading, at once a rejection of the inauthentic and the alienated, and an unearthing of the human which still lies buried therein. These 'Notes Written One Sunday in the French Countryside' may be set alongside Lefebvre's commentary on a passage from a book by Marc Bloch:

> But we are unable to seize the human facts. We fail to see them where they are, namely in humble, familiar, everyday objects: the shape of fields, of ploughs. Our search for the human takes us too far, too 'deep', we seek it in the clouds or in mysteries, whereas it is waiting for us, besieging us on all sides.[39]

This *archeological* mode of reading the everyday is also what characterizes Lefebvre's specifically sociological aims, and the consequences of this reach much farther than *Critique of Everyday Life*.

Everyday Life in the Modern World

If it was essential to recall the philosophical foundations, not to say the metaphysical prehistory, of *Critique of Everyday Life*, we should not lose sight of the fact that the book was intended first and foremost as a contribution to sociology, even if the originality of Lefebvre's sociology lies precisely in its philosophical roots. True, Lefebvre has a nostalgia for original *community*, but this is not so much the basis for his Communism as the inspiration for his early, partly empirical, research into rural sociology. We could go back as far as his youth, when while walking in the Pyrenees he came across some strange crosses with discs on them, and thought he had discovered the 'sun crucified', a primitive solar myth overlain by Christianity.[40] Above all, *Critique of Everyday Life* is contemporaneous of the research on the valley of Campan and agropastoral communities on which he was to base his doctoral thesis a few years later; he had begun this during the war, somewhat by chance, when he was hiding out in the Pyrenees, and spent his time rummaging through abandoned municipal archives. The conscious decision to study rural sociology dates, however, from 1948, when he joined the Centre National de la Recherche Scientifique (CNRS). Even if, apart from his doctorate in 1954 and a couple of articles, Lefebvre has not completed the ambitious projects he set himself in this sphere – like the *Traité de sociologie rurale* which was mysteriously stolen from a car, or the *Histoire rurale de la France* he was to have written in collaboration with Albert Soboul – the choice of sociology undoubtedly had a strategic significance.[41]

Lefebvre's critique of everyday life took up arms on two fronts: the first aim was to convince Marxists – at a moment when Zhdanovism was in full spate – of the value of an analysis of superstructures based on the concept of alienation; the second, to demonstrate to philosophers that the trivial should not be exempt from philosophical scrutiny. 'In so far as the science of man exists, it finds its material in the "trivial", the everyday.'[42] If the choice of the sociological field was strategic, this was above all because it was made at a moment when the entire range of the social sciences was witnessing a veritable explosion, whether in the domains of anthropology, demography and sociology, or in the shape of the revival of history by the history of 'mentalities'. A few key dates should suffice to prove this. The period between 1945 and 1949 saw the publication of major works by Friedmann, Dumézil and Bataille, as well as Braudel's *The Mediterranean* and Lévi-Strauss's *The Elementary Structures of Kinship*.[43] During the same period the institutions which were to assure the hegemony of this revival were set in place: the Institut Nationale des Études Démographiques and its review *Population*; the Centre d'Études Sociologiques at the CNRS, where Gurvitch produced the *Cahiers internationaux de sociologie*; and Section VI of the Ecole Pratique des Hautes Etudes, founded by Lucien Febvre, who, significantly, had just renamed his journal *Annales* (*Economies, Sociétés, Civilisations*). This explosion has been described as a 'change of paradigm in the social sciences' – even as a *critical* paradigm, and it is true that the social sciences were mounting a critique of speculative philosophy and of its abstract categories, thus making reflection on the destitution of the subject a possibility. At the same time they were leaning, if not to a directly political critique, then at least to a critique of society and history which sought to tear the veil from concealed or unconscious structures: *longue durée* economic cycles, collective psychology, the mythic and the symbolic. It is true that Lefebvre would launch an extremely violent attack on most of these trends in 1953 – the only moment in his career when opportunism led him to pay his political dues in this fashion – and denounced the 'police-force sociology' of the likes of Friedmann and Varagnac. It is a murky episode, but it should not deflect us from the fact that from Friedmann, whom he knew at the time of the *Philosophies* group, to Gurvitch, who secured him his place at the CNRS, Lefebvre was partly involved in the network which was to guarantee the expansion of the social sciences right up until the 1960s.[44]

But these French post-war years – the 'Trente Glorieuses' – were also the context for the impact of new technology and the consumer society as well as for the gradual disappearance of that rural world which had still been so dominant in the years between the wars. The period when André Varagnac was puzzling over traditional civilization and the spiritual world we have lost, when Gurvitch was sending his teams of sociologists out to investigate rural communities or religious behaviour, also saw the appearance of the first 4 CV, the first issue of the magazine *Elle*, the first Cannes Film Festival. Here we should compare the 'Notes Written One Sunday in the French Countryside' with 'Notes sur la ville nouvelle (Mourenx)' in *Introduction à la modernité*. When Henri Lefebvre moved from rural sociology to urban sociology, his thinking on the everyday was to become inseparable from his thinking about modernity. As he wrote in 1968 in *Everyday Life in the Modern World*, 'the quotidian and the modern mark and mask, legitimate and counterbalance each other. Today the universal quotidian ... is the verso of modernity, the spirit of our time'.[45] If modernity is the brilliant, even gaudy, side of the new, the everyday is its insignificant side, 'what is humble and solid, what is taken for granted and that of which all the parts follow each other in such a regular, unvarying succession that those concerned have no call to question its sequence'.[46] In other words, it is modernity which has *despoiled* the everyday life of former times, which never appeared save in its metamorphoses, as in *festival*, which embodied a genuine 'auto-critique' of the everyday; it is modernity which has caused everyday life to degenerate into 'the everyday'. Lefebvre's conception of modernity is both complex and contradictory, inscribed like Marx's in historical time, leading to a philosophy of progress, and, like Baudelaire's and Nietzsche's, anti-nomic to historical time, 'untimely' vis-à-vis its own present moment, leading to death and to the tragic. Modernity is the movement towards the new, the deployment of technology and rationality (which Lefebvre calls 'modernism'), but it is also the absence of any real transformation of social relations, and leads from the human towards the inhuman, towards barbarity. For Henri Lefebvre modernity and the everyday are historical categories, and if they cannot be dated precisely, at least they can be located at a moment of fundamental historical trauma: the failure of revolution, which was completed, at the very moment of the world crisis, by the advent of Stalinism and Fascism. With this failure of the world revolution, the moment of philosophy's 'realization' was gone, and it was modernity which, *in its own way*, was to complete the tasks that the revolution had been unable to bring to fruition; it was modernity that took on the responsibility of 'transforming the world' and 'changing life'.

Seen in this light, *Critique of Everyday Life* opens up yet another avenue, one that leads beyond rural sociology, beyond urban sociology, and beyond Lefebvre's later thinking on the production of space: the theme of the production of the everyday, of revolution as the revolution of everyday life. Producing the everyday, i.e. producing one's life like a work, is a thematic which in the 1960s led to Lefebvre's involvement with radical protest. In fact we need perhaps to go back here to 1948, when the Cobra group was founded, and to Constant, whose manifesto for an architecture of situations was explicitly inspired by *Critique of Everyday Life*. But above all we must offer some account of Lefebvre's relations with the situationist movement. They date back at least as far as the Research Group on Everyday Life which he organized at the Centre d'Etudes Sociologiques and, in particular, to the 'Department of Applied Sociology' which he created as a lecturer at Strasbourg University in 1961, and which in turn became the model for his Institute of Sociology at Nanterre in 1965. Before their brutal break with Lefebvre, the situationists, and first and foremost Guy Debord, acknowledged their debt to him; more precisely, they continued a dialogue with him from 1958 until the break in 1963. Conversely, the second volume of *Critique of Everyday Life*, *Fondements d'une sociologie de la quotidienneté*, in 1961, and equally his *Everyday Life in the Modern World* in 1968, were stimulated by the debate with the situationists. Subsequently Lefebvre and the situationists accused each other of plagiarism. Let us simply note the parallelism of their positions on certain crucial points, all present either explicitly or in embryo in *Critique of Everyday Life*. Most important among them is the idea that the use of everyday life is governed by the rule of scarcity, i.e. that it was detached from historicity at the height of the period of industrialization and accumulation. As Debord put it, 'everyday life is literally "colonized"' – a theme taken up again in the situationists' *De la misère en milieu étudiant*. This leads to the call for revolution in terms of 'revolutions in individual everyday life', a notion which is at the very origins of the theory of situations, and which subtends the identification of festival and revolution in Lefebvre's *Proclamation de la Commune* of 1965. In this book, which is the one the situationists accuse of plagiarizing their own writings, the idea that festival, like revolution, marks both a break in everyday life and a rehabilitation of the everyday, stems directly from *Critique of Everyday Life*.[47]

Of course it is impossible to deny Lefebvre's impact on the ideology of May 1968 itself, and it is astonishing that in France at least most studies should have underestimated Lefebvre's themes in favour of Marcuse or other even more exotic thinkers. Anglo-Saxon scholarship has concentrated on Lefebvre in a more serious and more sustained manner. We have written elsewhere of how the work of Perry Anderson, Mark Poster, Michael Kelly, etc., has restored Lefebvre to his rightful place among the great Marxist theoreticians of the twentieth century. We should mention, however, that it was in Germany during the 1970s that the debate on everyday life which sprang up in the context of the 'alternative' movement was the most firmly rooted in Henri Lefebvre's thought.[48] So much so that one might even begin making links with Habermas's distinction between *System* (specialized culture controlled by experts), for example, and *Lebenswelt* (lived experience and everyday life). Thus it becomes clear why we cannot fix our reading of *Critique of Everyday Life* in the context of 1947: it is not only an essential marker in Henri Lefebvre's philosophical and political evolution, but also one of the crossroads in the reorganization of the intellectual field of the second half of the twentieth century.

CNRS, Paris, March 1991

Foreword to the

Second Edition

I   In Retrospect

As it stands, this book[1] did not strictly speaking offer a new interpretation of Marxism. The following quotation from Lenin would have
made an appropriate epigraph:

> The whole point, however, is that Marx ... did not confine himself to
> 'economic theory' in the ordinary sense of the term, that, while *explaining*
> the structure and the development of the given formation of society
> *exclusively* through production relations ... [he] clothed the skeleton in flesh
> and blood. The reason *Capital* has enjoyed such tremendous success is that
> this book by a 'German economist' showed the whole capitalist social
> formation to the reader as a living thing – with its everyday aspects ...[2]

In this very important text, Lenin shows that Marx created scientific
sociology. He expressed similar ideas in many other places in his
writings:

> In his *Capital,* Marx first analyses the simplest, most ordinary and
> fundamental, most common and everyday *relation* of bourgeois (com-
> modity) society, a relation encountered billions of times, viz. the exchange
> of commodities. In this very simple phenomenon ... analysis reveals *all* the
> contradictions (or the germs of *all* the contradictions) of modern society.[3]

The fact remains that the *Critique of Everyday Life* was built entirely
around a concept which Lenin had left aside or neglected, the concept
of *alienation*.

The fact also remains that this book developed a generally neglected aspect of Marxism, the specifically *sociological* aspect.

When it appeared, the book was inadequately substantiated on both the philosophical and the sociological level. In the first place, it should have formulated and attempted to resolve the problem posed by the concept of alienation. It should also have explained what a Marxist sociology considered as a specific science could be (as method and object) in its relation with the other sciences (political economy, history, etc.) as well as with historical and dialectical materialism.

The fact is, however, that ten years ago these various problems were not sufficiently ripe. It was more or less impossible to formulate them correctly, let alone resolve them.[4]

Today we are only just beginning to glimpse the complexity of the questions the theory of alienation poses. These questions fall into several categories. *Historically*, we must discover what role this concept played in the development of Marxism, how (in his early writings) Marx took it from Hegel and Feuerbach, how he transformed and redirected it, and at what date. Thus it is appropriate to follow this transformation through the texts, and this means that a rigorous examination of the early writings, and notably of the celebrated *1844 Manuscripts*, is required.[5] *Theoretically*, we must determine what becomes of the *philosophical* concept of alienation in Marx's scientific and political works, notably in *Capital*, and understand whether the economic theory of fetishism is truly an extension of the philosophical theory of alienation onto an objective (scientific) level.[6]

Finally, the problem *philosophically* is of knowing what meaning and (critical or constructive) importance should be given at the present moment to the concept of alienation. To what extent should a philosopher take it up again, perhaps in a modified form, and put it at the centre of his thinking? This problem cannot be separated from the others although it can be distinguished from them. If it were true, as certain Marxists argue, that Marxism as such radically rejects earlier concepts, including those which helped to develop it – so that there was an absolute caesura in human thought at the moment of Marxism's emergence, and in Marxism at the moment when Marx became conscious of his doctrine – the problem of what the concept of alienation means now would not even arise. To take this position implies further positions, notably that Marxism is a completed system, and that philosophy's role and function are at an end. Such arguments must be deemed dogmatic and false.

Such vast and difficult questions had to ripen before they could be posed.

In particular it had to be possible to ask the question: 'Is alienation disappearing in socialist society? In the USSR or the countries which are constructing socialism, are there not contradictions indicative of new – or renewed – forms of economic, ideological and political alienation?'

As far as sociology as a specific science is concerned, there have been many moments of uncertainty to live through. The question of whether the Stalinist interpretation of Marxism was not mutilating it and depriving it of one of its dimensions has had to be faced; as has that of whether the Marxist notion of *socio-economic formation*[7] is not richer and more complex – since it involves the sociological study of social relations – than the currently favoured concepts of (economic) base and (ideological and political) superstructures.

The fact that these questions were absent from its argument explains to a certain extent the way the book was received when it was first published. What was the official, academic response? Utter silence. At that moment, in 1946, French philosophy had suffered a series of shocks from which it was only slowly recovering. The war and the Occupation had killed off several important currents of thought, notably Bergsonian anti-intellectualism, compromised by a vague relationship with German irrationalism, and Léon Brunschvicg's intellectualism,[8] which was poorly equipped to resolve the new problems. The generation of Hegelians[9] and existentialists was on the rise. But there were those who, though perfectly willing to respect and accept the notion of alienation on a speculative level, were probably less prepared to see it soiled by confrontation with actual human reality, with everyday life.[10]

So the professional philosophers generally ignored the book; for – starting with its title – it entailed relinquishing the traditional image of the philosopher as master and ruler of existence, witness and judge of life *from the outside*, enthroned above the masses, above the moments lost in triviality, 'distinguished' by an attitude and a distance. (There is nothing really exaggerated about these metaphors. The distance is called 'spiritual life' and the philosopher's attitude is called contemplation, detachment, 'epoche',[11] parenthesizing, etc.)

What about Marxism? If the traditional philosophers, still saturated with pure speculative thought or attracted by it, gave the book a cool reception, so did the Marxists.

In the enthusiasm of the Liberation, it was hoped that soon life would be changed and the world transformed. More than that: life had already been changed; the peoples were on the move, the masses were in a ferment. Their movement was causing new values to 'rise to the surface'. What was the point of analysing bourgeois everyday life, the style (or absence of style) imposed by the dominant class? What was the point of a philosophical or sociological critique? The weapon of criticism was about to be replaced, had already been replaced, by the criticism of weapons. In France, in the rest of the world, the proletariat was no longer an oppressed class. It was imposing itself on the nations as the ruling class. To talk about alienation was no longer possible, no longer permissible. The concept was just as outdated in France as it was in the USSR, in countries where socialism was on the march, or where the rumble of revolution could already be heard.

Thinking people were obsessed with the political drama. Rightly so. But they were forgetting that although the political drama was being acted out or decided in the higher spheres – the State, parliament, leaders, policies – it still had a 'base' in matters relating to food, rationing, wages, the organization or reorganization of labour. A humble, everyday 'base'. Therefore many Marxists saw criticism of everyday life as useless and antiquated; they perceived it as a reworking of an old-fashioned, exhausted critique of bourgeois society, little more than a critique of triviality – therefore a trivial critique.

For this reason philosophers today are experiencing difficulties of a kind unknown to their predecessors. Great or small, profound or superficial, their lives have lost that simplicity and elegance of line they attribute (fictitiously, no doubt) to the lives of their illustrious models. Philosophers and philosophy can no longer be isolated, disguised, hidden. And this is precisely because everyday life is the supreme court where wisdom, knowledge and power are brought to judgement.

II   What Has Changed in the Last Ten Years?

Under these circumstances, what is the point – after ten years of interruption – of resuming this task?

Firstly, during these years a certain number of young intellectuals have read the book with interest – with passion. Their expressions of appreciation have alleviated any feelings of bitterness the author may have had about the coolness of the book's 'official' reception.

But that is not all. During the last ten years the development of research in the social sciences has shown that the book was on target, that its point of view is well-founded. Problems of everyday life and studies of everyday life have become increasingly important in the minds of historians, ethnographers, philosophers, sociologists, as well as of writers, artists and journalists. Our very best informed and most 'modern' publications – daily and weekly newspapers, reviews – have started columns dealing with everyday life. There has been a proliferation of books about everyday life, and bit by bit a method to confront everyday life with ideas apparently far removed from it, such as myths, ceremonies, works of art, is being developed.[12]

For the historian of a specific period, for the ethnographer, for the sociologist studying a society or a group, the fundamental question would be to grasp a certain quality, difficult to define and yet essential and concrete, something that 'just a quarter-of-an-hour alone' with a man from a distant or extinct culture would reveal to us.[13]

Let us consider some areas very remote from the social sciences. Recently I read an article[14] which was something of a manifesto or policy statement for the idea that the modern theatre can only be 'a place where everyday life attains its highest degree of intensity; where the words and gestures of everyday life at last take on meaning'. A Soviet critic has made the same assertion about Chekhov's theatre: 'He [Chekhov] considers that theatre ought to represent everyday life'.[15]

We shall return to this idea.

Again, the monumental volume of *L'Encyclopédie française* devoted to *Everyday Life* was published recently. It is a considerable piece of work,[16] but one in which the descriptive and the technological points of view push the *critical* point of view into the background, and even obliterate it.

Indisputably the last few years have witnessed the application of the most modern of techniques to the way everyday life is organized, that is to say, to a sector which up until now has been paid scant attention. The way in which everyday life lags behind what is technically possible is and should be one of the themes of the *Critique of Everyday Life*. How could this theme possibly have lost its foundation or its meaning?

In *L'Express* of 8 June 1956 (p. 21) the following information was given on the 'interesting novelties' which its special New York correspondent had noticed, and which 'will inevitably end up coming to France':

> Kitchens are becoming less like kitchens and more like works of art ... The latest technique is the electronic oven ... The intercom (a system of loudspeakers linking every room) is becoming a standard piece of equipment in the home, while everyone is talking about a personalized little television network which will enable the lady of the house to attend to her chores while keeping an eye on the children playing in another room or in the garden ... The remarkable ubiquity of 'do it itself' [sic], the latest craze for the American husband ... includes all the household gadgets that go with it ... the latest development in the household industry? Swimming pools, which the manufacturers say they are about to mass-market ... Popular requirements as far as houses are concerned: at least seven rooms, with two bathrooms ...

In the next column, 'Madame Express' informs anyone who was unaware of it that:

> a woman needs cast-iron will-power to stop her hairdresser from cutting her hair short. Nothing is more persuasive than a hairdresser who has made his mind up. And they have some powerful allies: cover-girls, actresses, all the women for whom money is no problem and whose pictures, distributed every day, are more persuasive than any words could be ...

The remarkable way in which modern techniques have penetrated everyday life has thus introduced into this backward sector *the uneven development* which characterizes every aspect of our era. Manifestations of the brilliant advances in the 'ideal home' constitute sociological facts of the first importance, but they must not be allowed to conceal the contradictory character of the real social process beneath an accumula-

tion of technological detail. These advances, along with their consequences, are provoking new structural conflicts within the concrete life
of society. The same period which has witnessed a breathtaking
development in the application of techniques of everyday life has also
witnessed the no-less-breathtaking degradation of everyday life for
large masses of human beings. All around us, in France, in Paris itself,
there are hundreds of thousands of children, youngsters, students,
young couples, single people, families, living in conditions undreamed-
of by anyone who does not bring a sociologist's interest to bear:[17]
furnished rooms (increasingly expensive and squalid), slums, over-
crowded flats, attic rooms, etc.

The deterioration of the conditions of existence is spreading to a
great many French rural areas (notably in the southern half of the
country), to a large proportion of craftsmen, small shopkeepers and the
working class.

Agreed, it is not unusual to find peasants owning electric cookers,
but the houses they live in are still dilapidated; they manage to buy
gadgets, but cannot afford to repair their houses, and even less to
modernize their farms. In other words, the latter are given up for the
sake of the former. In the same way quite a large number of working-
class couples have a washing machine, a television set, or a car, but
they have generally sacrificed something else for these gadgets (having
a baby, for example). In this way problems of choosing what to buy –
or problems associated with hire-purchase, etc. – are posed within
working-class families, and these problems modify everyday life.[18] That
relatively poor peasants, or workers, should buy television sets proves
the existence of a new *social need*. The fact is remarkable. But it does not
tell us the size or the extent of this need, nor the extent to which it is
satisfied. Nor does it prove that this need has not been satisfied to the
detriment of another.

Far from suppressing criticism of everyday life, modern technical
progress *realizes it*. This technicity replaces the criticism of life through
dreams, or ideas, or poetry, or those activities which rise above the
everyday, by the critique of everyday life from within: the critique
which everyday life makes of itself, the critique of the real by the
possible and of one aspect of life by another. Compared with lower or
degraded standards of living, everyday life with all the superior mod
cons takes on the distance and remoteness and familiar strangeness of a

dream. The display of luxury to be seen in so many films, most of them mediocre, takes on an almost fascinating character, and the spectator is uprooted from his everyday world by an everyday world *other* than his own. Escape into this illusory but present everyday world, the fascination of ordinary objects which scream wealth, the seductive powers of the apparently profound lives led by the men and women who move among these objects, all this explains the momentary success these films enjoy.

Happily, contemporary cinema and theatre have other works to offer which reveal a truth about everyday life.

III   On Charlie Chaplin, Bertolt Brecht and Some Others

It is not Chaplin's clowning contortions and funny faces that make people burst out laughing. From his very first films, he stood out from such other film comedians as Fatty Arbuckle and Harold Lloyd. The secret of his comic powers lies not in his body, but in the relation of this body to something else: a social relation with the material world and the social world. Naïve, physically adept but spiritually innocent, Chaplin arrives in a complicated and sophisticated universe of people and things with fixed patterns of behaviour (where people behave like things − and in conjunction with things). The clown's physical suppleness, and his concomitant ability to adapt himself and his gestures with an almost animal rapidity, become humanized as they give way to an extreme awkwardness which both proves and signifies his naïvety. However, this awkwardness is never permanent; the original situation is reinstated; the clown has his revenge, he defeats the hostile objects − and the hostile people − only to fall back into momentary disarray. Hence visually comic moments when he cannot adapt are followed by moments of victory when he can, and this stops the 'mime−audience' relationship from breaking down, producing fresh gusts of laughter and assuring that the humour never becomes awkward or embarrassing. Like pleasure, like harmony in music, laughter is stimulated by a series of resolved tensions, in which moments of relaxation are followed by even higher tensions.

The point of departure for the 'vis comica' peculiar to Chaplin is therefore the simplicity of a child, a primitive and a wonderfully gifted barbarian, suddenly plunged (as we all are at every moment) into an everyday life that is inflexible and bristling with ever-new difficulties, some foreseeable, others not. In his first films Chaplin takes up battle – a duel which is always different and yet always the same – with objects, everyday objects: an umbrella, a deckchair, a motorbike, a banana skin ... Always surprised, always delighted by the strangeness and richness of things, always awkward when faced with ritualized practices (essential behaviour, necessary conditioning), Chaplin captures our own attitude towards these trivial things, and before our very eyes. He makes it appear suddenly amazing, dramatic and joyful. He comes as a stranger into the familiar world, he wends his way through it, not without wreaking joyful damage. Suddenly he disorientates us, but only to show us what we are when faced with objects; and these objects become suddenly alien, the familiar is no longer familiar (as for example when we arrive in a hotel room, or a furnished house, and trip over the furniture, and struggle to get the coffee grinder to work). But via this deviation through disorientation and strangeness, Chaplin reconciles us on a higher level, with ourselves, with things and with the humanized world of things.

Thus the essence of this humour is not to be found in pity, nor even in strangeness (alienation), but on the contrary in a triumph which is forever being renewed and forever threatened. The dog, the pretty girl, the child, are not cinematic props, but elements necessary to the more or less complete final victory.

Therefore Chaplin's first films may be seen as offering a critique of everyday life: a critique in action, a basically optimistic critique, with the living, human unity of its two faces, the negative and the positive. Hence its 'success'.

In Chaplin's feature films, the critique becomes broader, taking on a higher meaning. They confront the established (bourgeois) world and its vain attempts to complete itself and close itself off, not with another world but with a *type*. This type (a down-and-out) is the emanation of that other world, its expression, its internal necessity, its essence externalized and yet still internal (to put it abstractly and speculatively, which after all is how Marx expressed his discovery of the proletariat as a class).

As necessarily as it produces machines and men-machines, the bourgeois world produces deviants. It produces the Tramp, its *reverse image*. The relation between the Tramp and the bourgeois order is different to the relation 'proletariat–bourgeoisie'. In particular it is more immediate, more physical, relying less on concepts and demands than on images.

By its false and illusory and euphoric and presumptuous insistence upon the self, the 'free world' immediately creates its pure negative image. Thus the Tramp-figure contains certain characteristics of the image Marx presents of the proletariat in his philosophical writings: the pure alienation of man and the human which is revealed as being more deeply human than the things it negates – negativity forced by its essence to destroy the society to which at one and the same time it belongs and does not belong. And yet the 'positivity' of the proletariat, its historic mission, is not accomplished on the philosophical or aesthetic level; it is accomplished politically, and philosophical criticism becomes political criticism and action ... In the type and the 'myth' presented by Chaplin, criticism is not separable from the physical image immediately present on the screen. If therefore it remains limited, it is nevertheless directly accessible to the masses; it does not lead to revolutionary action or political consciousness, and yet it uses laughter to stir up the masses profoundly. Thus in his best films Chaplin's humour takes on an epic dimension which comes from this deep meaning. 'The image of alienated man, he reveals alienation by dishonouring it.'[19]

Here for the first time we encounter a complex problem, both aesthetic and ethical, that of the *reverse image*: an image of everyday reality, taken in its totality or as a fragment, reflecting that reality in all its depth *through* people, ideas and things which are apparently quite different from everyday experience, and therefore exceptional, deviant, abnormal.[20]

The type created by Chaplin achieves universality by means of extremely precise elements: the hat, the walking stick and the trousers, all taken from London's petty bourgeoisie. The transition from the mime to the Type marks a date and an expansion in Chaplin's work, an expansion within the work itself and one made possible by that work alone; suddenly he puts his own previously constructed figure (or image) at the centre of his films. In a very strong sense, he puts himself on the stage; as a result, a new development takes place.

Thus the critique of everyday life takes the form of a living, dialectical pair: on the one hand, 'modern times' (with everything they entail: bourgeoisie, capitalism, techniques and technicity, etc.), and on the other, the Tramp. The relation between them is not a simple one. In a fiction truer than reality as it is immediately given, they go on producing and destroying one another ceaselessly. In this way the comical produces the tragic, the tragic destroys the comical, and vice versa; cruelty is never absent from the clowning; the setting for the clowning is constantly being broadened: the city, the factory, Fascism, capitalist society in its entirety. But is the comedy defined by its underlying tragedy, or by its victory over the tragic? It is in the spectator personally that Charlie Chaplin constantly manages to unite these two ever-present and conflicting aspects, the tragic and the comical; laughter always manages to break through; and like the laughter of Rabelais, Swift and Molière (i.e. the laughter of their readers or audiences) it denies, destroys, liberates. Suffering itself is denied, and this denial is put on display. In this fictitious negation we reach the limits of art. On leaving the darkness of the cinema, we rediscover the same world as before, it closes round us again. And yet the comic event has taken place, and we feel decontaminated, returned to normality, purified somehow, and stronger.

To sum up, our analysis has seen Chaplin as a *type* rather than a *myth*, based on general characteristics (poor but full of vitality – weak but strong – ruthlessly seeking money, work, prestige, but also love and happiness). How can an image which so directly reveals what is significant about the so-called 'modern man' be called *mythical*?

In any case the interesting thing here is not a discussion of the Chaplin 'myth' and the mythical character of the image of life he presents; it is the very fact that an image with its roots deep in everyday life can be seen as *mythical*, and that the word 'myth' can be used to describe it.

Might this illusion be significant on a more general level? The most extraordinary things are also the most everyday; the strangest things are often the most trivial, and the current notion of the 'mythical' is an illusory reflection of this fact. Once separated from its context, i.e. from how it is interpreted and from the things which reinforce it while at the same time making it bearable – once presented in all its triviality, i.e. in all that makes it trivial, suffocating, oppressive – the trivial becomes extraordinary, and the habitual becomes 'mythical'. In the same way, a humble plant taken from the soil and from the plants around it, seen up close, becomes something marvellous. But then, once images like this have been separated from their everyday context, it becomes very difficult to articulate them in a way which will present their essential everyday quality. This is the secret of talents like Fellini's (*La Strada*) or that of the directors of *Salt of the Earth*,[21] and (perhaps) it offers a potential way ahead for realism ...[22]

Brecht – that great man of the theatre who recently passed away – tried to renew realism by proposing a revolutionary formula: *epic* theatre.

This formula has provoked more than one misunderstanding. On reading those words – in a country whose culture is traditionally referred to as 'humanist' – it is easy to imagine noble, violent actions unfolding majestically, and protagonists fighting for the crown, for their dynasty or their loves.

In fact what Brecht meant was a theatre in which action (and poetry) would be expressly and deliberately brought close to everyday life. When he tried to explain the meaning of the word 'epic', he used the example of a traffic accident, with witnesses discussing what happened and giving biased accounts of it, each implying a judgement (taking a stand, taking sides) and an attempt to make the listener share that judgement. 'The epic theatre wants to establish its basic model at the street corner ...'[23]

Brecht's great play about Galileo – that hero of knowledge – begins with a 'de-heroization':

GALILEO: (*washing the upper part of his body, puffing, and good-humoured:*) Put the milk on the table ...[24]

To understand this properly, we need to think about what is happening around us, within us, each and every day. We live on familiar terms with the people in our own family, our own milieu, our own class. This constant impression of *familiarity* makes us think that we know them, that their outlines are defined for us, and that they see themselves as having those same outlines. We define them (Peter is this, Paul is that) and we judge them. We can identify with them or exclude them from our world. But the familiar is not necessarily the known. As Hegel said in a sentence which could well serve as an epigraph for the *Critique of Everyday Life*, 'Was ist bekannt ist nicht erkannt.' Familiarity, what is familiar, conceals human beings and makes them difficult to know by giving them a mask we can recognize, a mask that is merely the lack of something. And yet familiarity (mine with other people, other people's with me) is by no means an illusion. It is real, and is part of reality. Masks cling to our faces, to our skin; flesh and blood have become masks. The people we are familiar with (and we ourselves) *are* what we recognize them to be. They play the roles I have cast them in and which they have cast for themselves. And I myself play a role for them and in them (and not only while they are watching), the role of friend, husband, lover, father which they have cast me in and which I have cast for myself. If there were no roles to play, and thus no familiarity, how could the cultural element or ethical element which should modify and humanize our emotions and our passions be introduced into life? The one involves the other. A role is not a role. It is social life, an inherent part of it. What is faked in one sense is what is the essential, the most precious, the human, in another. And what is most derisory is what is most necessary. It is often difficult to distinguish between what is faked and what is natural, not to say naïve (and we should distinguish between a natural naïvety and the naturalness which is a product of high culture).

The waiter in a café is not playing at being a waiter. He *is* one.[25] And he is not one. He is not selling his time (for working and living) in exchange for the role of a waiter. And it is precisely when he is playing at being a waiter (and a virtuoso in the art of carrying overladen trays, etc.) in front of his customers that he is no longer a waiter; by playing himself he transcends himself. Moreover, it is certain that a worker does not play at being a worker and could not transcend himself if he did. He is completely 'that', and at the same time he is completely other and something else: head of the family, or an individual eager to enjoy life, or a revolutionary militant. For him and within him, at his best moments and his worst, contradictions and alienations are at a maximum. For us, in our society, with the forms of exchange and the division of labour which govern it, there is no social relation – relation with the other – without a certain alienation. And each individual exists socially only by and within his alienation, just as he can only be for himself within and by his deprivation (his *private* consciousness).[26]

It would be too simple to tear off the masks and shatter the roles; to cry 'faces are nothing more than masks' is the answer of cynical irony, the solution a cartoonist might come up with. An irrelevant solution, since *they* are that – and *they* are not that – and thus *they* escape irony on two counts. Still, the very fact that irony is possible immediately reveals the impossibility of any true identification with 'beings' who are not identical with themselves. Now familiarity relies upon apparent identification, upon a belief in identification: upon a practical credulity. Irony begins breaking this belief up; without necessarily putting *a reasonable distance* between us and the people we live with, it allows us to begin appreciating the distance between them and their own selves, between them and us. Irony is necessary, it is a powerful weapon ethically and aesthetically, but it is not enough. It plays a momentary role in the critique that everyone makes – more or less – of their own everyday lives and it cannot be disregarded. In Brecht – in his poetry as in his plays – there is a constant underlying irony, yet this irony is always transcended by a more deeply serious intent.

There is an intense feeling which can be rare or frequent in life, according to who one is, but which is certainly frequent in narrative fiction, and which can be put more or less in the following way: 'He realized that this woman who had been sharing his bed for the last ten years was nothing more than a stranger to him ... Germaine looked at Roger in amazement; it was as though she was seeing him for the first time ...'

For the audience in a theatre, this surprise must be made to last. And the distance between the characters, as between the characters and their own selves, must be determined by the distance between the audience, the stage and the actors. They must be placed at a reasonable distance. But this is just a technical problem, at least as far as Brecht is concerned. No doubt the essential thing is that in the twentieth century the people we live with have nothing in common with classical *characters*, precisely because they play a *role* in life.

In the great classical dramas, by virtue of a contradiction for which they offer a magnificent solution, *characters* are not *characters*. They are utterly sincere, authentically sincere, even when they are pretending. They are not acting, and this is why actors are able to impersonate them completely. The audience can identify with well-defined 'beings' and 'natures'. Conversely, all around us, in real life, characters really are characters; plays which attempt to represent them (in other words to present what is hidden in life in a clear way and at a reasonable distance) must go beyond the classical concept of *character*. We are dealing with people about whom it is impossible to say either what they are or what they are not; about whom we cannot say that they are not – that they only appear to be – what they are, nor that they are or appear to be what they are not. They are undefined and yet they are, and with a vengeance. Presence–absence does not function on the level of the image or the imaginary, but in life. This is precisely why an awareness of what is familiar becomes transformed into an awareness of something strange. As soon as we get really close to someone, we say to ourselves: 'He's an odd type of chap ... She's an odd type of girl.' Every 'type', by which we mean every individual (the opposite of *typical*) is an odd type of person.[27] The following conversation could be about anyone: 'You're exaggerating. I don't think he's nearly as complicated as that.' 'That's because you don't know him well enough.' 'Honestly, he's really very nice.' 'Who to? His friends. His little clique. But as far as I'm concerned ...' 'It's her fault, the bitch.' 'Come on, don't be so hard on her ...' And so on ...

One possible outcome of this is Pirandelloism, which has been fashionable for so long that it must have a deep meaning. Pirandello initiated a theatre which is almost perfectly *static*, and which recently has become even more so.[28] Nothing happens but a series of interpretations and points of view which shed light on a past, absent or unknown event. Pirandelloism expressed in terms of the theatre the relativity – the absolute relativity – of characters and judgements, an important discovery of 'modern times' in bourgeois society. There are only points of view, perspectives, masks and roles. Truth is draped in veils; it can be defined only by an endless succession of points of view.

And yet there is something in life which Pirandelloism cannot contain and which escapes it: the action, the event, the decision, the final outcome and the necessity for a final outcome; actions, and judgements about actions, in the sense in which they involve decisions. Even when we are playing, or above all when we are playing, we have to make decisions.[29] To play is to transform our point of view into a decision by confronting chance and determinism in the absence of adequate information about our opponent's game. We must lay our

17

cards on the table, make our play. And quickly. We must make a decision. We do not have all the time in the world, either to shuffle the pack or to think about our partner's hand. In any case, would all the time in the world supply us with complete information? Would it exhaust chance and determination? Would it come anywhere near uncovering their unity? When we are not playing (in other words when we are living seriously) we also come to decisions in the absence of adequate information, confronting chance and determinism and therefore playing in the deepest meaning of the word.

At this point we may at last be defining and grasping something that Brecht understood profoundly. We are never really sure where actions, decisions or events spring from.[30] But, in all their stark reality, the results are *there*. What lies hidden within men and women is beyond our grasp; maybe these hidden depths are only an insubstantial mist, and not a profound substance (a *Grund*, a nature, an unconscious belonging to the individual or a group); it may only be a myth. Men and women are beyond us. But the battle, however confused, always has an outcome. There, before us, lies a child, a casualty, or a corpse; a marriage, a life together to organize or to disrupt, a place to live to be found; suffering to endure or avoid – pleasure to enjoy or spoil; a decision to hazard and accept with all its consequences (and this without adequate information, or having lost information en route, etc.).[31] Uncertainty is not without its charm or interest; it can never last long. It maintains ambiguity, keeping what is possible in a state of possibility, allowing us to take our pleasure in what Valéry called the whorehouse of possibilities; it can even oscillate between the comical and the dramatic, but we must choose. We weigh the pros and the cons, but there is no telling when something new on one side of the scales will come to outweigh the other. So decisions may ripen like fruit on a tree, but they never fall of their own accord; we must always cut the stem, we must even choose the moment of choice . . .[32] Hence the infinitely complex, profound and contradictory character of life is given an element which is always new, and which is indeed constantly being renewed by knowledge.

To put it more clearly or more abstractly, *ambiguity* is a category of everyday life, and perhaps an essential category. It never exhausts its reality; from the ambiguity of consciousnesses and situations spring forth actions, events, results, without warning. These, at least, have clear-cut outlines. They maintain a hard, incisive objectivity which constantly disperses the luminous vapours of ambiguity – only to let them rise once again.

Philosophers and psychologists have confused the issue by sometimes attributing this 'being-there' of results to consciousness or being, rather than to actions and decisions, and sometimes attributing ambiguity to philosophically defined existence rather than to the everyday as such.

Feelings and desires can hardly choose. They would like to choose, they would like not to choose, to possess incompatibles all at the same time: several skills, several possibilities, several futures, several loves. Practically, the requirement to act and to make decisions imposes choice. But to choose is to *make a judgement*. We have no knowledge of the human actions which go on around us; they escape us just as our own selves escape us. And yet we must *make judgements*. And even before or after the epic moment of decision or action, we must go on making ever more and more judgements. It is the only solid ground, the only unchanging requirement amid all life's ups and downs, its one axis. Such are the varied aspects of the everyday: fluctuations beneath stable masks and appearances of stability, the need to make judgements and decisions. But nothing is as difficult and as dangerous as making judgements. 'Judge not.' From the very beginnings of social life, men have been obsessed by the function of the Judge, and the powerful fight among themselves to exercise it. The Judge pronounces, makes irrevocable decisions according to the law as it stands, or in the court of appeal. He must embody justice, or Law, or the force of Truth. God passes for supreme judge, and the myth of the Last Judgement is a mighty image, the most striking in the most elaborate of all religions. The human masses sustain this great hope: the Judge will come. For ordinary men, every one of the innumerable little judgements required in life implies a risk and a wager. We are so used to making mistakes about our fellow man that good sense tells us to be wary of passing judgement, disapproves of hasty verdicts, and, quite rightly, denounces prejudice. As a result we find it easier to judge a global society than to judge men. Every capitalist is a man; within him, up to a point, the man and the capitalist are in conflict. Extreme cases – the capitalist who is the complete incarnation of money and capital – are rare. Generally, there are two or more contradictory spirits living inside the capitalist (in particular, as Marx noted, the coexisting needs of enjoyment and accumulation tear him apart). It is therefore both easier and more equitable to condemn a society than to condemn a man.

Brecht perceived the epic content of everyday life superbly: the hardness of actions and events, the necessity of judging. To this he added an acute awareness of the alienation to be found in this same everyday life. To see people properly we need to place them at a reasonable, well-judged distance, like the objects we see before us. Then their many-sided strangeness becomes apparent: in relation to ourselves, but also within themselves and in relation to themselves. In this strangeness lies their truth, the truth of their alienation. It is then that consciousness of alienation – that strange awareness of the strange – liberates us, or begins to liberate us, from alienation. This is the truth. And at the moment of truth we are suddenly disorientated by others and by ourselves. To look at things from an *alien* standpoint – externally and from a reasonable distance – is to look at things *truly*. But this strange and alien way of looking at things, disorientated but true, is the way children, peasants, women of the people, naïve and simple folk look. And they are afraid of what they see. For this many-sided alienation is no joke. We live in a world in which the best becomes the worst; where nothing is more dangerous than heroes and great men; where every thing including freedom (even though it is not a thing) and revolt, changes into its own opposite.

Brecht gave examples borrowed from everyday life. His *Verfremdungs-effekt* has become famous, but some technically inclined stage directors tend to turn it into a theatrical device; they achieve a specific effect with a couple of tricks of light and shadow, or with incidental music out of keeping with the real spectacle. When Brecht showed the strangeness of the everyday, pointing up that contradiction within the familiar, whereby it embraces both the trivial and the extraordinary, he was already protesting against this kind of technocratic interpretation. A lorry has just run over a passer-by. Policemen run to the scene, people gather round, discussing what has happened. They try to reconstruct the event, but are unable to do so. The witnesses disagree. The driver tries to exonerate himself, throwing the blame on the victim. The fact, the event, is there, in all its stark and gory reality. Everyone judges or tries to judge, everyone takes sides and makes his decision.

This is the approach historians – who must make judgements

sooner or later – still have towards criticizing evidence.

Brecht's epic theatre rejects classical transparency (as it happens, a deceptive transparency which in principle extends to the conflicts and problems presented, to the logical unfolding of the actions and events). If he starts from a 'commonplace', it is the opposite of the classical 'koinon',[33] and is taken from the everyday. He starts from disagreement, divergence, distortion. The play – or the scene – poses a complete problem which has not been resolved in advance, and which is consequently irritating, embarrassing. To begin with, Brecht confronts the spectator with an action or an event (the quarrel between the Kolkhozians in *The Caucasian Chalk Circle*, for example). He leaves the spectator in a (for him) disturbing externality. Instead of making him participate in an action or with defined 'characters', the stage action liberates him: it 'arouses his capacity for action, forces him to make decisions ... he is made to face something [by] argument'.[34] Called upon to make a judgement, obliged to come to a decision, the audience hesitates. And in this way the action is transferred to within the spectator. Without being aware of it, and although everything is clearly happening in full view, the spectator becomes the living consciousness of the contradictions of the real.

And is it really accurate to say that this theatre excludes emotion? It excludes emotion of a magical nature, the kind that allows or implies participation and identification. But maybe Brecht's theatre is aiming to bring forth new forms of emotion and images by actually ridding them of whatever magic the imagination has retained.[35] If this were not the case, if Brecht's theatre were restricted merely to evoking states of mind, this is where it would come up against its own limitations, and fairly severe limitations they would be. As it happens, it provides a model for art liberated from magic.[36] And that is a great innovation. Brecht unravels the contradictions of everyday life and liberates us from them. For magic plays an immense role in everyday life, be it in emotional identification and participation with 'other people' or in the thousand little rituals and gestures used by every person, every family, every group. But in practical life as in ideology, this magic only signifies the illusions men have about themselves, and their lack of power. And everyday life is defined by contradictions: illusion and truth, power and helplessness, the intersection of the sector man controls and the sector he does not control.

In Brecht's theatre, the protagonists are placed in the full glare of the stage-lights, but the very brilliance of the lights and the bareness of the dramatic space deliberately isolate and distance them. Thus the audience can identify neither with the dramatic development nor with such-and-such a 'hero' or 'character'. It is not even a bad thing – at least now and then – for the protagonist to be unsympathetic, irritating; this helps to accentuate the distance. The spectator weighs the pros and the cons; he waits for the play to offer him arguments, but it does so only in a way which delays judgement, or provokes judgement without laying down what it should be. A dialogue between the spectator and the spectacle (one dare not say author) is established which brings a growing tension, relieved by musical interludes (the 'songs').[37] The spectator cannot relax. He is not allowed to. He must take sides. Political, public, contradictory, the play is fundamentally no different from a meeting. The paradox here is that Brecht – who was never a politician, who was never a member of the Communist Party, who had difficulties with the East German authorities – nevertheless offers a model for a political art to which taking sides and making a stand are fundamental. Genuinely so: making the audience do so, without presenting it as a *fait accompli*, without explaining it or imposing it dogmatically. Hence the misunderstandings about him, which were as painful as they were ridiculous.

Far from attempting to purify passions and emotions – except in the most fundamental sense of delivering them from the realm of magic – Brechtian stage narrative stirs them up. Thus it condenses a becoming analogous with practical becoming: the exploration of potentialities, the transition from possibilities to actions and decisions. The denouement is the moment when a judgement is passed, a stand made, a side taken. Therefore the object of the play is something unknown and something strange: an event in the historical sense, a social man, rather than a 'plot' or 'situation' given or determinable in the relationships between the characters. Thus the action can very easily be cut up into distinct moments, into relatively independent 'scenes'. It loses the classical characteristics of unity and continuous movement, where a *coup de théâtre* is like a sudden blow on the kettledrums in a symphony: neither interrupts the unity of the whole. There is no internal conflict resolved by the supreme moment of denouement or death. The action is happening more inside the spectator than physically on the stage.

22

Let us sum up. Classical theatre transcended everyday life: by using heroes, situations, the formal logic of the Unities. It purified it; it represented it while filtering its impurities, investing it with noble, majestic outlines. It projected it along a continuous line and within a rigorous framework. It criticized it from outside, using metaphysical or religious norms (which historically were basically the 'values' of the dominant classes). It imposed an identification between the spectator and the Hero, his will, his conflicts, his struggle – an identification which included the espousal of accepted norms and values. It is precisely in this way that classical art sanctioned and consecrated one particular aspect of everyday life, a negative one: the magic of participation and ritual.

Brecht's epic theatre immerses itself in everyday life, at the level of everyday life, in other words at the level of the masses (not simply the masses of individuals, but the masses of instants and moments, of events and actions). Thus it appears as a democratic revolution in the art of the theatre. It breaks with the theatre of illusions as it does with the (Naturalist) theatre which imitates life. It does not purify the everyday; and yet it clarifies its contradictions. In its own way, it filters it. It throws its weak part away: the magical part. Thus the Brechtian dramatic image differs from what we called the *reverse image* in Chaplin. Brecht aims (and he has said so) at an image which will *master* the facts. Nevertheless he has used the reverse image procedure on occasion (in *Mahagonny*, for example).

Are Brecht's high ambitions justified? Did he achieve his goal?

There is no shortage of objections. In the first place his theatre is intended to be physical, direct, and thus popular, but parts of it appear to be excessively intellectual. Nowhere – even in Germany – does it seem to have become truly popular. The spectator wavers between an externalized judgement – an intellectual state which implies high culture – and an immersion in the image proposed. Perhaps this is what the dialectic of the *Verfremdungseffekt* is. The spectator is meant to *disalienate* himself in and through the consciousness of alienation. He is meant to feel wrenched from his self but only in order to enter more effectively into his self and become conscious of the real and the contradictions of the real. Unfortunately, there is a risk that this process will take on the disturbing form, worse even than classic identification, of *fascination*. Whether it be to compare them or contrast the two,

French partisans of Brecht's theatre nearly always refer to Antonin Artaud's theatre of cruelty. The violence of dramatic effects, of the lighting, of the images, make it even more impossible for the spectator to relax his mind and momentarily resolve his inner tension by identifying with the hero or by escaping into a kind of dream. There is a danger that unity will be re-established momentarily in the spectator's disorientated mind, caught up as he is by the image; for tension needs moments of respite; expectation demands to be satisfied, if only fleetingly. Unable to find this in a 'classic' completeness, there is a danger that he will look for them in a sort of bloody ecstasy. Therefore generalized strangeness entails a danger (which was avoided by Brecht, but not necessarily by the people who produce his plays or write about them). An art based on alienation must struggle against alienation; if not it sanctions it. Significantly some of his French commentators translate *Verfremdungseffekt* as 'effet d'aliénation'.[38] It would be another paradox, and a very strange one, if this new art were to sanction alienation by giving it all the glamour of violence. In *Danton's Death*, tragedy and fascination are grounded in the irremediable triviality of everyday life:

> DANTON: Time loses us. – This is very tedious – we put the shirt on first, then we pull the trousers up over it, and every night we crawl into bed, and every morning we crawl out again, and we always put one foot down in front of the other. And it doesn't look as if it's ever going to be any different.[39]

Criticism of life by death – surely the last word in lucidity.

We should add that the spectator cannot effectively be transformed into a historian of the event (or action or decision), since the historian's attitude is defined in terms of knowledge and not of art. Moreover, to make judgements – in life – is not the same as adopting the attitude of a Judge. The Judge's attitude excludes sudden surprises, amazement, expectation. The professional Judge pronounces according to written evidence, he applies the law, he takes the event as having actually happened. Impassive by definition, impartial by principle, he decides without taking sides. Such is his duty. And if he behaves otherwise, it is because he has fallen foul of the contradictions of the Law, of Justice, of truth. In which case it is the Judge's turn to be put on trial.

Thus it is that the functions of the critique of everyday life can be determined by reference to an art which immerses itself in everyday life. To be creative in art one must seek a certain pathway, committing oneself to it and pointing the way towards it. The philosopher still has a part to play, by pointing out the risks, the dangers; and how a straight line – a linear orientation, without deviations, without meanders – is generally a practical impossibility.

This is the place, or the moment, to mention one of the most gifted up-and-coming French authors: Roger Vailland.[40] This is not only because he has defended classicism against Brecht,[41] but also and above all because Vailland the novelist has his own problem: that of confronting everyday life with a 'vision', or with images, from somewhere else. Roger Vailland's formative reading was Stendhal and Laclos. He modelled himself on them, and still carries them in his head, even when he is no longer actually using them as models. Thus his attempts to grasp everyday triviality (real, apparent, or both) are honed by a sensibility derived from classical humanism, a carefully cultivated eroticism, an almost Romantic novelistic 'vision'. On top of that, he has read the Marxists. Such are the analytic tools with which he hopes to come to grips with the everyday. The resultant – fruitful – contradictions give his attempts great interest beyond whatever specifically literary qualities his books may have.

Thus *325,000 francs*[42] is a novel which is very close to the (apparently) most ordinary kind of everyday life: that of a moulder in a plastics factory. Someone has said that he wrote it for a bet: to write a romantic novel about overtime.

A simple, solid, healthy proletarian is in love with a girl (a working girl, but an isolated one, a dressmaker) who, after playing the field, uses her rather advanced feminine wiles to trap a husband. She teases him, and leads him on through the *classic* stages of courtship – almost of the *pays du Tendre*[43] – to force him to marry her. Roger Vailland thus manages to situate his refined eroticism at the centre of a novel dealing with the everyday life of the proletariat ...

Aroused, and very much in love (and yet aware of what the girl really is – and in this respect reminiscent of the hero of a classical play), the boy knows that to have the woman he loves he will have to marry her, and that to marry her he will have to leave his class. He would probably aspire to leave it anyway, but surely not at the risk of his life or health. Thus the woman plays the traditional female role – a role which is certainly still a real one – of an ambiguous figure who excites contradictory actions and thoughts.

The boy seeks fame and fortune in sport and becomes a racing cyclist. When this fails, he is forced to work night and day to earn enough to 'settle down' with his beautiful but demanding lady. It costs him a hand, his health, and his physical mobility.

The drama of everyday proletarian life is treated here with true artistry, and this makes the book a work of art. Roger Vailland has captured his subject in such a way as to make it at once flimsy, transparent and profound. The book is written like a musical composition, an opera, with an overture to whet our appetites, containing the themes, presenting the characters and foreshadowing the continuation and conclusion: a cycle race, watched by the girl who is also the prize, in which the boy makes a heroic effort, only to fall, injure himself, and lose.

In this book, as in Vailland's earlier novels, the author appears as such. He says: 'I'. He intervenes as a witness, designating the characters and situating them, entering into a dialogue with them, inviting the reader to decide what attitude to adopt towards them: what judgement to make. Here judgement is inseparable from event; it is rigorously included in the story. This authorial presence has various meanings, and not simply on the level of technique. It is Roger Vailland's way – and a very simple way it is – of resolving a difficult literary problem, that of novelistic consciousness or of consciousness in the novel. Who is speaking? Who is seeing, who saw the actions in the story? Who bridges the gap between the lived and the true? How has the speaker seen or heard about the things he narrates? How has he been able to foretell or sense what will happen next? Who has detected the characters' motives (hidden even to themselves)? And as he is drawn on by the great movement called 'reading', with whom does the reader identify, in whose consciousness does he participate?

Roger Vailland's solution, the novel as first-person evidence, is not without its drawbacks. It corresponds too closely to the general tendency to bring the novel nearer to journalism and autobiography. Inevitably, as soon as he begins extending his narration, the author will start introducing scenes from which he was absent; or else he will write sentences which are incompatible with his main guidelines and techniques. 'At the same instant, she saw her father's face again ...'[44]

The presence of the author situates the characters, placing them constantly before our eyes, not too near and not too far away: *at a reasonable distance*. For Roger Vailland this has the advantage of piquing the reader's interest. And yet the use of his own consciousness as a witness – and virtually as a judge – would remain contemplative and formal if it did not have a solid content: the totality of human and social relations as manifested in the everyday life of a village, a factory, a small industrial town. Conversely, this knowledge of 'modern' everyday life, superimposed as it is upon a great familiarity with classical culture, is characterized by a certain externality of consciousness on the part of the 'knower' or witness. The author's use of the first person thus has a deeper meaning than simply the solving of a problem of novelistic technique. The author is present because in himself he contributes something irreplaceable; because he comes from somewhere else; because he introduces into a certain kind of everyday experience a lucidity and a recognition which it did not previously contain. Consciousness presents itself in the novel in this way because this is how it occurs in life: at one and the same time *from without and from within.*

We could show here, not without a certain irony, that Roger Vailland the novelist is to some extent doing what Roger Vailland the writer on drama and the critic of Brecht is rejecting. He composes his novels in an 'operatic' mode. He inserts scenes which are almost independent, and which as it happens are virtually scenes from a play: weddings, dances, arguments or brawls in pubs, jealous rows, etc. As a witness he passes judgement, and makes the reader take sides: making him pass judgement. Supported by details borrowed from everyday life,[45] the narrative has a spontaneous tendency to become epic. As the critic of *L'Express* observed on 27 November 1954, *Beau Masque* is 'an excellent epic narrative'.

That Roger Vailland, with all his idiosyncratic qualities and faults, should be much closer to Brecht than he thinks is really rather curious. It must surely be indicative of one of the requirements of everyday life – or more exactly of the aesthetic representation – in drama or in the novel – of everyday life.

Ulysses demonstrates that a great novel can be boring. And 'profoundly' boring. Joyce nevertheless understood one thing: that the report of a day in the life of an ordinary man had to be predominantly in the epic mode.

Finally, to clarify a few ideas, and above all to amuse the reader, here are two extracts from modern Anglo-Saxon authors. The first attacks American everyday life with a black and chilling irony. By contrast the second, by a famous and talented English woman writer, uses an acute sensitivity to show the subtle richness of the everyday:

The subway, Archer thought, was the only place to read today's newspapers. Underground, in a bad light, at an increased fare, with all the passengers fearing the worst about each other. Everyone suspecting the man next to him of preparing to pick a pocket, commit a nuisance, carry a lighted cigar, pinch a girl, ask for a job, run for a vacant seat, block the door at the station at which you wanted to leave the train. Archer put the paper down and looked around at his fellow passengers. They do not look American, he thought; perhaps I shall report them to the proper authorities.[46] ... Archer walked down Fifth Avenue, past the shops with their windows full of dresses, coats and furs, and the women rushing in and out of the doors, their faces lit with the light of purchase. It is the new profession of the female sex, he thought – buying. If you wanted to set up an exhibition to show modern American women in their natural habitat, engaged in their most characteristic function, he thought, like the tableaux in the Museum of Natural History in which stuffed bears are shown against a background of caves, opening up honeycombs, you would have a set of stuffed women, slender, high-heeled, rouged, waved, hot-eyed, buying a cocktail dress in a department store. In the background, behind the salesgirls and the racks and shelves, there would be bombs bursting, cities crumbling, scientists measuring the half-life of tritium and radioactive cobalt. The garment would be democratically medium-priced and the salesgirl would be just as pretty as the customer and, to the naked eye at least, just as well dressed, to show that the benefits of a free society extended from one end of the economic spectrum to the other.[47]

One goes into the room – but the resources of the English language would be much put to the stretch, and whole flights of words would need to wing their way illegitimately into existence before a woman could say what happens when she goes into a room. The rooms differ so completely; they are calm or thunderous; open on to the sea, or, on the contrary, give on to a prison yard; are hung with washing; or alive with opals and silks; are hard as horsehair or soft as feathers –...[48]

IV Work and Leisure in Everyday Life

Throughout history, criticism of everyday life has been carried on in a number of ways: by philosophy and contemplation, dream and art, violent political or warlike action. By flight and escape.

These criticisms have a common element: they were the work of particularly gifted, lucid and active *individuals* (the philosopher, the poet, etc.). However, this individual lucidity or activeness concealed an appearance or an illusion, and therefore a hidden, deeper reality. In truth their work belonged to a time and a class whose ideas were thus raised above the everyday onto the level of the exceptional and the dominant. Hence the criticism of everyday life was in fact *a criticism of other classes*, and for the most part found its expression in contempt for productive labour; at best it criticized the life of the dominant class in the name of a transcendental philosophy or dogma, which nevertheless still belonged to that class. This is how we must understand the criticism of the 'world' and the 'mundane' carried out from the Middle Ages until the era – the bourgeois eighteenth century – when the 'mundane' element burst forth into art and philosophy.

In our era, one of the most recent forms which criticism of everyday life has taken is criticism of the *real* by the *surreal.* By abandoning the everyday in order to find the marvellous and the surprising (at one and the same time immanent in the real and transcending it), Surrealism rendered triviality unbearable.[49] This was a good thing, but it had a negative side: transcendental contempt for the real, for *work* for example (the long-inevitable rift between Surrealists and Marxists took place during a memorable meeting of the Association of Writers and Revolutionary Artists (AEAR) over the Soviet film *Road to Life*).[50]

And yet, be he an author or not, the man of our times carries out in his own way, spontaneously, the critique of *his* everyday life. And this critique of the everyday plays an integral part in the everyday: it is achieved in and by *leisure activities*.

The relation between leisure and the everyday is not a simple one: the two words are at one and the same time united and contradictory (therefore their relation is dialectical). It cannot be reduced to the simple relation in time between 'Sunday' and 'weekdays', represented as external and merely different. Leisure – to accept the concept uncritically for the moment – cannot be separated from work. After his work is over, when resting or relaxing or occupying himself in his own particular way, a man is still the same man. Every day, at the same time, the worker leaves the factory, the office worker leaves the office. Every week Saturdays and Sundays are given over to leisure as regularly as day-to-day work. We must therefore imagine a 'work–leisure' unity, for this unity exists, and everyone tries to programme the amount of time at his disposal according to what his work is – and what it is not. Sociology should therefore study the way the life of workers as such, their place in the division of labour and in the social system, is 'reflected' in leisure activities, or at least in what they demand of leisure.

Historically, *in real individuality* and its development, the 'work–leisure' relation has always presented itself in a contradictory way.

Until the advent of bourgeois society, individuality, or rather personality[51] could only really develop outside productive labour. In Antiquity, in the Middle Ages, and even during the period when bourgeois social relations still retained aspects of the social relations bequeathed by feudalism – in the seventeenth century of the *honnête homme* – the man who was able to develop himself never worked.

However, whether they were aristocrats, clerks still tied to feudalism, or bourgeois *honnêtes hommes*, such men only *appeared* to remain outside the social division of labour and social practice. In reality they were prisoners of the separation of manual and intellectual work. Moreover, directly or not, consciously or not, they had a social function, if only on the ideological level. Leonardo da Vinci was an engineer as well as an artist. Rabelais was a doctor and then a writer, at once an encyclopedic brain and an epic novelist. Montaigne worked in local government. And Descartes was an army officer before becoming a scholar ... In so far as the man of those times was *genuinely* separated from social practice and devoted to leisure alone – to laziness – he was doomed both in a personal sense and from the point of view of class.

Another element must be considered which makes the question even more complicated. In those eras, in those modes of production, productive labour was merged with everyday life: consider the lives of peasants and craftsmen, for example. What distinguishes peasant life so profoundly from the life of industrial workers, even today, is precisely this inherence of productive activity in their life in its entirety. The workplace is all around the house; work is not separate from the everyday life of the family. Formerly the imperatives of the peasant community (the village) regulated not only the way work and domestic life were organized, but festivals as well. Thus up to a point a way of living which strictly speaking did not belong to any one individual, but more to a group of men committed to the ties – and limits – of their community or guild, could be developed.

With bourgeois society these various elements and their relations were overturned: in one sense they became differentiated, separate, in another they came to constitute a unified whole. Bourgeois society reasserted the value of labour, above all during the period of its ascendancy; but at the historical moment when the relation between labour and the concrete development of individuality was emerging, labour took on an increasingly fragmented character. At the same time the individual, more and more involved in complex social relations, became isolated and inward-looking. Individual consciousness split into two (into the private consciousness and the social or public consciousness); it also became atomized (individualism, specialization, separation between differing spheres of activity, etc.). Thus at the same time a distinction was made between man 'as man' on the one hand and the working man on the other (more clearly among the bourgeoisie, of course, than among the proletariat). Family life became separate from productive activity. And so did leisure.

As a result there is a certain obscurity in the very concept of *everyday life*. Where is it to be found? In work or in leisure? In family life and in moments 'lived' outside of culture? Initially the answer seems obvious. Everyday life involves all three elements, all three aspects. It is their unity and their totality, and it determines the concrete individual. And yet this answer is not entirely satisfactory. Where does the living contact between the concrete individual man and other human beings operate? In fragmented labour? In family life? In leisure? Where is it acted out in the most concrete way? Are there several modes of contact? Can they be schematized as representational models? Or must they be reduced to fixed behaviour patterns? Are they contradictory or complementary? How do they relate? What is the decisive essential sector? Where are we to situate the poverty and wealth of this everyday life which we know to be both infinitely rich (potentially at least) and infinitely poor, bare, alienated; which we know we must reveal to itself and transform so that its richness can become actualized and developed in a renewed culture? ...

The discreteness of the elements of the everyday (work – family and 'private' life – leisure activities) implies an alienation; and perhaps at the same time a differentiation – certain fruitful contradictions. In any event, like all ensembles (or totalities), it must be studied in terms of the interrelation of its elements.

The social history of leisure shows that during the course of a development in which its various stages may have overlapped or contradicted each other, it has been transformed in fact as well as in theory,[52] and new needs have come into being.

At first, leisure gives rise to an undifferentiated global activity which is difficult to distinguish from other aspects of the everyday (family strolls on Sunday, walking).

On a higher level, leisure involves passive attitudes. Someone sitting in front of a cinema screen offers an example and a common model of this passivity, the potentially 'alienating' nature of which is immediately apparent. It is particularly easy to exploit these attitudes commercially.[53] Finally, on the highest level of all, leisure produces active attitudes, very specialized personal occupations, linked to techniques and consequently involving a technical element independent of any professional specialization (photography, for example). This is a cultivated or cultural leisure.

This brief examination immediately reveals the contradictory character of leisure, both in terms of itself and in relation to the everyday. Leisure embraces opposing possibilities and orientations, of which some tend to impoverish through passivity while others are more enriching. Some are undifferentiated (although they may still be worthwhile on a certain level), others very much the reverse. And while some involve escape into a vacuum, others rediscover 'nature', an immediate, sensory life, through what is sometimes a highly developed technical expertise (organized sports or amateur films, for example).

Therefore, with its fragmentation of labour, modern industrial civilization creates both a *general need for leisure* and differentiated *concrete needs* within that general framework.

Leisure is a remarkable example of a new social need with a *spontaneous* character which social organization, by offering it various means of satisfaction, has directed, sharpened, shifted and modified. In response to such new needs, our civilization creates techniques which nevertheless have an 'extra-technical' meaning and character. It produces 'leisure machines' (radio, television, etc.). It creates new types of play which transform the old ones, sometimes conflicting with other activities, sometimes overlapping (in the camping holiday, work and leisure are barely distinguishable, and everyday life in its entirety becomes play). Concrete social needs are determined in a way which increasingly differentiates them according to age, sex and group. They also fall spontaneously into the categories of individual needs and collective needs (for example, the distinction between individual sports and team sports).

There is no doubt that today – in capitalist, bourgeois *society*, which has its own way of manipulating the needs arising from a specific level of *civilization* – the most striking imperative as far as the needs of leisure among the masses are concerned is that it must produce a *break*. Leisure must break with the everyday (or at least appear to do so) and not only as far as work is concerned, but also for day-to-day family life. Thus there is an increasing emphasis on leisure characterized as distraction: rather than bringing any new worries, obligations, or necessities, leisure should offer liberation from worry and necessity. Liberation and pleasure – such are the essential characteristics of leisure, according to the parties concerned.[54] There is no more of a sense of genuine 'leisure' about a family get-together than there is about gardening or doing odd jobs around the house. So those involved tend to reject ambiguous forms of leisure which might resemble work or entail some kind of obligation. The cultural aspect strikes them as being irrelevant (which is not to say that *it really is so*). They mistrust anything which might appear to be educational and are more concerned with those aspects of leisure which might offer *distraction*, *entertainment* and *repose*, and which *might compensate* for the difficulties of everyday life. If we are to believe the subjective opinions revealed by surveys, this is as true for workers (proletarians) as it is for the other social classes.

It is thus not the work of art, in so far as it has a role to play in everyday life (the picture or the reproduction hanging in the bedroom), that is liable to constitute an element of leisure. Nor armchair reading, unless it provides thrills or escapism (travel books, stories about exploration, or crime novels), or relaxation (picture books, strip cartoons, or 'readers' digests' – evoking nothing so much as pre-digested food). The constitutive elements of leisure are more likely to be images and films. And images and films which are (or at least appear to be) as far away from *real life* as possible.

The first obvious thing that the so-called 'modern' man around us expects of leisure is that it should stop him from being tired and tense, from being anxious, worried and preoccupied. To use a term which is now very widely used by the public at large, he craves *relaxation*. There is a veritable ideology, and a technicity, and a technocracy of relaxation (which is obtained by a variety of procedures, some passive, ridding life of its content, creating a vacuum – others active, exerting control over actions and muscles). Thus the so-called 'modern' man expects to find something in leisure which his work and his family or 'private' life do not provide. Where is his happiness to be found? He hardly knows, and does not even ask himself. In this way a 'world of leisure' tends to come into being entirely outside of the everyday realm, and so purely artificial that it borders on the ideal. But how can this pure artificiality be created without permanent reference to ordinary life, without the constantly renewed contrast that will embody this reference?

There are plenty of examples in the past of art aiming to embellish everyday life by skilfully transposing it: presenting it in a flattering light, imposing a style on it while acknowledging its real achievements – Flemish and Dutch painting, for example. What is new today in bourgeois society is that a complete break has become imperative (a fact that constitutes a serious obstacle for any attempt at realism in art). Consequently the art of obtaining this break is now a specific and eagerly exploited commercial technique. Clever images of the *everyday* are supplied *on a day-to-day basis*, images that can make the ugly beautiful, the empty full, the sordid elevated – and the hideous 'fascinating'. These images so skilfully and so persuasively exploit the demands and dissatisfactions which every 'modern' man carries within himself that it is indeed very difficult to resist being seduced and fascinated by them, except by becoming rigidly puritanical, and, in rejecting 'sensationalism', rejecting 'the present' and life itself.

The sudden eruption of sexuality in the domain of the image – and more generally in leisure – calls for an investigation in its own right. Our era has witnessed the demise of a certain number of ridiculous taboos – which before becoming ridiculous were very serious indeed – which had imposed a ban on sexual matters, on clothes that externalized sexual characteristics, on bodies, on nudity. And yet it still produces a shock whenever this ban is transgressed, as though it were still in force. Images with a (more or less explicit) erotic meaning, or simply the display of a woman's body, are violently attractive. The excessive use of such images in advertising has not yet exhausted the effect they have on us, and we may conclude that they correspond to something profound. Displays of sexuality and nudity break with everyday life, and provide the sense of a break which people look for in leisure: reading, shows, etc.[55] On posters, in shop windows, on the covers of magazines, in films, everywhere there are unclothed women. It is a kind of escapism which from certain angles is more like a generalized neurosis: this sexuality is depressing, this eroticism is weary and wearying, mechanical. There is nothing really sensual in this unbridled sexuality, and that is probably its most profound characteristic. From this point of view, we will not criticize eroticism for being immoral, or immodest, or corrupting to children, etc. We leave that to other people. What we will criticize 'modern' eroticism for is its lack of genuine sensuality, a sensuality which implies beauty or charm, passion or modesty, power over the object of desire, and fulfilment. With 'modern' eroticism we step outside of the everyday, without actually leaving it: it shocks, it seems brutal, and yet this effect is superficial, pure appearance, leading us back towards the secret of the everyday – dissatisfaction.

Chaplin gave us a *genuine reverse image* of modern times: its image seen through a living man, through his sufferings, his tribulations, his victories. We are now entering the vast domain of the *illusory reverse image*. What we find is a false world: firstly because it is not a world, and because it presents itself as true, and because it mimics real life closely in order to replace the real by its opposite; by replacing real unhappiness by fictions of happiness, for example – by offering a fiction in response to the real need for happiness – and so on. This is the 'world' of most films, most of the press, the theatre, the music hall: of a large sector of leisure activities.

How strange the split between the real world and its reverse image is. For in the end it is not strange at all, but a false strangeness, a cheap-and-nasty, all-pervasive mystery.[56]

Of course, the fictional and mystifying 'world' of leisure is not limited to the exploitation of sex, sentimentality and crime. Sport too will have to be scrutinized.

Sport has developed by presenting itself as the culture of the body, of individual energy and team spirit: as a school for health. What have these lofty ambitions achieved? A vast social organization (commercialized or not) and a great and often magnificently spectacular *mise en scène* devoted to competitiveness. The vocabulary is not without its humour. People who go to the races and bet on their favourite horse are known officially as 'sportsmen'. Every football club has its 'supporters'[57] and a supporter can be someone who has never kicked a ball in his life. He goes to the match in his car, or by bus or the metro. He participates in the action and plays sport via an intermediary. He quivers with enthusiasm, he fidgets frenetically, but he never moves from his seat. A curious kind of 'alienation'. Sport is an activity which is apparently incompatible with illusion, and yet in fact it confronts us with a reverse image, a compensation for everyday life.

So the analysis of the relation between the needs of leisure and the other areas which globally make up everyday life presents many difficult problems. It is not sufficient simply to describe the facts. To obtain an analysis of content, we need a conceptual apparatus to supplement description. In particular the philosophical concept of alienation is essential. In a sense it has been introduced from outside, but placed in the context of sociology it becomes scientific and allows the sociology of everyday life to become a science as well as a critique.

Georges Friedmann[58] has undertaken a long and very richly documented investigation into human labour in which he has attempted to pose the problem of the relations between leisure and work.

In substance, this work (*Où va le travail humain*) identifies leisure with freedom and work with necessity. Every day the sum total of techniques is transforming the conditions of existence. 'Every instant of life is more and more penetrated by them' and the *technical environment* surrounding man is becoming more substantial by the day.[59] The notion of a technical environment generalizes the relation between man and machine and extends it to everyday life. However, the sciences of man, whose right to examine mechanization and its effects cannot be contested,[60] themselves modify the technical environment. They do this by an intellectual, moral and social reassertion of the value of labour which 'tightens the link of interest between the worker and society, by strengthening the incentives which justify his work, even if it is fragmented, and integrate him within a collectivity'.[61] The human problem is therefore a dual one: on the one hand how to organize labour rationally, and on the other how to organize leisure rationally – especially 'compensatory leisure', in which the workers can express their personality.[62] It would seem therefore that freedom in and through work comes principally from the intervention of psycho-technical or sociological theoreticians, in a word from an intervention of the 'sciences of man applied to industrial labour',[63] which assures freedom 'in so far as it exists in this domain' – which according to Friedmann is not very far. For the technical environment is following its destiny. It characterizes not only capitalist society,[64] but also industrial civilization as a whole.

Only the domain of leisure escapes the technical environment, escapes necessity, in other words, escapes depersonalization. In our leisure activities we are already beyond techniques. We achieve a leap from necessity into freedom, from the enslavement of the individual into whatever will permit his self-development.

Georges Friedmann has had the indisputable merit of posing problems and posing them in a wide-ranging way. He takes Marx's arguments about the worker alienated by a labour which is itself alienated and renders them concrete in terms of the era we live in. (For Marx, however, the alienation of the worker by fragmented labour and machines is only one aspect of a larger – a total – alienation which as such is inherent in capitalist society and in man's exploitation of man.)

It is certain that the development of the productive forces (in other words of techniques) has consequences within the *social relations* structurally linked to these techniques. Many Marxists have shut themselves away in a class subjectivism; their understanding of the social relations of production (in capitalist regimes) is restricted to and blinkered by the notion of class struggle. They have thus neglected to study the relations of production in so far as they are linked with the development of the productive forces. And this despite what Lenin had to say on the subject. Analysing monopoly capitalism, he demonstrated that 'underlying this interlocking ... its very base, are the changing social relations of production ... it becomes evident that we have socialisation of production ... that private economic and private property relations constitute a shell which no longer fits its contents'.[65] By starting from an abstract notion of the class struggle, some Marxists have neglected not only to study the recent modifications of capitalism as such, but also the 'socialization of production', and the new contents of specifically capitalist relations. Such a study could perhaps have modified the notion of class struggle, leading to the discovery of new forms of struggle.

These questions have been put by 'industrial sociology'. Has it resolved them accurately and completely? That is another matter. The undisputed fact is that since Marx's analyses, and since Lenin's, the productive forces have developed, and this economic fact cannot but have had consequences on the level of social phenomena.

Rather than resolving all the problems, Marx's statements about labour and its relation with leisure inaugurated an area of research. He predicted that work would become man's foremost need. The formula is only superficially clear. Objectively, for society, for the social man, for the 'collective worker', work has always been the foremost need. Does Marx mean that the *individual* man will transform this objective need into an essentially subjective one? So that by and in this work he will eliminate alienation? No doubt, but the formula is difficult to accept in relation to 'modern' fragmented labour. Moreover, if we put ourselves at the vanguard of technique and the modern productive forces, and consider the implications of automation, then we will need to interpret it afresh. For automation and transfer-machines tend to differentiate labour by splitting it into very highly skilled work and work for which no skill at all is required.

We may certainly affirm that work is the foundation of personal development within social practice. It links the individual with the other workers (on the shop floor, in the social class, in the social system) and also with knowledge; it is through work that the multi-technical education which controls the sum total of the productive processes and social practice is made possible, and necessary. And yet the fulfilment of these possibilities presents considerable difficulties. And under no circumstances can the 'bitty' character of labour be seen as conducive to the development of personality: whatever its social and political context, it is 'alienating'.

Elsewhere Marx wrote that 'this always remains a realm of necessity. *The true realm of freedom, the development of human powers as an end in itself, begins beyond it, though it can only flourish with this realm of necessity as its basis.* The reduction of the working day is the basic prerequisite.'[66] Therefore, according to Marx, the development of the need for leisure and the needs of leisure is deeply significant. Recent French sociology, and Georges Friedmann, have been right to bring this to the fore. But once that has been said, ought we to accept unreservedly the notion of leisure as the breakthrough of freedom into necessity? Or as a leap from necessity into freedom? As Marx said (and as Hegel said before him), necessity does not disappear in freedom, and freedom relies upon necessity. We cannot conceive of them as external to one other, except relatively. The notion of free leisure is valid up to a certain point. Beyond that point it is inadequate. If we push it too far we run the risk of forgetting that there can be *alienation in leisure just as in work* (and alienation precisely in so far as the worker is trying to 'disalienate' himself!).

Thus the dialectical analysis of leisure and its relation with work (an analysis which is an integral part of the critique of everyday life) would seem in some ways to complement the investigations of both the 'industrial sociologists' and the 'sociologists of leisure'.

Within the framework of bourgeois society (and the capitalist regime) work is lived and undergone by the worker as an alien and oppressive power. Not only do the technical division and the social division of labour overlap and impose themselves on him without his knowing the reasons why, but also he knows that he is not working for himself, either directly or indirectly. Moreover the fragmented character of individual labour is in fact interdependent with the increasingly complete socialization of productive labour. Fragmentation and socialization are the dialectically contradictory aspects of the labour process wherever the productive forces are highly developed. Fragmented labour can only be meaningful and productive within global or total labour. Thus for the worker a dual need develops in respect of his own labour.

On the one hand, the worker aspires to a *knowledge* of the system in which he plays an integral part: a firm, and also a global society. And this is already a means of not submitting, a freeing himself from imposed constraints, of mastering necessity. In capitalist firms this confused but real aspiration is answered in a mystifying way by 'human relations' and 'public relations'.[67] Marxists who have criticized these recent, originally American, institutions have made the mistake of merely seeing the ideology they embody, and of ignoring the fact that they correspond to a real *social need*, born precisely from the socialization of labour. They have disregarded this socialization of labour, imagining that it happens only in socialist regimes, whereas it is in fact also a function of the development of the productive forces. They have not understood that in socialism knowledge satisfies a need which under capitalism is answered by an ideology. Reciprocally, the mistake of the non-Marxist industrial sociologists has been that they have not always shown that these innovations (human relations, etc.) were responding to needs purely in order to harness them, twist them, deflect them from their meaning, by reducing them to the dimensions of the firm and to cooperation with the employers.

Moreover, the worker craves a sharp break with his work, a compensation. He looks for this in leisure seen as entertainment or distraction.

In this way leisure appears as the non-everyday in the everyday.

We cannot step beyond the everyday. The marvellous can only continue to exist in fiction and the illusions that people share. There is no escape. And yet we wish to have the illusion of escape as near to hand as possible. An illusion not entirely illusory, but constituting a 'world' both apparent and real (the reality of appearances and the apparently real) quite different from the everyday world yet as open-ended and as closely dovetailed into the everyday as possible. So we work to earn our leisure, and leisure has only one meaning: to get away from work. A vicious circle.

Thus is established a complex of activities and passivities, of forms of sociability and communication which the sociologist can study. Although he cannot describe or analyse them without criticizing them as being (partially) illusory, he must nevertheless start from the fact that they contain within themselves their own spontaneous critique of the everyday. They *are* that critique in so far as they are *other* than everyday life, and yet they are *in everyday life*, they are *alienation*. They can thus hold a real content, correspond to a real need, yet still retain an illusory form and a deceptive appearance.

Thus leisure and work and 'private life' make up a dialectical system, a global structure. Through this global structure we can reconstruct a historically real picture of man and the human at a certain step in their development: at a certain stage of alienation and disalienation.

Examples? Some are to be found in the present volume. Others will be analysed in the next. Let us list them briefly:

The café: generally an extra-familial and extra-professional meeting place, where people come together on the basis of personal affinities (in principle and at least apparently), because they have the same street or the same neighbourhood in common rather than the same profession or class (although there do exist cafés where the clients are pre-dominantly of the same class or profession). It is a place where the regulars can find a certain luxury, if only on the surface; where they can speak *freely* (about politics, women, etc.), and where if what is said may be superficial, the freedom to say it is fiercely defended; *where they play.*

The funfair: a people's event whose survival and indeed industrialization have occasioned much astonishment. The noise and the deafening music supply the required break. Here we enter a humble, restless microcosm, extraordinary and vulgar. And apparently cheap. Only things which might remind us of work are excluded from this microcosm. In it we find knowledge (the aquarium, anatomical displays), eroticism (naked dancers), travel, wonders, departures, sport, etc.

Radio and, even more so, television, the sudden violent intrusion of the whole world into family and 'private' life, 'presentified' in a way which directly captures the immediate moment, which offers truth and participation, or at least appears to do so ...

Here again we come up against certain characteristics specific to cultural or cultivated leisure. These forms of leisure have functions which are both new and traditional (comparable with reading books, listening to songs and poems, or perhaps dancing as it used to be). Their content is not only entertainment and relaxation, but also knowledge. They do not exclude productive activities – specialized techniques – but they control them. Sometimes it is a matter of techniques which have been rendered obsolete by production and which have become or are in the process of becoming sports (sailing, for example). Finally, as we have already mentioned, the ultimate characteristic of such cultivated leisure activities is that they lead us back towards the feeling of presence, towards nature and the life of the senses (or, as the experts would say, towards an audio-visual milieu revitalized by modern techniques).

Of all the leisure activities concrete sociology should scrutinize, there is one which nowadays seems particularly remarkable.

Everyone knows that for more than a century the French school of painting has enjoyed world-wide renown. But do enough people realize that in France painting is becoming a mass art? That France – for reasons which as yet remain obscure – is becoming a nation of painters? 'Sunday painters', people who spend their leisure time painting, exist in their tens and perhaps hundreds of thousands. Innumerable local or corporate 'art exhibitions' are held. Thus, at a very high cultural level, leisure transcends technical activity to become art. On this level it seems to be using a certain means of expression in order to re-establish a hold on life in its entirety. In this context leisure involves an original search – whether clumsy or skilful is unimportant – for a style of living. And perhaps for an art of living, for a kind of happiness.

To sum up, work, leisure, family life and private life make up a whole which we can call a 'global structure' or 'totality' on condition that we emphasize its historical, shifting, transitory nature. If we consider the critique of everyday life as an aspect of a concrete sociology we can envisage a vast enquiry which will look at professional life, family life and leisure activities in terms of their many-sided interactions. Our particular concern will be to extract what is living, new, positive – the worthwhile needs and fulfilments – from the negative elements: the alienations.

V   Some Overviews on the 'Modern World'

As I look up from writing these pages, I see before me one of the loveliest landscapes in the suburbs of Paris. In the distance, the long, lazy curve of the Seine, calm and blue, with its strings of barges. Rows of sparkling cars are driving across the pont de Saint-Cloud. A hill to the left, another to the right. On these hills, groves of trees, gardens, meadows, the last remnants of royal or princely domains. On their island, between the noble lines of these hillsides, I can see the concentrated power of the Renault factories. But nearer, tumbling down the groove of the valley of the Sèvre like insects, in a prosaic disorder, little houses separated by kitchen gardens where guard-dogs bark and cats wail at night. They are called 'pavilions', but no irony is intended. Between these pavilions lie alleyways, muddy paths where the puddles are never dry. Their owners' superficiality oozes forth in an abundance of ridiculous details, china animals on the roofs, glass globes and well-pruned shrubs along the miniature paths, plaques adorned with mottos, self-important pediments. From my window I can see a huge notice nailed to a tree in one of the kitchen gardens, proclaiming: 'Danger of death. Keep out.' On Sunday mornings, especially when the weather is fine, these little houses open their entrails to the sun with strings of red eiderdowns, sheets, blankets. They spread over the hillside like hundreds of dead chickens in an immense shop window.

Not much poverty here. The slums are farther down. And yet not only bourgeois and petty bourgeois live on these hillsides; there are also factory employees, workers. Your neighbour could be a taxi driver.

In the distance, tumult, power, creation, luxury – and poverty as well. Here the city has grown itself an appendix. In among the remnants of a mighty past it has established something terrifying: mediocrity. But for the Algerian workers at Renault, and for many others besides, going into one of these little houses would be like entering heaven.

Why should I say anything against these people who – like me – come home from work every day? They seem to be decent folk who live with their families, who love their children. Can we blame them for not wanting the 'world' in which they feel reasonably at home to be transformed?

Platitude. There are still contrasts here which give it a certain charm. A few more little developments, and even that will disappear. Mediocrity will have swamped this Parisian suburb just as it has swamped villages as much as ten kilometres away from the city. One has to go back to the office buildings in the centre of Paris to rediscover something of the beauty or charm of times gone by.

Will there ever be anything great which is not dehumanized – or a form of happiness which is not tinged with mediocrity?

The picturesque is disappearing with a rapidity which provides the reactionaries with an ample supply of ammunition for their pro-clamations and jeremiads. Above all it is being reduced to its vile essence: poverty. What used to be its spark of beauty – the primitive diversity of everyday man, the generosity of his nature, the many-faceted local eccentricities, the brutal, swarming tumult – that beauty has disappeared. It has become congealed into so many museum pieces floating on the muddy ocean of destitution. What disappoint-ments await the naïve traveller to the famous cities of the fabulous East! Were all those old story-tellers lying? Did they see things differently then? Can things and people have changed so much? The eagerly awaited wonders, the marvellous surprises, the ruins, the monuments, the stories from the Thousand and One Nights, the folksongs and dances – they are no longer enough to colour the spectacle and transform it for us. Naples, Baghdad, Calcutta: the same sun shines down on the same rags, the same running sores. The myths have disappeared, the rituals and magic spells have lost their glamour. All we can see now are the destitute masses, and the ignoble apparatus of domination which lies over them, the unlovely art of power. There is nothing left to seduce us. Everywhere a bare-faced display of force: rifles, armoured cars, policemen.

Wherever people are in the throes of liberation from the old oppressions, they are also sacrificing – there is no way they can avoid it – certain ways of life which for many years were great and beautiful. The tractor and the mechanical seeder must replace the gestures of the ploughman. Thus when backward countries move forward they produce ugliness, platitude and mediocrity as though that meant progress. And the advanced countries which have known history in all its greatness, produce platitude as though its proliferation were in-evitable.

So the New China, from the lowliest peasant girl to the highest Party chief, dresses up in blue overalls. She has given up the mandarins' silks, for hundreds of millions of peasants the direct opposite of their own rags. She has relegated them to museums or turned them into export items, along with the magic dragons and ivory buddhas. She is becoming austere, her mind bent on being victorious on the labour front. Solid Republics are founded on virtue.

In the USSR in September and October 1954 various articles appeared which presented some new problems. The *Kommunist* of 14

October suggests that the standard of culture in the Soviet Union and the handling of dialectical analysis were reaching a point where the simplified black-or-white, good-versus-bad view of reality which had been generally accepted hitherto would have to be abandoned. Thus writers, artists and philosophers needed to set about examining reality and life in all their aspects, distinguishing between their various elements, discerning the seeds of the new germinating in the old, separating the positive from the negative, but also grasping all the contradictions, even in what was new.

At the same time (and, to borrow a time-hallowed formula, this was no coincidence) the problem of *taste* was raised in the USSR for the first time. On 10 October the review *Novy Mir* writes: 'During the period of the construction of Communist society, the problem arises of how to elaborate a style of living in material culture which will best satisfy popular requirements.' There follows a comparison between 'the industrial aesthetic' of cars and railway engines, and the aesthetic anachronism of the objects on sale in the Moscow stores: sofas with fringes, beds with fruit-and-flower decorations, imitations of the mirrors and knick-knacks to be seen in the Savoy (a restaurant frequented by tradesmen under the old regime).

And the philosopher Alexandrov, who was then Minister of Culture, is quoted for his part as follows: 'everything surrounding man in his everyday life – houses, architecture, the organization of living space, furniture and household objects – is also part of culture, and influences taste ...'

The Soviets are thus discovering problems which we, who live in a capitalist country, have been aware of for a long time (which does not mean that we have solved them). As far as the style of everyday life is concerned, the Soviets have not progressed far beyond 1900. They are discovering *social needs* which are already known and which have already been explored (which is not the same thing as saying that they have been satisfied or fulfilled). They have attained petty-bourgeois mediocrity as though that were progress. How easily and quickly will they leave it behind them? Today the latest stop is the 'industrial aesthetic', an old chestnut which is liable to involve them in more than one lapse of taste ...

These observations are not intended to imply any hostility or even mistrust of the USSR, which remains the *objective* support of the democratic forces and the socialist movement. On the contrary: that a great civilization in the process of formation should express such problems frankly and lucidly can be considered a sign of its vigour and innovativeness. But nevertheless these facts give food for thought; we observe that socialism and the construction of socialism also involve criticism of everyday life. While not necessarily agreeing with Jean-Marie Domenach's conclusions, we can accept what he has to say on the subject of Yugoslavia:

> We have failed to pay enough attention in our analyses to this more immediate and less easily grasped reality of everyday life; let us not forget it, Marxism started from a concrete observation of alienation, and aimed to eliminate it. Nothing would be more useful today than a sociology of everyday life, separate from proclamations and official statistics, a sociology of the conditions of real existence in a socialist country: we could take a fresh look at the shortages and the sufferings which lead to unexpected explosions of unrest; by studying new alienations we could achieve a newly conceived revolutionary theory which would no longer be based exclusively on the poverty of the workers in 1850, but on the concrete sufferings of the men of 1956. Sadly, no such sociology exists as yet, in any of the popular democracies (although objective surveys on work, youth, etc. would help to avoid a good many wrong turns), and we have to make do with fragmentary impressions, naturally subject to chance, mood, and therefore extremely questionable ...[68]

This leads us in turn to pose yet more problems.

A few years ago, 'the new man', the socialist or Communist man, seemed radically and infinitely different from what 'we' are, 'we' who are immersed in capitalism and contaminated by the bourgeoisie even in terms of the way we struggle against it. This is how literature presented the new man: entirely positive, heroic, fearless and blameless in work, war or love. He was defined by his wholehearted devotion to (socialist) society and by the way he discovered the meaning of his individuality in dedication and self-sacrifice. That the individual was dedicated to society, that he was defined as well as determined by society, was never doubted for one minute, and this affirmation formed the basis for both an ethic and an aesthetic.

However neither this ethic nor this aesthetic was ever successfully or clearly formulated. Even less was anything definitive written, or a style of living developed, which might have imposed them. Is that not an indication, the visible sign of a flaw? The symptom of something lacking? In fact it became clear that the exaltation of the social man in socialist society was ending up as a set of perfunctory images of limited interest and certainly of limited use once they had outlived certain specific circumstances (the struggle for the Plan, production goals, or the war effort). So in place of the monotonous display of 'positive heroes' there was a demand for images of the real man, diverse, individual, complete with his conflicts and contradictions, and exemplified in his different types. There was even an official statement to the effect that certain negative types were not without interest – and that there were a great many men and women who experience within themselves the clash between the old and the new, the positive and the negative. Men and women in transition ...

Thus it is in his similarities with how men used to be that the new man becomes humanized. And we find the socialist or Communist man much more interesting when the distance between him and 'us' is reduced. He gains in sympathy and interest what he loses in terms of his ability to impress the naïve and the stupid. Even if the contradictions are different, even if they must be emphasized in different ways, even if over there they are fruitful while back here they are devastating, even if the attitude of the socialist man towards his work and society is totally different to 'ours', the contradictions allow us to understand, to know, to communicate. They enlighten 'us'. In the past an over-facile rhetoric has taken the 'socialist man' and the 'Communist man' over, comparing them to saints, to knights in shining armour. From our lowly positions we looked up in admiration at the Positive Hero. It was not possible to love him. Now that he has become contradictory, the socialist man is no taller than we are.

But this means we can ask him questions. But this means we become more demanding. We ask ourselves: 'What is socialism exactly? How does it intervene in everyday life? What does it change?' And the answer is unclear. The elimination of the bourgeoisie and class antagonisms? The suppression of capitalist relations of property and production? These are only negative definitions. We find the picture of a bourgeois society without a bourgeoisie neither reassuring nor satisfying. We think that there is, or will be, something else. But what? Accepting one's work, making it – willingly if possible – one's first priority, working harder, willing productivity to increase rather than merely putting up with it? These ideas are fine as far as they go. Admittedly they are probably all essential, very important for the social relations of production, and perhaps they would go some way towards defining a mode of production economically. But as a definition of a culture, a civilization, a humanity, a joy of living which are really *new*, they are inadequate. Nor can they define a worthwhile way of living which could come into being thanks to its own powers of persuasion.[69]

The problem is not limited to ethics and aesthetics. It forces us to return to the theoretical and scientific principles of Marxism. What is the exact role of the productive forces in society? Unquestionably production in the USSR and in the other countries of the socialist camp is growing at an increasingly rapid rate, and above all so are the means of production (Marx's Department I).

It is ludicrous to define socialism solely by the development of the productive forces. Economic statistics cannot answer the question: 'What is socialism?' Men do not fight and die *for* tons of steel, or for tanks or atomic bombs. They aspire to be happy, not to produce. What is more, both production (global or per capita) and labour productivity are even higher in the USA than they are in the USSR.

The productive forces do not define socialism. For socialism, it is necessary for the productive forces to be at a high level, as the example of the USSR shows, but that is not enough to institute it, as the example of the USA shows. And yet if 'life is to change' it is essential for the productive forces to reach a certain level. Moreover, change in the political superstructure (in its class nature: here the bourgeois State – there the proletarian State, controlling the means of production, the dictatorship of the proletariat, its leading role embodied in and exercised by the Party) does not *ipso facto* imply a concrete change in the way people live. In the capitalist countries, the superstructures (the 'shells' in the sense Lenin used the word in the text quoted earlier) are in contradiction with the living contents, because they *lag behind* them, whether it be the State or legal relations of property. This super-stuctural backwardness acts as a brake. And it will be the task and the meaning of the political Revolution to destroy these shells, to release their contents, and to rebuild new superstructures from the bottom up. In the countries which are building socialism today, the political and ideological superstructures start off *ahead of* the social relations and the economic base. In the backward countries this is what the Revolution is all about. But how is the contradiction resolved? How is a change which in these backward countries begins at the top, in the stratosphere of society, passed downwards through an immense apparatus into the humble depths of everyday life? Will it not sometimes come to a halt on the way? Will not whatever comes between the base and the apex slow it down or divert it?

To put it another way, socialism (the new society, the new life) can only be defined *concretely* on the level of everyday life, as a system of changes in what can be called lived experience.[70] Now, half a century of historical upheavals have taught us that everyday relations between men – 'lived experience' – change more slowly than the structure of the State. And in a different way, at a different rate. Thus in the history of societies modifications in the different sectors take place unevenly, some ahead of their times, others lagging behind. The fact that one sector is ahead does not mean that there is immediate progress in another. And vice versa. According to the productive and technical forces, certain social needs arise in bourgeois society which capitalism is unable to satisfy; they modify everyday life in a positive way, while at the same time introducing negative elements such as dissatisfaction, disappointment, alienation. On the other hand, in the socialist countries, or in the countries in which socialism is being built, the real social needs – which socialism should both stimulate, detect and satisfy – lag behind ideology and the superstructures.

Let us summarize and put what we have said into perspective. Today, the Revolution has lost its mythical meaning and the now-outmoded aspects of its former romanticism. In 1917, as in 1789, the revolutionaries thought they were entering straight into another world, an entirely new one. They were passing from despotism to freedom, from capitalism to Communism. Just one sign from them and life was going to change like a stage set. Today we know that life is never simple. There are no magic wands. We have been taught to look at necessary Revolution in a hard, realistic light. Still inadequately controlled by human will and freedom, necessity has produced a historical result that Marx did not foresee. The political Revolution which is a necessary condition for the transformation of the world, was first accomplished in the backward ('under-developed') countries. The incalculable consequences of this fact are springing up all around us, filling our era inexorably with tension and discord. This relationship of confrontation between two politically opposed 'camps' or 'worlds' is extending and amplifying the class struggle to world-wide, historical dimensions. But only a shamelessly absurd logic could mistakenly conclude from this contradiction, this 'coexistence' in antagonism, that the men in these two camps, and the way they actually live, had nothing in common.

In his lectures at Sverdlovsk University in 1924, Stalin defined the spirit of Leninism as the synthesis of Russian revolutionary enthusiasm and American pragmatism. Since then, now that the romanticism has faded away, the balance has possibly tipped in favour of the American sense of business, yield, results. Is this a bad thing? Certainly, if it is, it has its positive side. It is true that one of the camps is on the decline while the other is expanding; the latter may well be able to incorporate whatever is best or more effective in the former.

But to define 'the new' by sifting out everything that distinguishes it from the old is not as easy as the dogmatists with their lack of dialectic used to believe. Our era is truly an era of transition; everything about it is transitory, everything, right down to men and their lives. The informed observer will be as struck as much by similarities as by differences, as much by the unity within contradiction as by contradiction itself. The one must not eliminate the other! (A little example, quoted from a comedian: there are secret police in democratic countries as well as in reactionary or Fascist countries. In the democratic countries police chiefs are changed very often; in the socialist countries sometimes they even shoot them. Under Fascism they last as long as the regime!)

Today, despite the extreme unevenness of development, a sort of vast world-wide levelling process is taking place. The myths and the ideologies are falling; they are nothing more than shells concealing — very badly — facts, results, needs. Backward social structures are collapsing, giving way to demands that the social average be raised to the average level achieved in the developed countries. From one side of the world to the other questions are being asked about production and productivity, power of consumption, distribution of the gross national product, diversification of investments (and the 'socialist' countries realize that one day or another they will be obliged to do voluntarily and consciously what the capitalist countries have done involuntarily and blindly: invest in the production of consumer goods). So everywhere we see that advanced automated machines, power stations and atomic energy, tractors and combine harvesters are being perceived as a hope and a solution. But the 'man–machine' relation is only one aspect of the question. Men and women everywhere are aspiring to build their everyday lives on a solid basis, to escape from insecurity and poverty. These are mass problems, problems of social aspirations and social needs. The face of the world is changing; everywhere the everyday nature of life asserts itself, conscious now of its own weakness and its own value. Life is appearing in all its nakedness. The result for this period of transition is an appalling outburst of platitude which is in singular contrast to the other characteristics of this self-same period: inordinate ambitions, failures on a par with those ambitions, tragedies, threats, an ocean of blood and mire – and with brutal stupidity and platitude thrown in for good measure.

Should we attempt to escape from platitude through the past, the tragic and the mythical, the surreal or the transcendental? Or through the marvellous, in other words through the trumpery of lost illusions and miracles? In the course of our study we will attempt wherever possible to demonstrate the new marvels which are being born at the very heart of mediocrity. They are simple, human marvels. Let us name one of them without further ado: *trust.*

It is as old as social life itself; very close to naïvety, to foolishness; always abused from childhood on (trust in one's parents, in masters and bosses, priests and gods, faith and destiny, love); always changed into a distrust which is almost as unexpressed as the initial naïvety – today trust in life is taking root in life and becoming a need. In the contradictory dualism 'trust–distrust' – contradictory in an embryonic, suppressed way, more ambiguous than antagonistic – trust is slowly getting the upper hand. In spite of the most dreadful trials, the most awful illusions, it is getting stronger. Today trust is bursting forth, today trust is growing. We will see how it is at work deep in the heart of the everyday, and how it works through its opposite, doubt – the restless need for material security. This will be one of the themes of the second volume of *Critique of Everyday Life.*[71]

VI Once Again, the Theory of Alienation ...

Now let us return to several questions which we touched upon at the beginning and elucidate them more thoroughly. A certain number of Marxists, and notably the 'official' Marxists, gave this book a rather bad reception when it was first published. Why? In the first place, at that time in France there was a widespread prejudice against *sociology*. Due to the fact that certain theoreticians of the kind generally described from the political point of view as 'right-wing socialists' had reduced Marxism to a sociology, Marxist revolutionaries had drawn the hasty conclusion that sociology does not exist as a science. Indeed, in the USSR sociology is not included among the social sciences. When the term is used there, it is in reference to societies generally, either ethnographically or ethically, or even simply administratively. That there are ideologues – notably in Germany (Weber, Mannheim, etc.) – who have reduced the historical and social sciences, together with philosophy and the theory of knowledge, to sociology, is offered as an irrefutable argument; but this is merely a way of avoiding, by pure and simple negation, the real difficulties the sociologist encounters when he wants to situate and determine the object and method of his discipline.

We should add that the disappearance of sociology from the USSR and from revolutionary Marxism surely has another, deeper significance. We have already quoted an important text by Lenin which demonstrates how the materialist analysis of social relations in Marx goes beyond political economy (by renewing it). Far from excluding a scientific sociology which would study social relations (or certain aspects of them), the notion of *socio-economic formation* demands and requires it. We may note that the concept of *socio-economic formation* has almost disappeared from Marxist writing, to be replaced by the simplified scheme: *'economic base – political superstructure'*. Theoretically, Marxist thought and method have become impoverished. Practically, neither capitalist society nor socialist society in the process of formation has been studied in a concrete way. Economic statistics on the one hand, and observations attacking or defending ideology and the political apparatus in the two 'camps' on the other, have been deemed sufficient. This reveals an extremely serious development: *the growing break with objectivity* which in our view characterizes the Stalinist interpretation of Marxism.

This dogmatic and schematic simplification of Marxism, with its elimination of sociological research, went hand in hand with a simplification of philosophy. Why was the concept of *alienation* treated with such mistrust? Why was the Hegelianism in Marx's early writings rejected? Where does the tendency to separate Marx from his roots, and his mature scientific works from his early writings, come from? Or the tendency to date and determine the formation of Marxism from his political writings? Analysis shows that behind all this lies that murky mixture of simplistic empiricism, pliant subjectivism and doctrinaire, authoritarian dogmatism which is the philosophical basis of the Stalinist interpretation of Marxism. In Soviet society, *alienation could and must no longer be an issue.* By order from above, for reasons of State, the concept had to disappear. Why? Was it because alienation (economic, ideological, political) really had disappeared? The divorce between Stalin's decree and the reality, between ideology – brought into line with propaganda – and the objective truth, could only get wider.

This was why the Marxists who imported this Stalinist interpretation into France – not merely uncritically, but actually shooting down the slightest hint of criticism as though it were treason – could not accept sociology as a science, or the philosophical concept of alienation, or even philosophy as such. They had to be reductive, simplistic, schematic, dogmatic. And of course the Stalinist interpretation of Marxism,[72] which had already been pedagogically and politically simplified, and bent in the direction of a State ideology, could only become even more desiccated. So dogmatic was their attitude that all they could see in the *Critique of Everyday Life* was an attempt to analyse certain aspects of bourgeois society *sociologically*, without actually making a stand against it. They imagined it was taking a step backwards, that it was giving up political economy, and even dialectical and historical materialism. (Sectarian and dogmatic Marxist criticism frequently begins by isolating texts from their context, and then from the author's other works, in order to pin down some 'formula' or other.) They considered my sociological point of view to be narrow and depoliticized; as if the sociology annihilated all ideological or political criticism. (Sectarian Marxists have nothing much to say – and everything they have to say they say over and over again; when they were unable to find what they were looking for immediately in my book, they insisted that I had deliberately left it out!)

These attacks were spoken rather than written, and took place more by word of mouth behind my back than in actual discussions with me. Here are some extracts from a letter written by a young Marxist who was otherwise sympathetic towards the book:

> Your critique ends up being a theory of the decline of everyday life, of the growing alienation of a naïve way of life in which you sometimes appear to see the remains of a golden age for humanity ... Alienation in production consists above all in the fact that the worker is deprived of a share of the product of his labour. Mystification (the superstructure) also deprives the workers of an objective vision of the relations of production. This superstructure, this ideological alienation is complex (human relations hypostatized in religion – justified in ethics – explained by the pseudo-social sciences, by the political ideology of the dominant classes, etc. ...). But it cannot be said that social man has undergone a process of increasing alienation, for example by passing from slavery to serfdom and the proletariat ... Some of your propositions suggest that you believe that the analysis of everyday life can only begin with the theory of ideological mystification ... You say that the scientific study of society and of the proletariat begins by tearing away the veil of ideologies, and that Marxism describes and analyses the everyday life of society. But this is all grist to the mill of those who maintain that you are limiting Marxism to a sort of materialist phenomenology of the superstructures ... It would be worth your while to actually say that you are writing a theory of the super-structures ... You also seem to be saying that all the parts of Marx's writings are of equal importance. Your enemies have used this declaration that Marxism constitutes a whole, and is therefore a science and a philosophy, to conclude that you see economic facts and ideologies as having equal importance. That accusation of phenomenology again ... And it is telling!

This letter is a good illustration of how confused the ideas and discussions were (moreover they were never openly discussed in public or explored in any depth).

Before replying briefly, this is an appropriate place to emphasize another shabby polemical procedure associated with sectarian Marxism. In fact, whether historically or today, Marxist thought and the Marxist thinker cannot exist in isolation from each other. Absolute Marxism and the purely Marxist manner of thinking are intellectual entities created by dogmatism; this dogmatism has become entangled

in the very contradictions it has unwittingly created; in fact Marxism
asserts that thought – all thought – can only express itself historically,
socially, contextually. I (using the pronoun generically) am a French
Marxist who writes and thinks in French; who has been formed by
French culture. One would not have to go very deeply into my
dialectical thinking to find a predilection for lucid, well-organized,
clearly articulated ideas, for *analysis*. Clearly I have a rationalist and
Cartesian background. It is indeed conceivable that at one time or
another these tendencies of mine may conflict with the materialist and
dialectical thinking which, despite its differences with my background,
is my starting point; and I know this. It is equally conceivable that I
have resolved this conflict, or that I will resolve it, in a creative way.
And what could be more natural than such a conflict, given that
everything is contradictory and that we only move ahead in and
through contradictions? But here comes the sectarian, dogmatic
Marxist. Frowning, threatening, contemptuous, or indifferent, he
smells something he disapproves of, something incompatible, something impossible: one cannot be both a Cartesian and a Marxist;
Marxism is radically different from Cartesianism in respect of its
theory, its content and its aims. Therefore he will define me as a
Cartesian, fixing me for ever, labelling me, nailing me to the whipping
post of Cartesianism. And he will be very pleased with himself: he will
have served the cause of Marxism and the proletariat. And if I answer
back, he will brand me with other labels, other epithets. In fact he will
have transformed a problem, in other words a real conflict – and
therefore a creative one in so far as I am able to resolve it – into an
irresolvable, unproductive antinomy. He will have burdened living
reality with a parasitic growth: his interpretation. And he will have
been drawn unwittingly into a contradiction between the 'point of
view' of Marxism and the proletariat, and the 'point of view' of
acquired culture and national tradition; between the point of view of
the 'new' and that of the 'old'. It is true that subsequently the sectarian
can save face by jumping nimbly from one point of view to the other.
He can even maintain that there is no contradiction between the
'points of view'; which is true, since it is he who introduced the
contradiction in the first place, exaggerating it to the point of antagonism when necessary, and dismissing it when no longer required!
And now we are gradually isolating a process of degeneration in

dialectical thought: 'points of view' and the jump from one point of view to the other.

Thus it is fashionable for the dogmatists to use dominant modes of thought from outside Marxism against anyone who attempts to introduce new ideas. If phenomenology is fashionable, then they see phenomenology in every idea which does not duplicate the proven 'formulas'. If Hegelianism is in fashion, then they will find Hegelianism wherever they want to find it, etc. And maybe, indeed certainly, there is something true in all this, since, after all, phenomenology, Hegelianism or Cartesian analysis also correspond to something around us and within us. If not they would have lost all meaning, or would not have meant anything in the first place! And this is one of the worst aspects of dogmatism: as soon as it touches a sore point it turns it only too easily into a global condemnation, using a constant process of superfluity and imperturbable logic instead of analysing works, situations and men dialectically.

Dogmatism is a great evil which comes in countless forms. If we are to exterminate it we must hunt it down in every nook and cranny and drag it from its hiding place by the tail like a rat.

The amusing thing is that the man who wrote the letter quoted above begins by rejecting this form of criticism; then he appears not only to accept it but actually to overshoot the mark by seeming to embrace a theory of superstructures which is a theory of superstructures and nothing else. Thus he wavers between dogmatism and theoretical opportunism or eclecticism.

Sectarian criticism also forgets that the economic and the ideological as they are expressed in everyday life only attain the level of political consciousness at moments of revolutionary crisis. This is something Lenin wrote about at length in his analyses of the political crisis. At such moments all the elements of social practice, of spontaneous consciousness, and of the life of the masses and the classes are condensed and concentrated in political life. Outside of such moments, social practice splits up into discrete and even divergent areas; notably into the economic and the political. In everyday life, from that point on, the immediate and the ideological join forces to form a shell in which economic reality, the operation of the existent political superstructures, and revolutionary political consciousness are all contained and concealed.

So to reach reality we must indeed tear away the veil, that veil which is forever being born and reborn of everyday life, and which masks everyday life along with its deepest or loftiest implications.

There is no reason not to quote Lenin again: 'The beginning – the most simple, ordinary, mass, immediate "Being": the single commodity ('Sein' in political economy). The analysis of it as a social relation. A *double* analysis, deductive and inductive – logical and historical . . .'[73] Thus the simplest event – a woman buying a pound of sugar, for example – must be analysed. Knowledge will grasp whatever is hidden within it. To understand this simple event, it is not enough merely to describe it; research will disclose a tangle of reasons and causes, of essences and 'spheres': the woman's life, her biography, her job, her family, her class, her budget, her eating habits, how she uses money, her opinions and her ideas, the state of the market, etc. Finally I will have grasped the sum total of capitalist society, the nation and its history. And although what I grasp becomes more and more profound, it is contained from the start in the original little event. So now I see the humble events of everyday life as having two sides: a little, individual, chance event – and at the same time an infinitely complex social event, richer than the many 'essences' it contains within itself. The social phenomenon may be defined as the unity of these two sides. It remains for us to explain why the infinite complexity of these events is hidden, and to discover why – and this too is part of their reality – they appear to be so humble.

Is it truly a question of the superstructures? Is it the superstructures alone that matter? No: it is a question of superstructures only in so far as they are created at each instant of everyday life and social practice – in so far as they are constantly coming down to penetrate these realms from above. And also only in so far as the superstructures are linked to society as a whole, to social practice as a whole, although everyday practice is dispersed, fragmented – be it in terms of an individual or a specific and determined social activity: in them the whole is represented by the part, and vice versa.

It is therefore not only a question of the superstructures. In truth it is a question of *sociology*, in other words of a science which studies an aspect or sector of social relations.

And now the new reader – or the old one who reads this book again – will be able to judge for himself. Did it contain a theory of *increasing* alienation, based upon a fundamental naïvety, and with archaic contents left over from some golden age (to put it more scientifically: from primitive community – or from direct, immediate person-to-person relationships)? If it did, then the author must have expressed his thoughts badly. He believes that philosophically the process of social development involves two sides: *the increasing fulfilment of man* – and also an *increasing alienation* up to and including capitalist society. The one in the other. The one via the other. On the one hand *objectification*, in other words the more-and-more real, objective existence of human beings, both in the human world of products and works, and in the human strengths and powers developed throughout history; and on the other hand, and equally on the increase, externalization, an uprooting of the self, a split, an estrangement.

In capitalist society this contradictory process – this tearing – is at its maximum. This society and the concepts which express it (for example the idea of *social labour* discovered by classic bourgeois economy) shed light on the march of history, the past and the future. And this is why the objective analysis of it as a totality[74] undertaken in *Capital* is a decisive one.[75] The ever-unfinished development of the productive forces – in economic terms – has the philosophical implication of a new stage in human fulfilment, of limitless possibilities. But the corresponding alienation here is just as all-encompassing. It encompasses life in its entirety.

In capitalist society, money – the externalization of relations between human beings by means of commodities – takes on an absolute power. But this is merely economic alienation: *money-as-fetish*, objectified outside of men, functioning by itself, and as such one of the objects studied by the science called political economy. This economic alienation, though an integral part of total alienation, is but one of its aspects. Although the volume which follows contains certain quotations, let me clarify matters now by quoting some long extracts from the most important text by Marx on this question.[76] Obviously some of Marx's observations were only valid for his own times. One may still find workers living in hovels – even in France. But it cannot be said that this is the general rule, much less a law.

VII   Alienated Labour

The worker becomes poorer the more wealth he produces, the more his production increases in power and extent. The worker becomes an ever cheaper commodity the more commodities he produces. The *devaluation* of the human world grows in direct proportion to the *increase in value* of the world of things. Labour not only produces commodities; it also produces itself and the workers as a *commodity* and it does so in the same proportion in which it produces commodities in general.

This fact simply means that the object that labour produces, its product, stands opposed to it as *something alien*, as a *power independent* of the producer. The product of labour is labour embodied and made material in an object, it is the *objectification* of labour. The realization of labour is its objectification. In the sphere of political economy this realization of labour appears as a *loss of reality* for the worker, objectification as *loss of and bondage to the object*, and appropriation as *estrangement*, as *alienation* [*Entaüsserung*] ...

It is the same in religion. The more man puts into God, the less he retains within himself. The worker places his life in the object; but now it no longer belongs to him, but to the object ... What the product of his labour is, he is not ... The externalization [*Entaüsserung*] of the worker in his product means not only that his labour becomes an object, and *external* existence, but that it exists *outside him*, independently of him and alien to him, and confronts him as an autonomous power; that the life which he has bestowed on the object confronts him as hostile and alien ...

Political economy conceals the estrangement in the nature of labour by ignoring the direct relationship between the worker (labour) *and production.* It is true that labour produces marvels for the rich, but it produces privation for the worker; it produces palaces, but hovels for the worker ... It produces intelligence, but it produces idiocy and cretinism for the worker ...

After all, the product is simply the résumé of the activity, of the production. So if the product of labour is alienation, production itself must be active alienation, the alienation of activity, the activity of alienation. The estrangement of the object of labour merely summarizes the estrangement, the alienation in the activity of labour itself.

What constitutes the alienation of labour?

Firstly, the fact that labour is *external* to the worker, i.e. does not belong to his essential being; that he therefore does not confirm himself in his work, but denies himself, feels miserable and not happy ... Hence the worker feels himself only when he is not working; when he is working he does not feel himself. He is at home when he is not working, and not at home when he is working ... [His labour] is therefore not the satisfaction of a need but a mere *means* to satisfy needs outside itself ... Just as in religion the spontaneous activity of the human imagination, the human brain and the human heart detaches itself from the individual and reappears as the alien activity of a god or of a devil, so the activity of the worker is not his own spontaneous activity. It belongs to another, it is a loss of his self.

The result is that man (the worker) feels that he is acting freely only in his animal functions — eating, drinking and procreating, or at most in his dwelling and adornment — while in his human functions he is nothing more than an animal.

It is true that eating, drinking and procreating, etc., are also genuine human functions. However, when abstracted from our other aspects of human activity and turned into final and exclusive ends, they are animal ...

This relationship is the relationship of the worker to his own activity as something which is alien and does not belong to him, activity as passivity [*Leiden*], power as impotence, procreation as emasculation, the worker's *own* physical and mental energy, his personal life — for what is life but activity? — as an activity directed against himself, which is independent of him and does not belong to him. *Self-estrangement*, as compared with the estrangement of the *object* [*Sache*] mentioned above ...

Nature is man's *inorganic body*, that is to say nature in so far as it is not the human body. Man *lives* from nature, i.e. nature is his body, and he must maintain a continuing dialogue with it if he is not to die. To say that man's physical and mental life is linked to nature simply means that nature is linked to itself, for man is a part of nature.

Estranged labour not only (1) estranges nature from man and (2) estranges man from himself ... it also estranges man from his *species*. It turns his *species-life* into a means for his individual life. Firstly it estranges life-species and individual life, and secondly it turns the latter, in its abstract form, into the purpose of the former, also in its abstract and estranged form.

For in the first place labour, *life activity, productive life* itself appears to man only as a *means* for the satisfaction of a need, the need to preserve physical existence. But productive life is species-life. It is life-producing life. The whole character of a species, its species-character, resides in the nature of its life activity, and free conscious activity constitutes the species-character of man. Life itself appears only as a *means of life*.

The animal is immediately one with its life activity. It is not distinct from that activity; it *is* that activity. Man makes his life activity itself an object of his will and consciousness. He has conscious life activity. It is not a determination with which he directly merges. Conscious life activity directly distinguishes man from animal life activity. Only because of that is he a species-being. Or rather, he is a conscious being, i.e. his own life is an object for him, only because he is a species-being. Only because of that is his activity free activity. Estranged labour reverses the relationship so that man, just because he is a conscious being, makes his life activity, his *being* (*Wesen*], a mere means for his *existence* ...

It is true that animals also produce ... But ... they produce one-sidedly, while man produces universally; they produce only when immediate physical need compels them to do so ... while man is capable of producing according to the standards of every species ... hence man also produces in accordance with the laws of beauty.

It is therefore in the fashioning of the objective that man really proves himself to be a *species-being*. Such production is his active species-life. Through it nature appears as *his* work and his reality. The object of labour is therefore the *objectification of the species-life of man*: for man reproduces himself not only intellectually, in his consciousness, but actively and actually, and he can therefore contemplate himself in a world he himself has created. In tearing away the object of his production from man, estranged labour therefore tears away from him his *species-life*, his true species-objectivity, and transforms his advantage over animals into the disadvantage that his inorganic body, nature, is taken from him ...

An immediate consequence of man's estrangement from the product of his labour, his life activity, his species-being, is the *estrangement of man from man*. When man confronts himself, he also confronts *other* men ...

In general, the proposition that man is estranged from his species-being means that each man is estranged from the others and that all are estranged from man's essence ...

The *alien* being to whom labour and the product of labour belong ... can be none other than *man* himself ... a *man other than the worker*.

Thus Marx does not limit alienation to exploitation, to the fact that a share of the product is taken away from the worker individually or collectively (the working class) by the individual and the class which controls the means of production. He analyses alienation under several headings:

(a) the alienation of the worker as an *object* (the alien power which turns him into an object);

(b) the alienation of productive activity, in other words of labour itself (which is divided and split up by it);

(c) the alienation of man as species-being, member of the human species – as a system of *humanized species-needs*;

(d) the alienation of man as a being of nature, as a set of *natural needs*.

A little farther on, in other texts, Marx introduces some new elements: 'The machine accommodates itself to man's *weakness*, in order to turn *weak* man into a machine.'[77] Or again: 'The *division of labour* is the economic expression of the *social nature of labour* within estrangement.'[78] And again:

> *just* as society itself produces *man* as *man*, so it is *produced* by him ... The *human* essence of nature exists only for *social man*.[79] ... Each attempts to establish over the other an alien power, in the hope of thereby achieving satisfaction of his own selfish needs.[80] Estrangement appears not only in the fact that the means of *my* life belong to *another*, but also in the fact that *my* desire is the inaccessible possession of *another*, and also in the fact that all things are *other* than themselves, that my activity is *other* than itself, and that finally – and this goes for the capitalists too – an *inhuman* power rules over everything.[81]

These texts make the polyscopic, omnipresent character of alienation as a concept, a reality and a *philosophical* theory linked to the social *sciences*, more than abundantly clear, and this as much in regard to productive forces and social relations as in regard to ideology, and even more profoundly in regard to man's relation *with nature* and with *his own nature*.

The main quotation (from 'Estranged Labour') shows that for Marx work constitutes man's essence as a creator: a being of needs who creates his own needs; and it is precisely work that alienation humiliates, atomizes, overpowers.

The theory of impoverishment is an integral part of Marx's theory of alienation. And yet the two concepts are discrete; thus the facts relating to them must be studied separately, the latter being a more extensive area than the former. Therefore if one emphasizes the idea of alienation it means that one does not reject a priori the theory of the *tendency* towards impoverishment. The economic laws formulated by Marx always deal with tendencies, and are thwarted by other forces, other activities and other laws. As long as it is not backed up by scientific analyses of the life and the needs of the proletariat, compared by region, type of industry, and country, the analysis of impoverishment, like the analysis of alienation, is just so much hot air. A priori it is probable that here, as elsewhere, differences in development play an important role. It is becoming essential to undertake not only an economic analysis, but also a sociological one (dealing with basic or differentiated needs, the degrees and the structures of those needs, be they old or new, hidden or unsatisfied, etc.).

There are other texts by Marx which show clearly that in his view the crowning element in the inhuman power which reigns over all social life is the State; it consolidates that power, and sanctions it. In one sense *political* alienation (with the *political superstition* by which the State is actually endowed with a life superior to the life of society) is the most serious type of alienation. In another sense, it also determines the sphere in which the struggle against alienation ('disalienation') and radical criticism, its auxiliary, will be most effective, most necessary and most directly possible.

It is equally clear that Marx sees the *division of labour* as the cause of alienation. Now he never suggested that the political Revolution, on the level of the superstructures – nor socialism, on the level of the relations of production – could bring an end to the division of labour. He merely imagined that after a transitional period of unspecified length, Communism could supersede the division of labour. During this transition, the forms of alienation (the law, for example, and of course the division of labour) would carry on. Therefore Marx never limited the sphere of alienation to capitalism; and never did he suggest that socialism, or the proletarian Revolution, would bring alienation to an absolute and immediate end.[82] Alienation persists, or is even born again in new forms, along with its contradictory process, the process of 'disalienation'. But here we are broaching new problems which go beyond our immediate concerns, and maybe beyond the concerns of the book itself. For these are philosophical problems: the philosopher may well go so far as to ask himself whether all realization, all objectification, does not involve an alienation as its own deep-seated negativity.

And so there is still more to be said about the theory of alienation.

But before we proceed, we should clear up a difficulty which is linked to this theory, but distinct from it. A letter the author received shortly after the book was published said:

You demonstrate an analogy between acting, theatre and life ... You emphasize the importance of mask and character ... But what about the new man? Doesn't he supersede the opposition between acting and being serious? ... In my opinion, he no longer wears a mask for other people, not even the mask of irony ...

Oh, how wonderfully optimistic we were after the Liberation! It was zero hour for history, the man of old was disappearing, the new man was bursting forth in all his beauty and undeniable authenticity! What has become of this beautiful and naïve image? And this beautiful and naïve confidence? The new man, the new life, these were the images, the hopes, the myths at the moment of the Liberation, replacing the myth which had inspired the struggle in October 1917: the (almost) immediate transition to Communism. Significantly, the hope of the Liberation focused itself on everyday life and expressed the need to make a break – which we have encountered at the microscopic level of day-to-day worries and preoccupations – at the level of society. Indeed we could ask ourselves why this naïve expectation expressed itself as it did on the ethical level. And why it found it so easy to abandon the aesthetic level, where masks and acting are not considered necessarily bad. Would there still be theatre in art if there was no longer any theatre in real life? And if 'personalities' no longer put on their act – for themselves and for other people? The naïve belief that the new was at hand made it easy to sacrifice the aesthetic for the ethical. For better and for worse, this expectation of an absolute ethical authenticity was completely disappointed, a misfortune from which aesthetics came out very well – proving that the best things come to those who wait. Events have surpassed even Shakespeare for buffoonery and tragedy; history has gone even farther than the trials in Brecht's plays. What theatrical production could compete with the Rajk trials? What stage effect could rival the Khrushchev report?[83] What mask, what character in fiction, could compare with Stalin's?

The *new man* was not completely absent from this book. However, he only appeared in the conceptual and philosophical shape of the *total man*, entirely developed, entirely won back from alienation. In my critique of everyday life I was wary of bringing this concept too closely into confrontation with given everyday life. The philosopher's vocation is such that he is almost entirely and almost always above the naïvety of the passing moment. The new man, the Communist man, the total man: it would have been only too easy to confuse these terms. And in fact we have seen people who excel at sticking what they consider to be appropriate labels on others sharing these titles out amongst themselves. For all their assaults on huge historical truths, such dogmatists insist that they are world-historical men, contemporaries of the future. Because they are Communists in the mid-twentieth century, they see themselves as members of the Communist society of the future, with all the qualities of the Communist man (sometimes, in fits of critical and autocritical sincerity or self-deception, they reproach themselves for *not* having these qualities, and beneath the seriousness of their masks a set of new comic characters is born).

The concept of the *total man* comes from some brief comments Marx made. Notably this one: 'Man appropriates his integral essence in an integral way, as a total man.'[84]

In this brief phrase Marx limits himself to defining the philosophical problem of universality as a function of human development and of another fundamental concept, that of appropriation. This means that his observation would need to be much elucidated and developed before being treated as a genuine philosophical theory.[85]

It is particularly important to note that the famous theory of the leap from necessity into freedom offers an all-too-easy justification for the new strain of utopianism and idealism we have briefly outlined above. This theory tends to support the great modern myth of the Revolution as total act, radical break, absolute renewal. It is therefore appropriate to emphasize that the shift from necessity to freedom and from alienation to fulfilment requires a lengthy period of transition. What the classic Marxist theorists have somewhat laconically called a 'leap' occupies a vast period in history and implies the resolution of numerous problems and contradictions. The end of non-human history and the beginning of human history inform a process of becoming in which elements of discontinuity and continuity, a multitude of factors on the decline or on the rise, and complex quantitative questions are all interwoven. The classic account based on quantity and quality is too simple – as if in reality everything could always be reduced to a confrontation between quantity and quality. The transitional man cannot be avoided. And the transition is evident all around us. As much in capitalist society (and the reader is directed to the final pages of *Imperialism, the Highest Stage of Capitalism*) as in socialist society. It is impossible to cross over this period in a single bound. The critique of everyday life analyses 'life', as it is, without making an obscure entity of it; it studies the negative and positive elements which confront one another; it studies the new conflicts and the new contradictions in what is new, knowing that the new is (more or less) everywhere ... Thus it knows that the new man must resolve his own contradictions in order to develop as a man.

Man and the human have always constituted a whole: in and through contradictions, i.e. alienations. As for the total man – *universal, concrete* and alive – he can only be conceived of as a limit to the infinity of social development.

To what extent do the stages of transition fall into the philosophical category of alienation? Merely to ask the question shows that interest is shifting towards transition and man in transition, but in so far as he is moving towards the total man, in other words crossing through alienation – and perhaps alienation at its maximum – the transitional man is 'disalienating' himself. So we can keep our philosophical concepts, as long as we make them concrete and see them historically and sociologically, thus extending the developments undertaken by Marx, who concretized the initially philosophical concept of alienation by situating it in economic objects. This obliges us to search documents and works (literary, cinematic, etc.) for evidence that a consciousness of alienation is being born, however indirectly, and that an effort towards 'disalienation', no matter how oblique and obscure, has begun. For the era of transition should be the one in which the philosophical concept enters life and consciousness, whether spontaneously or introduced from outside; otherwise, that concept will remain philosophical and nothing more.

In any event, it is very important for the critique of everyday life to know (and to know that the masses know) that the transcendence of the internal splits and contradictions in the human realm (intellectual versus manual work, town versus country, private versus social) can no more be reduced to a simple act, to some decisive and 'total' moment, than revolution itself. The *total man* is but a figure on a distant horizon beyond our present vision. He is a limit, an idea, and not a historical fact. And yet we must 'historicize' the notion, thinking of it historically and socially. And not naïvely, like those who believed that the new man would suddenly burst forth into history, complete, and in possession of all the hitherto incompatible qualities of vitality and lucidity, of humble determination in labour and limitless enthusiasm in creation.

However, the dialectic of knowledge shows us a 'historicity' and a becoming united with universality. All historically acquired knowledge is approximate, reversible, provisional: *relative*. And yet only the notion of the *absolute* gives this partial, divided, contradictory knowledge a meaning. The absolute is present in the relative (and the relative in the absolute) in a dual way. On the one hand, the absolute is *in* the relative as we receive it historically: every piece of knowledge (every concept, every proposition, every statement) contains a grain of truth, which can only become clear in the context of an ongoing evolutionary process; though an integral part of this process, it will retain a degree of invariability even as the contradictions immanent to historical develop-ment are successively confronted and resolved. On the other hand, the absolute is *outside of* the relative: this is the idea that there will be a completion of knowledge, a fulfilment which is impossible and yet implied by the total becoming of knowledge, therefore placing a limit to infinity (the asymptote of the total process). Dialectically, the absolute is a limit to the infinity of the relative – and yet there is *already* something of the absolute in the relative. In all limited, contradictory and subjective knowledge there is already an element of total objec-tivity. Only the notion or idea of the absolute gives a *sense* (in other words both a *meaning* and a *direction*) to historically acquired knowl-edge. Only the (materialist) dialectic enables us to demonstrate the *historical* character of knowledge without making it entirely relative. Only the dialectic will enable us to define an advance (a progress) while at the same time criticizing the illusions which arise whenever progress is made, and which cause us to take every step forward, every discovery, every new law or theory for the finished form of some particular sector of knowledge. (This is another 'gnosiological' underpinning of the dogmatic approach.)

It is the same for the human. Either one thinks philosophically in order to found humanism, or else one neglects and rejects such an intellectual development, thus abandoning humanism to contingency and chance. Human advance and progress only take their sense (in other words both their *meaning* and their *direction*) from the notion of the *total man.* Every moment of history, every stage accomplished through history, constitutes a whole; so does every partial activity, every power which has been achieved practically; every *moment* also contains its grain of human reality which will appear more and more clearly during the subsequent process of development. At the same time the *total man* is a limit to infinity.

Only if we posit this limit as a universality can we assert that, despite the conflicts and the contradictions, there is a profound if still unrealized unity between domains of activity, poetry and science, art and knowledge, etc. Just as learning, without the idea of the absolute, falls into pure relativism – so, without the notion of the total man, humanism and the theoretical conception of the human fall back into an incoherent pluralism. Thus the theory of the fundamental *is* and *is not* in history. It integrates history, and integrates with history, in a coherent dialectical way.

Is this theory Hegelian, or neo-Hegelian? Let us look at it more closely. It is certain that for Hegel the absolute foundation of existence, of history, of the dialectic, was the alienation of the Idea. In his system this alienation is the initial and absolute condition for development. The Idea leaves its self, becomes alienated, the dispersed *Other*, itself a constantly alienated existence, incapable of apprehending itself without entering into opposition with itself. The ascending stages of Being (nature, mechanism, society, art, religion, philosophy) establish themselves by the Idea successively regaining control over itself. None of these stages, none of these shapings or configurations of consciousness, succeeds in being its own truth in itself and for itself. They thus remain in the domain of alienation. *In Hegel, then, contradiction is nothing more than an implication of alienation.* To know and to understand oneself, to reflect upon oneself, is to resolve contradictions while provoking new alienating contradictions.[86] The Idea is at once the motive force of contradiction and its outcome. It is both that which opposes itself and that which uses contradiction to rediscover – and to recognize through reflection – its unity with itself.

The movement of Logic appears to reconstruct the universe: in fact, it rediscovers and recognizes the descending and ascending emanations of the Idea. The Being which seems the absolute beginning of the real and of reflection (of consciousness) is in truth only the absolute limit of the Idea, at once inferior and superior, from below and from above, from the side of nature, feelings, abstraction – and from the side of Spirit. Thus Logic, which in Hegel appears at first to produce the world, is in truth only the human method for attaining the Idea (which is why it can rid itself of the Idea and the absolute in the Hegelian sense, and change course so as to enter Marxism). And yet in Hegel the absolute tearing apart of the Idea – its alienation – is indispensable if this Idea is to create self-consciousness and to become conscious of itself as it creates (by means of its reflection, in which it *is reflected*). Hegelianism likewise views the tearing apart of reality, of life, of consciousness (and its *unhappiness*) as irreducibly given.[87]

By abandoning the concrete analysis of these divisions, these separations, that tearing apart of actions and consciousness which are the real facts of real life, certain of Hegel's exponents have ended up in mysticism. They maintain that the tearing apart is an absolute drama: a drama within the absolute. In their view human actions illustrate this absolute drama, and can only be understood in terms of its image. Post-Hegelian mysticism develops the vision of the 'Speculative Good Friday'; it starts with the hypothesis that Hegel developed a new series of concepts in order to rationalize the irrational, that he succeeded up to a point, but that beyond that point he failed, thus authorizing them to resume the task from where he left off, precisely by giving prominence to the mystical essence of the residue of irrationality.

Yet it is also possible to show that in Hegel – and this even in his system-building – there was an attempt to enclose totality within the reflecting Individual, and that for him this attempt involved an explicit struggle against mysticism. For this is the sense and the goal of the Hegelian system: to allow an individual – the philosopher and his followers – to dominate the universe by thought; and the system is also the justification for this goal, the history of this Individual. Marx extended Hegel's contradictory attempt to rationalize, resolving its contradiction and breaking his system while at the same time retaining its element of rationality. Marx has demonstrated how dialectical reason arises precisely from the supposed irrationality constituted by nature, by practical and social activity, by man as he is in everyday life.

It is thus that the residue of irrationality in Hegel – the theory of alienation – becomes integrated within historical and dialectical materialism, and is transferred onto a level which is both practical and rational. In Marxism, *alienation is no longer the absolute foundation of contradiction. On the contrary: alienation is defined as an aspect of contradiction and of becoming in man.* Alienation is the form taken by dialectical necessity in human becoming. Thus Hegel explained contradiction by alienation, while Marx explains alienation by dialectical contradiction. This is what the well-known reversal whereby the Hegelian dialectic has been 'set back on its feet' consists of. This transformation does not exclude the theory of alienation, it encompasses it.

Feuerbach thought he had brought human alienation to an end in one fell swoop (by a radical and total philosophical act or decree). He proclaimed that theology, religion, metaphysics, are all alienations of man (and no longer of the Idea). But by defining man once and for all as an individual physiological entity – by rejecting the dialectic and the historicity of the human – he was destroying the foundation for a concrete theory of alienation. And he was also admitting the bourgeois individual as an anthropological principle – as an unconsidered presupposition.

Marx rejects the form taken by Feuerbach's materialism: his anthropological postulate. He does not think that man as such is a simple fragment of nature. But, on the other hand, he rejects the idealist postulate that thinking man emerges from nature and sets himself up above it by virtue of his thought, of the mere fact that he thinks. In this way he succeeds in superseding previous philosophies, the picture of man they presented and the relation they defined between man and the universe. Marx wants to think of man's essence dialectically: for him man is a being of nature in the process of self-transcendence, a being of nature struggling with nature in order to dominate it, a being emerging from nature, but doing so in such a way that in the very process of emerging from and dominating nature its roots are plunged ever more deeply therein.

In the prehistory of man (therefore up until the present) man was first of all a being of nature. Now in material and biological nature, becoming appears as fragmentation, dispersion, externalization, ex-clusion and reciprocal destruction. The natural *other-being* is essentially the enemy-being. In this prehistory, which was his natural history, man was precisely *that*. But in so far as he was a social being he was already becoming *something else*, in such a way that in his natural history nature within him was the profound reason and ever-present cause for his alienation, constantly renewed; for his internal contradiction.

This history of humanity presents us with a collection of strange facts and events. Institutions and ideas were external to the human, oppressive, exclusive, mutually contradictory. They were mutually destructive, and it was necessary to destroy them if they were to be superseded. And yet these institutions and these ideas were the indispensable expression of the development and the acquisition of human practice and human powers, essential in order to organize and formulate these and to render them conscious.

This contradiction is at the heart of Marxist thought as far as the historical development of man is concerned. But it is not a contradiction in Marxist thought itself.[88] It is an internal contradiction in history itself, and only the general theory of alienation can elucidate it. It alone can help us to understand how men constructed history while being caught within history, within their own history; and how they constructed it without knowing they were doing so, blindly at first, but more and more consciously, on several differing but convergent levels (economic, political and ideological struggles); and how finally revolt and violence and chance were only apparently an irrational and absurd factor in history. Things progress (in other words certain things disappear) with their bad side forward.

This tearing apart shows that in the growing control that man has over nature, nature as such keeps control over man. His products and his works function like beings of nature. He must *objectify* himself, and social objects become things, fetishes, which turn upon him. Man as a collective subject exists after the fashion of nature, yet man tends to supersede nature and to build a specific environment in which contradiction in its natural form (spontaneous, blind, necessary) will itself be superseded, controlled, known and mastered. The moment man invented tools and began to work he stopped being an animal, and entered the realm of historical and human contradictions. But these contradictions extend the contradictions of nature, and particularly in their necessary, blind aspect; if man has humanized himself, he has done so only by tearing himself apart, dividing himself, fragmenting himself: actions and products, powers and fetishes, growing consciousness and spontaneous lack of consciousness, organization and revolt.

Alienation may be defined philosophically as this single yet dual movement of objectification and externalization – of realization and derealization. But this movement must be seen in its dialectical profundity. *That which realizes is also that which derealizes. And vice versa*: whatever derealizes – dissolves, destroys, negates – also realizes by supersession. Obstacles, uncomfortable difficulties, disquiet, apparently insoluble problems, contradiction pushed to the point of antagonism, these are moments of progress: the step forward, the birth of a reality and a higher reflecting consciousness through the dissolution of what exists. *The positive is negative, but what is most negative is also what is most positive . . ..*

And this becoming may be expressed, in a way which is all the more striking for being concrete, practical and alive, as *the discreteness yet inclusiveness of the individual and the social.*[89]

This unity is the foundation of all society: a society is made up of individuals, and the individual is a social being, in and by the content of his life and the form of his consciousness. Now from the direct and physical rituals of primitive societies to the lived abstraction of self-consciousness (*private* consciousness) this unity has only expressed itself in mutilated, fragmented, singular ways.

It cannot be expressed outside of the contradictions which have ensnared it, splitting it and making it problematic, unstable, destined to be superseded. The social, for and in the individual, is always embodied in rituals, in particular words or expressions,[90] which are full of meaning and at the same time relatively meaningless in themselves, thus insignificant and symbolic.

According to the moment and the angle from which we perceive him, the individual is at one and the same time what is most highly concrete and most remotely abstract. He is what is most changing historically and what is most stable, what is most independent from the social structure, and most dependent upon it. Conversely, the social is abstract, since it is defined only by the individuals who make it up; and it is what is most supremely concrete, since it gives these individual existences their unity, their totality, and since it determines the content of their lives and their consciousness. For each individual, the unity of his consciousness and unity with his consciousness is his reality, and the rest is mere destiny, externality, necessity. However, from the point of view of its foundation and social content, the very unity of the most intimate individual consciousness is determined from outside. Thus what is most internal is also what is most external (*private consciousness* for example) – and conversely, what is most external is what is most internal (the sense of a 'value', for example).

Past ideologies tried to find answers to some very diverse questions and problems, to offer solutions to a multitude of contradictions, but most of all they addressed the problem of, and the contradiction between, individual and social. They recreated it in new forms, deeper and more hopeless, until such time as these were eliminated by violence or by gradual erosion, in the name of a new social content. Thus religions, theological or metaphysical projects, were *authentic* attempts to reconcile man with himself, the human with nature, the individual with the social. They achieved both their internal coherence and their entry into life from these attempts, in the form of actions, and the search for a style. Religious fervour and belief in a God gave symbolic expression to the unity of the elements of the human, and projected this unity outside man.

In fact, however, at the very moment ideology was creating this unity by becoming a coherent doctrine and discovering a style of living, it was also perpetuating the inner division, in the form of good and evil, sin and salvation, God and the Devil. Religion as institution maintained a social unity by separating the sacred and the profane, and by oppression. As for direct or indirect communion with nature, ecstatic contemplation, for the oppressed and even for a proportion of their oppressors, was merely a diversion; the intensity of the mystical states attained was an index of nothing but real powerlessness, and an absence of any creative appropriation.

As soon as the unity between the individual and the social begins a process of renewal, alienation takes the form of an antagonism between the private consciousness and the social consciousness. In modern society this self-same alienation has taken other forms. Every time it is possible to proclaim the externality of the whole and of the part – either that the part is superior to the whole, or that the whole transcends the part – there is always an ideologue on hand to do the job. And the resultant ideology is always influential: machines for machines' sake, or conversely man versus machine – reason for reason's sake, or conversely art reduced to a mere utilitarian technique, etc.

Man's unity with himself, in particular the unity of the individual and the social, is an essential aspect of the definition of the total man.

In these circumstances we must either abandon trying to formulate a coherent theory and proclaim pluralism – which is simply the expression of this abandonment – or instead construct a system of categories which will grasp *nature and man* at the same time, in their movement, in their contradiction and in their interpenetration.

Before dialectical materialism every 'system' which wanted to be total (which wanted to be philosophical, thus systematic and coherent) merely used unconscious social categories to grasp the universe. For the philosopher, for the ideologue in general, society was a given accepted naïvely along with its content and in the ideological forms it had spontaneously adopted at the moment the thinker started to reflect; in other words, he accepted it together with its profoundest assumptions. Thus Plato accepted slavery, Descartes and Spinoza accepted commerce and mercantile capitalism and Hegel accepted the bourgeois individual. So in these doctrines, and in their search for internal coherence, there was a radical duplicity, more often than not concealed by sophistry or mysticism: *thoughts based on unconsidered data and presuppositions.* Certainly throughout the history of philosophy we can see the (ambiguous and contradictory) pathways which in the eighteenth century crystallized as materialism and idealism. But that is just one aspect of the history of ideologies and philosophies in relation to the development of history and society. In our view past philosophies and their history, on the one hand, and Marxist philosophical thought on the other, cannot be reduced to a few glibly systematized observations on matter and spirit. They are richer and more complex than that. The elaboration of categories constitutes another aspect of the development, one which has its own complexities. For the categories had practical, historical and social origins; at the same time they underwent a theoretical elaboration aimed at formulating and defining them, and determining the connections between them. Specifically philosophical categories can only be separated from social categories a posteriori. In the wake of Marx (in *A Contribution to the Critique of Political Economy*), we have already noted the importance of the objectivity of the categories by which bourgeois society expresses itself and its criticism of previous socio-economic structures. For example, the category of *social labour.* At a certain stage in its development, society began to examine critically the categories which expressed it: this was when Marx inaugurated (as a function of bourgeois society seen in its becoming and its totality, and therefore as a function of the existence of the working class) the critique of the categories of bourgeois society itself. Thus Marx defined the bourgeois nature of the Individual, which hitherto had been taken as an absolute. For Marx the category of social labour discovered by the classic economists became that of *alienated* labour; need was revealed as *alienated* need; it was through critical reflection that the *fetishistic* character of commodities and money was arrived at; in this way a higher and decisive stage in objectivity was reached. Once the origins of these categories were made conscious, it became feasible to represent the universe and history coherently and in a way which really allowed the elements of the human their unity. In a way in which society and the human were consequently no longer in opposition, but integrated in a whole, each retaining its specificity.

If this unity is to be fully developed a painstaking and extensive critical analysis of the categories in every sphere of art and science will therefore be needed. In philosophy as well. This immense undertaking will provide us with a better grasp of what is still only abstract, and will enable us to introduce what is still only theoretical and ideological into *everyday* life and consciousness. Marx merely set this task in motion. Notably in the *Contribution to the Critique of Political Economy*, the importance of which is often totally neglected in favour either of his earlier writings, or else of *Capital.* His work is a model, a guide, a beacon. In no respect is it a completed system, a vision or a conception of the world in the traditional meaning of the terms!

At the same time this examination of categories and the elaboration of their relations and of their theoretical unity constitutes a critique of superseded ideologies, their concepts and categories; notably of those ideologies that sanction the directly experienced discreteness of the individual and the social (their real contradiction) by hypostasizing it in the form of an imagined discreteness which puts all the stress either on the one or on the other.

The profound Hegelian distinction between *understanding* (or intelligence) and *reason* takes on a new meaning. Understanding must be defined as a historical and theoretical stage in thought and consciousness. It analyses, separates and situates determinations in a reciprocal externality; it determines properties and relations in isolation. It undergoes determinations; it accepts them according to a given culture, a given society, with its class struggles and its social structure and its oppressive institutions. It seeks unsuccessfully to work out a coherent (logical) discourse on the universe.

Dialectical reason criticizes understanding and dispels its determinants but only so as better to grasp the unity behind its contradictions. It understands categories in their real historical development and their connections. It is defined by the *critical movement* of these categories. *It is the function of the universal* and of the *totality* operating through negation, and through contradictions, that are known and dominated. It relativizes categories in order to grasp the universal within them more surely. At the same time, whereas understanding always hopes to close and conclude its discourse on the universe, dialectical reason knows that *its* work can never be completed.

The notion of alienation may be grasped on the level of understanding. And that is the level on which we all receive it and grasp it initially, then try to conceptualize and apply it. But the problem is to move to the highest level of dialectical reason: to think the notion dialectically, in a universal and concrete way, in other words by determining it in all the breadth of its universality and by grasping it in the minutiae of everyday life.

Moreover, the effort of the philosopher does not and cannot stay on an isolated philosophical level, in a separate consciousness, sphere or dimension; the source of his theories is social practice, and he must direct them back towards life, be it through his teaching or by other means (poetry? literature?). Dialectical thought can and must transform itself into dialectical consciousness of life, in life: unity of the mediate and the immediate, of the abstract and the concrete, of culture and natural spontaneity. In this way it will pass from ideology and specific knowledge into culture, language, perhaps into direct perception of the world – in any event, into everyday life!

Conclusion: the theory of alienation and of the 'total man' remain the driving force behind the critique of everyday life. They allow us to represent social development as a whole and to determine the direction in which it is going. They also allow us to analyse this becoming, boring down within it for samples, penetrating its details and linking it with the overall system. These notions must be handled with extreme caution, however. We cannot give them an ontological meaning like the concepts in use in traditional philosophy. To use them inconsiderately – speculatively – is extremely hazardous; for example an *idea* (which expresses all the parts of the process and its limit to infinity) can become an *image of the future* or, even worse, an already accomplished *reality*. There is a perfunctory kind of Marxism which believes itself capable of seeing into the future or of asserting that the present – a given individual man in particular conditions, such as socialist society or militant action – represents the future.

And yet non-Marxist philosophers, psychologists and sociologists carry out exactly the same operation, even though they do so – apparently – in a more abstract way. They declare that man, or the human, or the social, or the historical, make up a whole. At the same time they declare that this totality is already with us, present, describable and fully graspable. They use the category of *totality*, a philosophical category, in a non-critical manner. They use it non-dialectically, in a way that is both logical and speculative. Thus investigations which ought to be pursued coherently using the category dialectically end up at sixes and sevens, pulling in different directions, representing themselves as opposing systems. Sometimes man and the human appear to be wandering aimlessly and endlessly through history; history and everyday life appear complex, but ambiguous, at the mercy of radical contingency and pure relativism; the concrete face of freedom is reduced to the minuscule dimensions of individual choice, and disappears as far as the meaning of history is concerned. At other times history is given a goal and personality a meaning according to a traditional theology: God and religion are the foundation of totality, of total life. And at other times again the hypothesis that totality is effectively present is used to certify its absence; and so it becomes a question of 'detotalized totality', something which emphasizes splitting and breaking, separation and the tragic, as a way of consecrating them.[91]

Thus, when taken *in isolation*, in other words speculatively, outside of *praxis*, the theories of alienation and totality become transformed into systems which are very remote from Marxism – into neo-Hegelianism. The operation which consists of leaving social practice and its analysis in order to engage in speculation, only to come back to reality armed with a pseudo-concept, leads to a variety of contradictory representations; their externality creates an illusion, and makes us believe in the richness of philosophy, whereas what we have before us is the image of its incoherence, its powerlessness, its poverty.

Another aspect of the question. Taken in isolation, non-dialectically, the concept of alienation is open to strictly individual manipulation.

Anyone at all can take it over and declare that such-and-such an activity alienates and externalizes him, and turns him into a thing – work, for example, or a profession, or love, marriage, children. There may be an element of truth in this, but the person concerned will use this partial truth to construct superfluities, exaggerations, disturbing interpretations. From this false point of view, it is no longer consciousness which is alienated, it is consciousness which does the alienating; and the first schoolboy who comes along will be able to say that the way he is taught at school (especially if he really is being badly taught) and the work he has to do there are turning him into a thing. In the same way, it will no longer be a particular type of work which is alienating, or social labour which is alienated, but work in general which will appear alienating. And the theory of everyday life, together with its critique, will be metamorphosed into a philosophy of idleness.

Thus this difficult and rigorous theory can become a principle of facileness; the implement for a positive critique becomes the implement for hypercriticism, for entirely negative pseudo-criticism. What form of life, what partial content is there, which could not be taken as being totally alienating? Not only religion, but love too; every form of art, not simply purely abstract art, or art for art's sake; not only State oppression, but any discipline within society; not only the *private* man, but the citizen; not only the systematic disordering of the senses,[92] but knowledge itself. Thus all self-realization – which can only be partial, and must therefore involve alienation at a more-or-less deep level – appears to be, and becomes, total alienation. Thus in recent years the theory of alienation has become widely available in a form which is both speculative and arbitrary; this is above all because in this guise it permits the 'free' and empty affirmation of the self – in other words a return to the bourgeois individual, as well as to pessimism, to individualism. But despite appearances, we are still within the parameters of neo-Hegelianism. I say 'despite appearances' because this interpretation does conflict with the political and state-controlled claim that only by political action and activity on the level of the State can alienation be avoided, the human realized and the individual humanized. The fact is that the two interpretations (individualist or political, anarchistic or state-centred) are interdependent; the one relies on the other, the one justifies the other, and neither goes beyond the Hegelian framework.

Thus of necessity theory and concepts (such as alienation, totality, the total man) become meeting points and areas of discussion for divergent doctrines; and an excuse for polemics. On the theoretical and ideological level it is a situation which calls for extra vigilance. We have reached the core of the problems of our era: the core of all our problems.

The danger is that we may use philosophical concepts and categories speculatively. But how can we determine how to use them legitimately?

Marx gives us the example and the model. In his writings the theory and the concept of alienation are integrated into the development of his thought while retaining their philosophical meaning. They become transformed. Though no longer discernible *as such* in economic science, they nevertheless constitute its basis and its philosophical meaning. The theory of alienation becomes transformed into the theory of fetishism (fetishism of commodities, money, capital). Social relations are enclosed and concealed within these economic objects, which are also objects of political economy. Taking on the appearance of things, the products of social activity in effect become things invested with power over men.

In my opinion, in his early writings, particularly in the *Economic and Philosophical Manuscripts of 1844*, Marx had not yet fully developed his thought. It is there, however, germinating, growing, becoming. Certainly, the interpretation of these texts is problematic, but the problems need to be properly formulated. My view is that historical and dialectical materialism *developed*. It did not come into being abruptly, with an absolute discontinuity, after a break, at *x* moment, in the works of Marx (and in the history of humanity), and to think that it did produces false problems. To begin with, Marxism is made to appear like a system, a *dogma*.

This is not to challenge the newness of Marxism. On the contrary, it represents it in a more profound manner. Any radical newness must be born, must grow and take shape, precisely because it is a new reality. A brutal break is highly unlikely to produce something with genuine life; rather it creates a pure, abstract idea, or a dogmatic decree. The thesis which puts a date on Marxism, or tries to, seriously runs the risk of desiccating it, and of interpreting it in a one-sided way. What is more, how can Marxism be envisaged outside of its own categories —

becoming, development? This would be to enclose it in a contradiction; or worse: to represent it as external to the reality for which it provides the key; to apply it from outside, dogmatically.

These problems have their philosophical side; they involve exegesis, scholarly apparatus, but they also contribute to living research. It cannot be simply a matter of confronting text with text; the texts must also be confronted with living reality. Therefore there is generally no ready-made solution to the problems presented; or else the problem presented is not the real one, but a prefabricated, dogmatic schematization. The mistake, the false option which must be avoided, is to *overestimate* or else to *underestimate* Marx's early writings. They already contain Marxism, but as a potential, and certainly not *all* Marxism (a term which in any case has no clearly defined meaning). It is false (and anti-dialectical, and anti-Marxist) to consider that Marx's thought was born like Minerva springing forth from the head of Jupiter; and it is absurd to consider that Marxism begins with the *Manifesto* or *Capital*. The early writings contain great riches, but riches still confused, riches half mined and scarcely exploited. That Marx should subsequently abandon or transform such philosophical concepts as alienation does not prove them to be meaningless, nor does the advent of political economy mean that the role of philosophy is at an end. We may take them up again and use them – as Marx did – to criticize their social origins and speculative interpretations of them. What is more, Marx shows us the dangers of using them metaphysically. He integrates them within a specific science, political economy. Thus the problem is as follows: there is more to *Capital* than political economy. It contains history; it contains deep insights into *sociology* (notably the fundamental concept of 'socio-economic formation'). Are we really betraying Marx's work if we integrate the concept of alienation into a sociology which has been explicitly constituted as a science?

Certainly, it is not clear what use the concept of alienation can have for the historian. But in fact that proves nothing; maybe historians will have something to say about this, and they are perfectly entitled to do so. The same question goes for psychologists and psychiatrists. But if we can form a clear idea of the use the *sociologist* may make of the concept, then we can *legitimately* conclude that such a use follows the fundamental tendencies of Marxist thought.

Let us make an even more general point. The content of concrete life has produced forms which conflict with it, smother it, and which consequently collapse from this self-inflicted lack of substance and roots. The separation of form and content does not date from today or yesterday; it turns up in most ideological mystifications. And it produces an error which dialectical thought must carefully avoid. The danger in separating form and content is that their unity will be forgotten. There is no form without content, no content without form. It is impossible to grasp a content *as such* without giving it a form, or without using an existing form as a starting point in order to come to grips analytically with its content. Any separation of form and content involves a certain amount of illusion and superficiality; for form it means not an absence or formal purity, but rather a loss of content. Conversely, to determine content in terms of itself is an indication of dogmatism, and more often than not a confidence trick. This having been said, nowadays (needless to say, in the speeches and writings of 'thinkers' and authors) forms do appear as purified and purely formal, as striving to become self-sufficient, to supplant content, to take its place; which, being translated, means the destruction of content. This active formalization becomes an attack on form itself, which is destroyed by its consequent emptiness; unless, of course, it can still be used to present a 'content' outside of itself, which has no relation to the form, but which needs a deceptive language in order to appear as a figure.

Let us make a (provisional, incomplete) list of these conflicts:

(a) *rationalism versus reason* (formal rationalism, bourgeois intellectualism, never going beyond the level of understanding – versus living, concrete, dialectical reason);

(b) *nationalism* (the old, 'classic', right-wing variety) *versus nations and versus its own nation* as a living thing, on the march towards democracy and socialism;

(c) *individualism* (the individualism of the bourgeois individual isolated and isolating himself in his *private* consciousness and his own aloofness) *versus the individual,* the real individual, active, alive, solving problems, starting with his own;

(d) *objectivism* (the kind which thinks 'neutrally' and 'impartially', which endlessly weighs the pros and the cons or jumps from one point of view to another, which takes facts in isolation and information out of context) *versus thorough objectivity,* where thought is allied with practice to grasp every aspect of a contradictory reality, its complex becoming, its hidden tendencies . . .;

(e) *aestheticism of pure form* (technicality in art, the pursuit of pure style and pure plasticity), completely detached abstraction or formalism, *versus form*;

etc.

This list of 'isms' could go on and on. We have given enough examples to demonstrate the general present tendency of thought, ideology and culture in bourgeois society; a tendency which is concealed by the technical and technocratic airs adopted by most activities in a specific area – and also by the existence of conflicting aspirations, procedures and efforts to rediscover or create a content.

Surely this general formalism means that human activities and capabilities are being alienated in a multiplicity of ways, heterogeneous and yet drearily monotonous, that while shapes external one to the other and external to living man are being projected, human activities and capabilities are being split apart. It is a general alienation, coming to the surface in the overall structure of society and brought forth by the movement of that structure, but constantly turning back towards and into day-to-day living. Might this not give us a potentially vital guide to the critique of everyday life?

We began by showing the danger of using the notion of *alienation* in an abstract (isolated, speculative) way. The philosopher has no right to elaborate this notion in itself, to examine it outside actual alienated or alienating situations. He has no right to isolate the domain of philosophy. Once he has established the notion and its universal significance, he must move over into other well-defined areas – political economy, sociology – and above all he must confront the notion with concrete situations in everyday life. Here, however, basing ourselves upon practice, and on the real – contemporary – situation, we may rediscover generalities – and thus halt the decline of knowledge into the mere observation of facts, into mere empiricism or mere pragmatism.

This theoretical development does not give us the right to postulate – by decision or 'option' – one activity as essentially human and another (which we find unpleasant or boring) as dehumanized, alienated or alienating. The critique of everyday life does not make life's problems any simpler. It requires and determines a critical and self-critical consciousness which is higher than the consciousness exerted when we make the occasional uncomplicated choice. Anyone who wishes to found an ethic – and his personal ethic – on the notion of alienation needs to have a precise and analytic tool and a consciousness that has been finely honed by the dialectic at his disposal. Only then will he be able to find his way through the labyrinth which is all social life and through the jungle which is bourgeois society; only then will he distinguish between what is 'life-enhancing' and what is obscurantist and static in his life. Thus everyone may perhaps be able tightly to embrace *their own* lives, and to love them, without evading any task, fruitful conflict, or useful risk.

In short, we have returned to the level of philosophy, a philosophy tested by life. It is as much a question of ethics as it is of sociology. But before we can broach the ethical problems we will need to put our concepts to the test, to verify them and develop them more thoroughly, and not just once.

VIII   Philosophy and the Critique of Everyday Life

Philosophy is going through a very difficult period; and so is the philosopher. He draws comfort from the thought that he is not the only one. One wonders: 'Is it growing pains, an adolescent crisis, or a terminal illness?', ('one' being first and foremost the philosopher).

One of the most curious symptoms of this crisis is philosophy's increasing importance. Who is there who does not long to have his say about 'important problems'? Specialists from the various sciences, men of action, men of state – they all yearn to launch into vast reflections, and by doing so to justify themselves in grandiose terms. This is an outpouring of philosophy in which the philosopher himself disappears; and the more obscure he becomes, the more disturbing he is (assuming always he persevers in being a philosopher). It becomes easier and easier for him to inspire fear in people. The promotion of philosophy to the status of an ideology – of a weapon in the great struggles between classes, nations, peoples – is not without its drawbacks. It is subjected to appalling pedagogic or political simplifications. Over a period of twenty or thirty years we have been forced to witness the schematization of the dialectic: the Stalinist interpretation has reduced this subtle way of thought first to a robust and popular common sense (and that was the heyday of Stalinist interpretation, the era of *Anarchism and Socialism*), then to the permanent seven-point plan: four points for the dialectic, three for materialism. With the definition of matter, and of consciousness as a reflection of it, philosophy comes to an end. Everyone thinks he is a philosopher, and sets off cheerfully for life's fray armed with this possibly useful but somewhat light-weight equipment. The role of philosophy is over. The general, world-wide crisis has certainly not spared non-Marxist philosophy (that was the sector where it began); it has also affected Marxist philosophy. But the symptoms are different. On one side, the non-Marxist side, the symptoms are obscurity, jargon, technicality, illusory profundity. On the Marxist side they are false clarity, pedagogy which takes itself as a measure of thought, desiccated dogmatism and skeletal schematization, propagandist exploitation of ideological themes. Philosophy is in its death throes: it is being killed off, or perhaps it is the philosopher who is committing some second-rate hara-kiri.

In the period of the last twenty-five years, have the philosophers in the Soviet Union been blind or merely unwilling to see? Have they been in hiding? What analysis of the real, or what elements for an analysis of the real, have they contributed? What worthwhile books have they produced? Certainly not the glossaries, dictionaries or encyclopedias, in which the 'formulations' have changed only according to the political situation. We cannot even say to their credit that these official or semi-official philosophers used the kind of ruses by which other philosophers (Lukács, for example, but not only him, since the reader may enjoy looking for a few such ruses here in this book!) managed to introduce a few new ideas into the general debate. Today, even the most prudent, the most official 'Marxists' admit that a new analysis of this period is needed. Now the aridity of Marxist philosophy – and that in the very countries where it should have grown and developed – cannot be separated from the sum total of the events that have taken place. It is an aspect of the situation, and must be analysed and studied. Marxists must open their eyes and examine the fact closely: Marxism has become *boring*. It has been a disappointment;

young people are disappointed with it because it bores them.

If the philosopher can no longer be accepted as typifying man, or as the mediator between heaven and earth – between the relative and the absolute – then what role has he to play? If in the last analysis it is the masses which judge, if philosophy becomes accessible and turns into a force, if the political leader speaks (legitimately when like Lenin he has attained authentic and incontrovertible greatness) as a philosopher, what use can the philosopher have? As a funeral director, a pall-bearer for the past, in other words as a historian for out-of-date philosophy? As a secondhand scholar, following painfully in the footsteps of genuine scholars? As a latter-day encyclopedist? As a vulgarizer, compiling glossaries and manuals? None of this is worth even an hour's effort. So the philosopher is beset with self-doubts. He lets himself be outclassed by literary hacks whose best-sellers bring them fame and fortune. He gives in to the temptations of literature or politics, and abandons philosophy – yes, philosophy too – to platitude and mediocrity.

This leads us to the point when we need to ask ourselves what the 'critique of everyday life' means. To confront philosophers with life – simple life – and its problems, to immerse them in this human raw material and to ask their help in mastering it, in scraping away the coating of mud to reveal the gems within, would that be a breakthrough, a new direction? How should we situate the critique of everyday life in relation to classic philosophy? Is there room in Marxist philosophy for a critique of everyday life considered as a philosophical discipline? Are we dealing with a *sociological* undertaking in the narrow sense of a specialized discipline, or of an undertaking with a *philosophical* meaning and a set of concrete contents and social objects to support it?

It is not enough simply to examine the concept of alienation and its *actuality* (in the dialectical meaning of the word). For here we are talking about philosophy as an activity, and of the philosopher as such – of his function, his situation – rather than about philosophy as a set of concepts and as the development of those concepts.

As an activity, philosophy used to be precisely one of those exceptional and superior activities through which men who could devote their lives to leisure[93] could step outside of everyday life, and which involved criticism of everyday life, implicitly or explicitly. Among these activities we can also include: dreams, the imaginary, art, play, ethics, political life, etc.

In terms of these activities, the first definition of everyday life is a *negative* one. If in our minds (by a sort of abstraction) we remove the highly specialized occupations from man and from the human, what is left? An apparently very scanty residue. In reality this so-called residue contains a 'human raw material' which holds hidden wealth, as our study shows. The higher activities derive from it, they are at one and the same time its ultimate expression, its direct or indirect critique and its alienated form – albeit an alienation embodying a more-or-less conscious and successful attempt to achieve 'disalienation'.

Would the aim of a critique be to systematize the various perspectives offered by these higher activities and by the indirect criticisms they imply? Or conversely to exclude them systematically and to separate the exceptional moments from the everyday by way of an apology for the latter? Neither. The second of these objectives would abandon everyday life to vulgarity; it would bring back a sort of populism into philosophy; thus it would grant art, science, ethics and philosophy the inordinate privilege of constituting superhuman – and therefore inhuman – 'worlds'. It is therefore an interpretation we must formally reject. On the other hand the first objective would limit itself to confronting what is possible with what was been accomplished. It would delve into poetry, or play, or ethics, in search of images from beyond everyday life which could be used in evidence against it. It would add little to works of the past, which can be looked upon as indirect criticisms of everyday life. So neither objective is valid. And yet they both are. For we must be careful neither to abandon the (acquired or potential) wealth of the content, of the 'human raw material'; nor to lose whatever was achieved in the highest, most intense moments. The problem is therefore to define the reciprocal relation of these activities and realities: the simple moments and the highest moments of life.

Superior, differentiated and highly specialized activities have never been separate from everyday practice, they have only appeared to be so. Their consciousness of being separate from it was in itself a link; they implied an indirect or implicit criticism of the everyday only inasmuch as they raised themselves above it. Thus French eighteenth-century philosophy, literature, art, ethics and politics corresponded to *the everyday life* of the bourgeoisie: the new pursuit of happiness, pleasure, luxury, profit and power. In the same way eighteenth-century rationalism corresponded to the everyday attitude expressed in 'commonplace books'. And every time a scientist comes up with a formula or a law, he is of necessity condensing a long experience in which the lowliest assistant and the simplest tool have had their part to play.

And yet these appearances (like all appearances) contain a certain reality. Specialized activities (considered *as* activities, with their 'products', or works) genuinely did develop outside and above the everyday. Only by controlling it through this externality were they able to condense it, to concentrate its meanings and achievements. There is a cliché which with a certain degree of justification compares creative moments to the mountain tops and everyday time to the plain, or to the marshes. The image the reader will find in this book differs from this generally accepted metaphor. Here everyday life is compared to fertile soil. A landscape without flowers or magnificent woods may be depressing for the passer-by; but flowers and trees should not make us forget the earth beneath, which has a secret life and a richness of its own.

The indirect criticism of the everyday in works of the past which emerged from that everyday appeared only too frequently to *devalue* it. People who gather flowers and nothing but flowers tend to look upon soil as something dirty. Practical activities were always the basis and the foundation for 'pure' thought, and even for its most extreme form, pure contemplation. What does the contemplator contemplate, if not – from afar – the everyday, the crowd, the masses, all the things from which his 'epoche'[94] holds him aloof, and which he will try in vain to rediscover?[95] And yet the situation is eventually reversed. The day dawns when everyday life also emerges as a critique, a critique of the superior activities in question (and of what they produce: *ideologies*). The devaluation of everyday life by ideologies appears as one-sided and partial, in both senses of the word. A direct critique takes the place of indirect criticism; and this direct critique involves a rehabilitation of everyday life, shedding new light on its positive content.

We have already demonstrated how the worker, as a human being, constitutes a whole. To consider him as such means that the *separation* between the human factor and the technical factor in private life and in leisure is ruled out, but not as a result of analysing the *contradictions* between the elements which make up the whole. The fragmented character of modern industrial labour both encloses and conceals the social character of all the work done in any one firm and of the total labour in society (the growing *socialization* of labour and the relations of production). Thus the worker's consciousness of the *social* character of labour comes to him largely from outside rather than from *his own* individual work, notably from his political life. It is a consciousness which he expects and demands from *his own* work, which he needs in order to understand that work and the place it holds, and yet it does not come from his work alone. We need to study the life of the worker in its varied aspects, its conflicts, its contradictions. The consciousness of the worker involves – together with the content of his own practical experience – numerous ideological elements, some justified, others illusory; some atavistic (coming for example from the peasant or artisan classes); others deriving from objective but partly outmoded conditions of capitalism (the 'free' labour contract in competitive capitalism, the 'classic' forms of the class struggle); still others derived from the new conditions within capitalism (monopolies, and new content contradicting the monopolistic form of capitalism; trade union action and new forms of class struggle); others deriving from socialism, and finally others coming from individual limits or the limits of the group the worker in question belongs to (corporatism, professional solidarity, etc.). If we consider the overall life of the worker, we will see that his work and his attitude towards work are linked to social practice *as a whole*, to his experience as a whole, his leisure activities, his family life, his cultural and political goals, as well as to the class struggle. What is more, this 'whole' must be taken in the context of a specific country and nation, at a specific moment of civilization and social development, and as involving a certain set of needs. And this brings us back to the critique of everyday life.

Let us turn to another very precise example: *political* activity. It can be founded on already established authority, or on constituted law, on mystification and violence, or on knowledge. In so far as it is founded on knowledge, it requires the most scrupulous attention to everyday life. The progressive or socialist politician must know the life and the needs of the people whose immediate or essential interests he is defending. If he strays from this duty, he is no longer qualified for the task. He is progressive or socialist only in so far as he has this knowledge. The simplest matters concerning housing, roads, children's playgrounds, public transport etc., have their place in a hierarchy of requirements which may lead to the transformation of the State. The politician's talent rests on his ability to grade the elements in this hierarchy, and to address whatever is essential at any given moment.

And yet if true politics involves a knowledge of everyday life and a critique of its requirements, conversely everyday life involves a critique of all politics. Political life is by definition lived out in the stratosphere of society: in the sphere of the State and on that level. The problems posed in political life are both abstract and concrete, but they have an aura of technicality which makes them appear totally concrete (questions of law, finance, budget, etc.). However, their abstraction can conceal both the fact that they will influence many human lives and interests, and that any solution proposed will be class-specific.

More generally, in the modern State, the *citizen*, in so far as he is separate from the *private* man and the *productive* man, becomes externalized in terms of his own self. He plays a part in a political community in which he sees himself as social. Whereas he is also social, and more so, in another context. The citizen – the man who is well-informed about public matters, who has reasoned opinions, who knows the law – has become a political fiction; for there are necessarily political fictions just as there are necessary legal ones ('ignorance is no defence in law'). At this point we could define concrete democracy as the reduction of the role of political fictions to a minimum. The externality of the citizen in relation to his own everyday life becomes of necessity projected outside of himself: in models, in fanaticisms, in idolizations, in fetishisms. Wherever it appears, the cult of personality has a political sense and can never be reduced to a peripheral ideology; it is bound up with the nature of the State; it signifies both a democracy and a lack of democracy: a political fiction which is in danger of becoming a crushing reality. The externality of the citizen and his projection outside of himself in relation to his everyday life is part of that everyday life.

'[The] *German*[96] conception of the modern state, which abstracts from *real man*, was only possible because and in so far as the modern state itself abstracts from *real man* or satisfies the *whole* man in a purely imaginary way',[97] wrote Marx, in one of the rare and precious texts in which he talks to us about *the total man*; and what was valid for the monarchical State, for enlightened despotism and for Hegel's ethically based State remains valid for any State which establishes itself above society. The man who holds power becomes the only 'total man' and at the same time embodies the fiction of the total man in the eyes of every individual: its deceptive image. From this analysis Marx drew a decisive conclusion about the State:

> Only when real, individual man resumes the abstract citizen into himself and as an individual man has become a *species-being* in his empirical life, his individual work and his individual relationships, only when man has recognized and organized his *forces propres* (own forces) as *social forces* so that social force is no longer separated from him in the form of *political* force, only then will human emancipation be completed.[98]

Wherever there is a State, it is in the State that individual man will find his generality, his generic existence as a man, and this he does by becoming an imaginary member of a fictitious community. Within every class-based society the constraints that one class imposes upon another are always a part of the inhuman power which reigns over everything. On that level, the individual sees himself 'divested of his real individual life and filled with unreal universality'.[99] How does the individual see himself when faced with the enormous mass of the State? Like a minute speck, like a shadow. He becomes *for himself* an unreal appearance; but at the same time, by an absolute contradiction, the political fiction sanctions the *private* man, *qua* selfish individual with personal interests, as the supreme reality. This division assigns reality to egoism and abstract form to the citizen. Therefore a political revolution can take place without the State's natural basis, real social life – the 'world of needs' or of private law – being submitted to a critique and completely transformed. And if the political transformation subsequently 'revolutionizes' certain of these elements – after having dissociated them and thus particularized them *as* elements – it may leave certain others intact. For example, it might leave the world of needs to one side, or likewise the law, despite having transformed 'private' interests or the way labour is organized. Thus there is alienation by politics wherever the State has not yet withered away, for the Marxist critique of the State attacks all States. If certain texts are specifically directed against the Hegelian State or the bourgeois democratic State, others specify the 'political State' in general, in its relation with civil society. In no respects do the texts quoted by Lenin (in *The State and Revolution*) on the smashing of the bourgeois State apparatus, the constitution of a new State and its decline, invalidate the earlier texts. Rather, they confirm them as a function of concrete political situations. But if politics alienates, and contains alienation, it can also be disalienated, and this through political activity – in and through struggle on the political level and in and through the conflict between life and politics. Here again we recognize a complex of contradictions within a unity. In a sense bourgeois democracy in capitalist society, for example, entails a maximum of alienation: total alienation, complete political alienation. It perfects the opposition between the public and the private, between community and slavery. It mystifies every individual by granting him a place both in slavery and in community, in fiction and in reality. It allows him an apparent independence, because he takes 'the *unbridled* movement of the spiritual and material elements which form the content of his life'[100] for total freedom. The individual becomes totally subservient, and totally dehumanized. At this point the only link between all these social atoms and fragmented activities seems to be the State. It is not irrelevant to point out here that right from the start of his career, Stalin fell foul of what Marx calls political superstition: the illusory idea that the State cements society together, whereas it is the functioning of civil society and its cohesion, even in the apparent anarchy of its activities, which support the State.[101] The individual realizes that in bourgeois society the way he represents himself, for others and for himself, is contradictory, in that it splits him in two. On the one hand it isolates him as 'private' , atomizing him, dividing him; and this is a false image: atoms have no needs, they are self-sufficient, without needs, contented, perfect. Then on the other hand the individual realizes that each of his activities, his 'properties', his impulses, involves a *need*. This need brings him into relationship with other people. No matter how alienated need, natural necessity and man's essential properties may become, they still form a link between the members of this society. Thus these needs in everyday life are a cohesive force for social life even in bourgeois society, and they, *not political life*, are the real bond. So the individual tends to transcend his own separation from his self, his illusory image, his real appearance and false reality, his artificial atomization, his duplicity. He recognizes himself, and even by recognizing himself as an egoistic individual he has transcended political superstition.

Let us sum up. There is a set of elements to consider, and to the ones we have already examined we must add this complex contradiction: the citizen, the public man, the member of a State versus the real man, the private man. It is a complex system, for the public man and the citizen are at one and the same time fictitious and real; in so far as they are real, they pull the reality of man into the fictitious realm. As for the 'private' man, he is also both real and fictitious.

Everyday life includes political life: the public consciousness, the consciousness of belonging to a society and a nation, the consciousness of class. It enters into permanent contact with the State and the State apparatus thanks to administration and bureaucracy. But on the other hand political life detaches itself from everyday life by concentrating itself in privileged moments (elections, for example), and by fostering specialized activities. Thus *the critique of everyday life involves a critique of political life, in that everyday life already contains and constitutes such a critique*: in that it *is* that critique.

Let us now consider the structure of consciousness. A man's consciousness is determined by his (social) being. To coin a phrase, it *reflects* it. The word 'reflection' can lead to many confusions, and above all to many simplifications. If we are to avoid them, all we need do is notice that in nature reflections are profoundly different from what they reflect; and the image in the mirror only appears to be a reproduction of whatever is in front of it. The theory which maintains that on the one hand there are things and on the other their reflection in men's minds, and that the one reproduces the other, is philosophically puerile. A reflection in a consciousness, or a reflection which constitutes a consciousness, can be incomplete, mutilated, inverted, distorted, mystified; it is a reflection and yet in the generally accepted sense it is not a reflection. Let us consider the individualist individual's consciousness – under classic capitalism: the bourgeois individual's consciousness. In no way does it reflect the social complex to which he belongs: bourgeois society, capitalism. It is in the very nature of 'free competition' that an overview of phenomena and their laws is beyond the scope of the individual consciousness; and that is why there had to be economists, and Marx, to discover and understand these laws! The bourgeois's (the capitalist's) individual consciousness *reflects* his private interests in competition; it therefore conflicts with society as such, in that it is a *social consciousness*. The capitalist individual sees the other members of society – be they bourgeois or not – as outside of himself, and in opposition to himself. His consciousness only reflects the fact that competition separates one individual from another in such a way as to constitute a society which is beyond the grasp of any individual consciousness. But having said that, we should add that up to a point the capitalist embodies Capital and its functions, and this personification may be more or less successful. The *typical* bourgeois would be the perfect incarnation of Capital. But Capital is an economic fetish, and cannot in itself define a human being, with a human being's consciousness. Every bourgeois is *also* something else: a private man, with private passions – a father, who loves horses, or music, etc. As Marx has said, within every bourgeois two souls are locked in Faustian combat: the need to enjoy and the need to accumulate, thus on the one hand man's 'private' needs, and an aspect of his 'private' consciousness which now and again he gives in to – and on the other the need imposed upon him by the requirements of his money, his capital. What is more, in so far as he is a private man, or a father, or even a sensualist (in other words an egoist), he needs other people; now his consciousness reflects this tendency, now it reflects his secret or avowed opposition to it. Thus consciousness joins forces with the need for other people which is determined by the situation the individual is in; together they transform needs into desires, decisions into actions; or, conversely, the one inhibits the other.

This consciousness is therefore determined by *objective* conditions (economic, social, but also physiological, etc.); however, it is unaware of these conditions; and it is, precisely, inasmuch as it is unaware of them that it is determined. Such a complex and contradictory situation gives rise to a multitude of problems. The individual (in this case the bourgeois individual) must solve them; he looks for a solution, consciously. He looks to ideologies and moral doctrines for an image of himself. The solutions and possibilities thus revealed and represented – through a mixture of ideological fictions and moments of awareness – are true or false, illusory or valid; they lead to more-or-less complete failures or successes, and also to combinations of success and failure. It is possible for the success to have no objective relation with ideology. For example, take a believer who is a successful businessman; he is supported by his faith; he will see his success as a blessing from God (which is how religion is generally perceived in the USA: as a factor in success). Thus activities of an exceptional nature only *appear* to be beyond everyday life; they are used to solve problems – or not to solve them. The externality of ideology involves a measure of illusions.

All this means that the simplified notion of reflection is inadequate as an analytic tool. Consciousness reflects and does not reflect: what it reflects is not what it seems to reflect, but *something else*, and that is what analysis must disclose. Precisely because the activity that produced ideologies was exceptional and specialized, they came out of social practice – of everyday life – in two senses: it produced them and they escaped from it, thus acquiring in the process an illusory meaning *other* than their real content. The problem of ideologies is as follows: how can consciousness at all levels (individuals, groups, classes, peoples) be mistaken about itself and its content – its being – when it is that very content and that very being which determine it? Only by taking the formal structure of consciousness and its content as inseparables and submitting them to a complex analysis will we be able to understand any particular form of consciousness, or any particular ideology.

And here we are faced once again with a problem which is fundamental for the critique of everyday life. It is a problem which the first volume of this study failed to pose clearly. Many men, and even people in general, *do not know their own lives very well, or know them inadequately*. This is one of the themes of the critique of everyday life, confirmed by the spectacular failures of subjectivist sociology (based solely on interviews, questionnaires or surveys). Men have no knowledge of their own lives: they see them and act them out via ideological themes and ethical values. In particular they have an inadequate knowledge of their needs and their own fundamental attitudes; they express them badly; they delude themselves about their needs and aspirations except for the most general and the most basic ones. And yet it is their lives, and their consciousness of life; but only the philosopher, and the sociologist informed by the dialectic, and maybe the novelist, manage to join together the *lived* and the *real*, *formal* structure and *content*. Thus ideology is at one and the same time within everyday life and outside of it. It is forever penetrating everyday life, forever springing forth from it, uninterruptedly. Yet at the same time it interprets it, adds to it, transposes it, refracts it (more or less clearly, more or less deceptively).

Man's being is at once natural and historical, biological and social, physiological and cultural (which does not exclude possible or real conflicts between these elements and aspects – on the contrary, it involves them). Man thinks because he has a brain (a superior activity of the nervous system), and because he has hands, and because he works and because he has a language. Therefore consciousness *reflects* these manifold interactions; it not only 'reflects' the outside world, and things, but also human activity, practical power over nature. It not only reflects a given objective environment, but the equally objective conflicts between man and the 'environment', between the human world and nature, between individuals in the human world. A thing in isolation can only be defined as a *product*, and consequently as corresponding to a more-or-less consolidated *power*. Even when a consciousness reflects a thing, in truth it is reflecting a power together with the imperatives of action and its *possibilities*. And this involves the leap forward, the unending escape from what has already been accomplished towards images and the imaginary, towards a realm beyond the everyday, and thence indeed back into the everyday so as to take cognizance of it.

And yet it is in everyday life and in everyday life alone that *the natural and the biological are humanized* (become social), and, further, that *the human, the acquired, the cultivated, become natural.* Here there is a constant interaction between *the controlled sector* (controlled by knowledge and practice) and *the uncontrolled sector* (unknown, or unbounded by knowledge, so that blind necessity holds sway over man's helplessness and ignorance). It is in everyday life and everyday life alone that those interpenetrations which philosophers and philosophy define in general and abstract terms are concretely realized. Thus when the philosopher turns back towards real life, general concepts which have been worked out by means of a highly specialized activity and abstracted from everyday life are not lost. On the contrary, they take on a new meaning for lived experience. The philosopher discovers that exceptional activities benefit from the richness acquired on the level of everyday life; sometimes they contribute to that richness, at other times they prey upon it and suck it dry; they do not produce it. It is in and through everyday life that organs (eyes, genitals) are humanized. They have been transformed by history, by work, by social life and culture. This transformation operates in the everyday realm, it flows from the everyday and concludes within it. Otherwise it cannot exist.

Here the fundamental notion becomes appropriation, a philosophical notion which Marx extracted from the work of the economists, and criticized; he then integrated notion and criticism and incorporated them in the theory of Capital and property, but without ever fully developing them. Through social practice, man appropriates nature (an elementary thesis of Marxism); he also appropriates *his own nature*. Thus the human eye is no longer the organ with which an animal, nervous or replete, always on the look-out, explores a nature ever filled with danger, ever filled with prey. It becomes the mediator between a consciousness and a formed, welcoming world. By thus becoming a means, it becomes an end: joy, rest, fulfilment. And communication.

Rest can only be regarded simply as an interruption of activity – or the opposite of activity – in a fragmented and alienated life, and within a non-dialectical conception of life. In fact, the totality of the conscious being – even while he is resting, even in his exceptional activities – benefits from work, itself considered as a total activity, in other words as the power of man over nature (and his own nature).

Material labour (to which intellectual work contributes the essential tools – techniques, concepts, knowledge) creates *products*. Some of these products are means of production, others are objects or consumer goods. Taken together, products and works make up the 'human world'. But where and in what sphere is the relation between living men and objects of consumption actualized? Where do they become *goods* in the concrete sense of the term? How are they *appropriated*? In everyday life, that sphere where needs and goods meet.[102] And yet, where do needs come from? Where are they formed? How? And how do they find what they are looking for? Do needs make up a system? Is there a 'system of needs' or a structure of needs? What is this structure?

Alongside the scientific study of the relations of production which is the province of political economy, there is thus a place for a concrete study of *appropriation*: for a theory of needs. Such a study enfolds philosophical concepts and makes them concrete; in a sense it renews philosophy by bringing it back into the sphere of real life and the everyday without allowing it to disappear within it. But it also belongs to a specific science which we have called *sociology*.

The social relation between individuals and products (and works) embodies modalities and various aspects which can be distinguished by analysis. It cannot be reduced to the economic study of the processes of production and circulation (or as vulgar economics has it: distribution). It involves a sociology and even a psychology. It has ideological, cultural and even ethical aspects which the economist may glimpse but which he is unable to grasp. The notions of *need* and of *good* affect political economy on the one hand, and ethics, the theory of social classes, the critique of society and the definition of society, culture and civilization on the other. Thus they affect concrete philosophy.

Therefore we need to develop the notion of need and to formulate a theory of needs. This will be one of the aims of the next volume of this *Critique of Everyday Life.*

Everyday life, in a sense residual, defined by 'what is left over' after all distinct, superior, specialized, structured activities have been singled out by analysis, must be defined as a totality. Considered in their specialization and their technicality, superior activities leave a 'technical vacuum' between one another which is filled up by everyday life. Everyday life is profoundly related to *all* activities, and encompasses them with all their differences and their conflicts; it is their meeting place, their bond, their common ground. And it is in everyday life that the sum total of relations which make the human – and every human being – a whole takes its shape and its form. In it are expressed and fulfilled those relations which bring into play the totality of the real, albeit in a certain manner which is always partial and incomplete: friendship, comradeship, love, the need to communicate, play, etc.

The substance of everyday life – 'human raw material' in its simplicity and richness – pierces through all alienation and establishes 'disalienation'. If we take the words 'human nature' dialectically and in their full meaning, we may say that the critique of everyday life studies human nature in its concreteness.

So then how are we to define the function of the philosopher? Will philosophy still retain a meaning as a specialized activity?

Yes, it will. Once the philosopher is *committed to life,* he will watch over its meaning and its development from within. He will not set himself up above the everyday, in the sphere of exceptional activities, in the domain of ideologies and of the State. At the very heart of the everyday, he will discover what is hindering or blocking the march forward. He will remain a witness to alienations, and their judge. Keeping his vigil by night and day, the philosopher will not be satisfied simply to study the development of 'human nature'; he will want to help it, negatively at least – but the negative is also positive – by removing whatever may obstruct its fragile seeds. And the more life is in jeopardy, the more vigilant he will be. An overall picture of the universe? A cosmology? An ontology? A theory of knowledge? It is not on such a traditional level that the philosopher will rediscover his lost concrete universality. To rediscover it he must confront looming alienations as a critic and an implacable enemy. Wherever they come from.

This duty has its dangers, both for the philosopher as individual, and also for the effectiveness of his role, in that it will always run the risk of turning into an aberrant activity and an irrelevant by-product The philosopher must accept these risks. The critique of everyday life does not mean exemption from self-criticism.

IX   Plans and Programme for the Future

In principle this present volume was only intended as an introduction to the *Critique of Everyday Life.*

The first draft of the second volume was abandoned for a number of reasons.[103]

The second volume was intended to include a methodical study of little magic spells in everyday life: words, sayings, interjections – familiar gestures, rituals – minor superstitions, archaisms, countless relics of ideologies and customs whose 'base' has disappeared. These detailed observations were to have been the starting point for an analysis of myths and remains of myths in emotional, erotic and sensual life, and even more generally in images of the cosmos, as well as in the sphere of human relations in general, in literature (including bad literature, melodrama, serials), on the radio, etc.

The plan had one serious drawback: the external – and therefore arbitrary – way it was systematized. The book ran the risk of becoming a work of philosophy rather than a piece of concrete sociological research.

One fine day, once I had become aware of this objection and the risk involved, I realized that I had at my disposal a vast amount of material in which my object of study was concretely embodied: the *romantic press*, the so-called *women's* press. In it we find survivals, superstitions, rituals, myths and modern mythology, formulated and systematized in accordance with new (and obscure) needs; and that in the fullness of the everyday, in a direct expression of the preoccupations and aspirations of the most immediately practical kind of everyday life. Moreover, this press represents an extraordinary sociological fact, which cries out to be analysed. It is precisely over the last ten years that it has achieved its world-wide success and importance. In France its three million copies per week are read by ten million women (and men ...). What does this enormous success mean? What new need does it reveal? Is it profound or superficial, valid or spurious? What structure of consciousness does it reveal? What contents?

Thus the second volume of *Critique of Everyday Life* will include:

(a) an attempt at a *theory of needs* which will develop the observations included here, and in the works of contemporary sociologists, economists and demographers;

(b) an *analysis of the romantic press*, not on the economic level, as a commercial organization, but on the *sociological* level (an analysis of the formal structures of consciousness, of ideologies, and more profoundly of the contents and the needs in so far as one can grasp them through their public expression);

(c) the outline of an analysis of *class* relations and attitudes in everyday life – of the contents and needs which these attitudes and conflicts reveal.

Obviously I will not be able to isolate these different 'chapters'. Moreover, the final section – on class relations – could become the subject of a special volume if it at last became possible to carry out precise, concrete and broad-based surveys in France.[104]

Paris, December 1956 to February 1957

CRITIQUE OF EVERYDAY LIFE

Introduction

1

Brief Notes on some

Well-Trodden Ground

Numbers have lost nothing of their mystical glamour. Between 1880 and 1900, in a confusion worthy of the panic which greeted the year 1000, most artists and writers considered themselves to be 'fin de siècle' and 'decadent'. By the same confusion the writers who appeared on the literary scene after the 1900 Exhibition slipped effortlessly into the role of renovators. For the public, and in their own eyes, they represented the 'New Century'. Decadence was no longer in fashion.

But decadence stopped being a fashion at the very moment it was becoming a reality, when so-called 'modern' civilization was entering its convulsive death-throes. Peacefully and blissfully nurtured during the years before the First World War, this 'New Century' generation was nevertheless able to dominate the tormented times which followed, and at this moment in time (1945) it is still peddling its 'values' – so that for more than half a century France has suffered a 'spiritually' stultifying continuity in which until now wars and defeats have seemed mere episodes, untroubling to philistine and aesthete alike.

To this generation we owe a certain worldly *awareness*. Although we have become extremely *cynical*, on the positive side we see things more sharply, more lucidly, and we have refined our intellectual and literary techniques.

Most of the pharisees of political and social life come from the petty bourgeoisie: as oppressor or victim, the petty bourgeois likes situations he can vindicate. By 1900 (and the coincidence between the number and the historical significance of the date is purely fortuitous) the haute bourgeoisie no longer needed to vindicate its political actions to itself (although it still knew how to pull out all the stops when rehearsing the gamut of its 'values'), and it won a decisive victory over the petty bourgeoisie, which ceased to play any determining political role.

The minds of the petty bourgeois were crammed with prejudice, boredom, ideals. But after 1900 immoralism became the order of the day. It was immoralism, not the invention of a new morality, that replaced outgrown moral categories. To a certain extent questions of sexuality became less shrouded in secrecy. Clarity and abstraction took over from preaching. A kind of intellectualized sensuality made its appearance; intellectuals and aesthetes began to discover – and to disinterested eyes the spectacle was one of high comedy – that they could be thirsty, that they could be hungry, that they could feel desire. This discovery was greeted with demonstrations of joyful and emotional surprise: poetic hymns to thirst, to hunger, to desire, to fountains, to taverns, to fruits of the earth ...[1]

At the same time, from its very beginnings the era of finance capitalism was characterized by the extreme abundance of unfixed capital on the move, seeking investments – or avoiding them in a series of *exoduses*, some unobtrusive, some turbulent, towards some safe haven.

This wealth of availabilities, whether pecuniary or human, proved very profitable for the literary hacks and the artists. Shortly after 1900 the boom in paintings, rare books and luxury editions coincided with a revival in snobbery. Writers and artists began to find life more beautiful, more 'free'. Almost totally indifferent to the fact that they were putting themselves up for sale along with their works – theirs was an alienated consciousness transformed into commodities without their even knowing it – they disregarded the terrible events which were looming on the horizon, even and above all when they brought the new, abstract, metaphysical themes of 'adventure' and 'risk' to the fore. It is of little importance here whether or not we would deem this irresponsible. The important thing is to establish that the underlying themes had not changed, and that the literary twentieth century is a myth, an illusion. Had the themes of adventure, risk, immoralism and sexual freedom in any way modified those far more serious and tenacious themes and realities – pessimism, doubt, weariness, despair, loneliness – which first appeared in our literature towards the middle of the nineteenth century? No, on the contrary, in the 'new' climate of dry lucidity, improved verbal technique and icy cynicism, the resonance of these themes merely grew stronger, deeper and more clear-cut. What does the theme of adventure really imply? The dissolution of social relations in decadent capitalist society.

If he avoids complicity in the deceptions, the complacent optical illusions, the self-interested mutual congratulations and the posturings of critics who pronounce on the 'importance' of works which have only been out a week, the objective critic will be able to unravel the deeper network of themes lying beneath the surface decorations. His conclusion will be that:

> the literary and 'spiritual' nineteenth century began with Nerval and Baudelaire and Flaubert. Romanticism goes back to Rousseau with his sentimental rhetoric and an individualism which he could still be complacent about, since it perceived no barrier between itself, nature and the divine, and since it had not been seriously tested as yet by loneliness and anguish. Stendhal too was an eighteenth-century man, optimistic and full of confidence in mankind, nature and the natural. With Baudelaire and Flaubert we enter another era, in which we are still living . . .

According to this objective critique, what are the characteristic themes of that intelligent but sombre nineteenth century? We will limit ourselves to three, only one of which – the third – need concern us here, and all of which are linked by more than one painful thread.

THE THEME OF FAILURE AND DEFEAT

Cf. *Sentimental Education*, 'Fusées',[2] 'My Heart Laid Bare', etc.

THE THEME OF DUALITY

Spleen and ideal, action and dream, flesh and soul, etc.[3]

THE THEME OF THE MARVELLOUS

Under the banner of the marvellous, nineteenth-century literature mounted a sustained attack on everyday life which has continued unabated up to the present day. The aim is to demote it, to discredit it. Although the duality between the marvellous and the everyday is just as painful as the duality between action and dream, the real and the ideal – and although it is an underlying reason for the failures and defeats which so many works deplore – nineteenth-century man seemed to ignore this, and continued obstinately to belittle real life, the world 'as it is'.

It was Chateaubriand who invented 'the Christian marvellous',[4] which was as coldly academic as the antique marvellous had become, constructed as it was of gods borrowed from Homer's pantheon. Then came Romanticism, which had to make do with a mediocre compendium of witches, ghosts and vampires, of moonlight and ruined castles, a vast petty-bourgeois waxworks. It remained for Victor Hugo to invent the most inept brand of the marvellous yet, the *moral,* which only his extraordinary poetic vitality rescued from total risibility: 'As you are my witness, O mountains clad in the candid purity of ageless snows, I say this man is wicked!', exclaims the Aigle du Casque, in a sudden burst of moral energy.[5]

With Baudelaire, and with him alone, the marvellous takes on a life and intensity which were totally original: this is because he abandons the metaphysical and moral plane to immerse himself in the everyday, which from that moment on he will deprecate, corrode and attack, but *on its own level* and as if from within. His insight into man's failures, his duality, his loneliness and ultimate nothingness is not merely intellectual, it is intensely physical.

Take for example 'The Painter of Modern Life', which more than one commentator has singled out as being particularly important. In it Baudelaire announces the presence in each object – even the most familiar – of a second nature, abstract, symbolic:

> If an impartially-minded man were to look through the whole range of French fashions, one after the other from the origins of France to the present day ... and if to the illustration representing each age he were to add the philosophical thought which that age was mainly preoccupied by or worried by, a thought which the illustration inevitably reflects, he would see what a deep harmony informs all the branches of history ...'[6]

To Baudelaire the unity of the world appears in the narrow, abstract form of the symbol hidden behind the thing. He says elsewhere that beauty always has 'a double composition'.[7] This duality of art is a consequence of the duality of man: on the one hand an eternal element, on the other a 'circumstantial' element, which will be separately or at one and the same time 'the period, its fashions, its morals and its appetites'. When the eternal appears in the circumstantial – the marvellous in the familiar – the result is a beautiful work of art. According to Baudelaire, who wrote the article as a eulogy to his work, Constantin Guys had the ability to extract the phantasmagorical from within nature.

Among the various aspects of man's duality, that of art and nature corresponds to those of town and countryside, make-up and unpainted skin, clothes and body. The duality of the eternal and the circumstantial, of spirit and matter, is also the duality of good and evil, of the individual and the crowd. Baudelaire, who did not discover duality and who never pretended to have done so, is mainly concerned with intensifying it until it reveals a sort of unity within its extreme and painful tensions: a confused unity – not conciliation, or synthesis, or supersession, but more of a scholarly confusion where contradictions are resolved through a painful, relentless struggle so intense that it leaves the mind in ruins. What does he expect of the painter of modern life? That he should embrace the hostile crowd, contemplate the 'stone landscapes' of great cities as though they were a new nature at the heart of art and artifice, that he should perceive the eternal in the transitory, and above all in the most fleeting of moments. He wants the artist to confront the everyday – and even if necessary to tear through it to reveal the living spirit enshrouded within, not above, or beyond, but within – and in doing so to liberate something strange, mysterious and bizarre ... And then, confusing the most differing categories and groupings, and becoming the first writer to eulogize mental illness, Baudelaire calls on thought itself to supply the shock, the physical spasm which will give birth to the Bizarre. And in the process he rejects Man, maturity, strength, in favour of the myth of Childhood, which is the corollary of the Marvellous:

> Let us hark back, if we can, by a retrospective effort of our imaginations, to our youngest, our morning impressions, and we shall recognize that they were remarkably akin to the vividly coloured impressions that we received later after a physical illness ... The child sees everything as a novelty; the child is always 'drunk' ... But genius is no more than childhood recaptured at will, childhood equipped now with man's physical means to express itself, and with the analytical mind that enables it to bring order into the sum of experience, involuntarily amassed. To this deep and joyful curiosity must be attributed that stare, animal-like in its ecstasy, which all children have when confronted with something new.[8]

The power of seeing the mystery traced like a watermark beneath the transparent surface of the familiar world is only granted to the visionary. The Angel of the Bizarre merely brushes the surface of the child's mind, but for the invalid or the convalescent he penetrates the very soul, opening the world up to reveal its secret treasures. Is it an illusion, or is it reality become more real? For Baudelaire, as yet, this is not a question that needs asking.

All he asks is the pleasure, the organized confusion of the mind which words can so delightfully supply, particularly words of different natures: 'These great and beautiful ships ... with their out-of-work, homesick air'[9] – 'Spiritual and physical pleasure.'[10] Baudelaire demonstrates a kind of dialectic of opposites[11] which always ends abortively: 'a sketch for a lyrical or fairy extravagance for a pantomime ... Supernatural, dream-like atmosphere of the *great days*. That there should be something lulling, even serene, in passion. Regions of pure poetry.'[12] Or again: 'Cruelty and sensual pleasure are identical.'[13] This explains the admission: 'I have cultivated my hysteria with delight and terror.'[14]

In this confusion (at the basis of which we may discern not an anti-intellectualism, but on the contrary an excess of intellectualism, a cerebralism, an over-excitement of the mind whereby he tried to *think* the everyday world of the senses instead of merely perceiving it, and so to uncover its second, abstract truth), words still have power, they are the only remaining support, the last social reality. In Baudelaire may be found all the formulae which were henceforth to become ever-repeated passwords for successive clans of turbulent and neurotic poets – but from his pen they have an honesty which can produce such thoughts as 'only the brute gets a proper erection'.[15] 'Of language and writing, considered as magical operations ...'; 'A magic art'; Magic 'as applied to ... evocation', he announces in 'My Heart Laid Bare'.[16] And in his essays on the theatre he is careful not to forget 'drama, the marvellous – the magical and the romanesque'.[17]

When Flaubert set out for the Orient – Flaubert the petty bourgeois who hated the petty bourgeoisie (they all hated and despised one another) – he was unaware that the journey would change nothing, that he would end up once more living on his private income in some provincial backwater – with his ageing mother – and with nothing to show for it but oriental bric-à-brac and incipient syphilis – just as Baudelaire, that half-starved bohemian clown, lived with his memories of tropical islands, black women and a pampered childhood. The theme of failure is no less poignant in Flaubert's books and letters than it is in Baudelaire's intimate notebooks. Failure of one love, of one man: *Sentimental Education*; failure of one woman, failure of love itself: *Madame Bovary*. The contrast between the oriental splendour of *Salammbô* and the bitter, ludicrous precision of *Bouvard and Pécuchet* is a striking example of duality (even though Flaubert's genius was not sufficiently lucid to realize it). Thus it is that Flaubert shares with Baudelaire the thankless distinction of having inaugurated the literary nineteenth century.

But the denunciation of reality and its transposition into literary themes – in particular childhood illness and the dissolution from within of a type of individuality which corresponds to so-called 'modern individualism' – does not concern us for the moment. The call to unconscious, elemental, primitive forces which were supposedly capable of freeing this individuality from its impasse by offering it a content and a meaning and revealing hidden 'depths' was but one aspect of its decay.

After Baudelaire, after Flaubert, literature became increasingly involved in cerebralism and hyper-intellectuality.[18] There was no need for Rimbaud to return to childhood: he was a genius as a child, and when he was no longer a child, the genius left him. He never reached maturity, the sphere of distinctions between intelligence and reason, the senses and the mind, things and concepts.

It has been said time and time again that Rimbaud – like many children – practised simple hallucination. He poeticizes the real by directly seeing one thing in the place of another. Where his eyes perceive faces, clouds or landscapes, he 'sees' animals, angels, incredible cities. He casts aside any halfway stages between the thing and the other thing (the image). He eliminates the comparative conjunction which was traditionally used in classical and romantic writing to introduce metaphors, similes and 'images'. With Rimbaud the word 'image' takes on a new meaning, working on two levels, that of the senses and that of the mind or the dream. In this heightened confusion of the abstract and the concrete, symbol and sensation are no longer distinguishable, although Rimbaud's symbols are so intellectually refined that they take on a metaphysical dimension; and he identifies himself boldly with the thing, with the symbol: 'Sweeter than the flesh of sour apples to children, the green water penetrated my pinewood hull ... and sometimes I saw what men thought they saw ...'[19]

In this way 'The Poet becomes a seer by a long, prodigious and rational disordering of all the senses ...'[20]

The poet splits into two, intolerably, for 'I is someone else',[21] and he knows it. But on the level of basic, physical life, and in confusion – in cultivated neurosis – he regains a kind of formless unity. 'Unspeakable torture', as he calls it in the famous letter, since the poet 'searches himself and consumes all the poisons within',[22] and every form of suffering and madness.

The alchemy thanks to which the real becomes transformed into poetry by means of words operates on the level of everyday reality. And in the *Songs of Maldoror*, it is precisely the unexpected juxtaposition of two familiar objects – for example an umbrella and a sewing machine on an operating table – which provokes the effect of surprise, of simultaneous shock to the mind and the nervous system, wherein Lautréamont discovers what he still calls beauty.

But subsequently the modern theme of the marvellous underwent a curious and rather confused disassociation.

Magic realism[23] attempted to express the mysterious meaning of the real world in a way that would make it appear insubstantial, like a perfume. Thus in *Le Grand Meaulnes* the apparently trivial life of a penniless schoolboy gradually reveals a mystery, a magic spell. In this way the real becomes 'transfigured', or, to put it more simply, more decorative and acceptable, at least on a literary level.

More explicitly, *Surrealism* set out to divert interest away from the real and, following Rimbaud's lead, to make the other world, the imaginary infinite, spring forth from within the familiar.

The magic realists had rather reactionary aims, whereas the Surrealists thought themselves to be revolutionaries, but both shared a common desire to belittle the real in favour of the magical and the marvellous. This coincidence of aims, this complicity, is very significant. In each case the concerted attack directed against everyday life and human reality is identical. The paths of literary and political reaction – and pseudo-revolution – have converged.

'The marvellous is always beautiful, anything marvellous is beautiful, in fact only the marvellous is beautiful', proclaimed Monsieur Breton in the *First Manifesto of Surrealism*.[24] The tone is characteristic: solemn, authoritarian and intimidating – to impressionable adolescents, that is. The aim of the Surrealists was to ensure that no form of the marvellous would be neglected. But Antonin Artaud's preface to his translation of Matthew Lewis's *The Monk* puts it better than I ever could:

> Yes, let them all slip back once again into that closed world where, like their excreta, only what is organically and sensuously demonstrable is valid, let them feed off the routine detritus and mental excrement of what they call *reality*, for my part I will continue to regard *The Monk* as an essential work, one which vigorously challenges that reality, dragging sorcerers, apparitions and phantoms before me in the most perfectly natural fashion, making the supernatural a reality like any other ... I know that I believe in ETERNAL LIFE, and that I believe in its complete meaning. I regret living in a world where sorcerers and soothsayers must live in hiding, and where in any case there are so few genuine soothsayers ... as far as I am concerned, I find it astounding that fortune-tellers, tarot-readers, wizards, sorcerers, necromancers and other REINCARNATED ONES have for so long been relegated to the role of mere characters in fables and novels, and that, through one of the most superficial aspects of modern thinking, naivety is defined as having faith in charlatans. I believe whole-heartedly in charlatans, bonesetters, visionaries, sorcerers and chiromancers, because all these things have being, because, for me, there are no limits, no form fixed to appearances; and because, one day, God – or MY SPIRIT – will recognize his own.[25]

This attack on the real and on everyday life is energetic, agreed, but how compromising it is!

After all, it may well be that the historians of modern life will come to look upon 'Surrealism' as a great moment for the intellect, born in an era when events were many and thoughts so few.

Already there are some very impatient historians scrambling to get their hands on this little corpse. (Moreover, rather than being a proof of richness and creativity, the current plethora of biographies, appraisals, judgements and learned tomes devoted to illusory 'contemporaries' is an indication of poverty and exhaustion.)

Without a doubt, the young disciples of Surrealism brought with them *a great desire for purity*. They wanted to live, to live according to themselves – freely, in the purity of 'the spirit'. Revolt, protest against an insufferable reality, refusal to accept that reality, despair, hope that human redemption was immediately possible, ever-repeated departures in search of the marvellous, an imminent world of images and love, all this was mingled in a confusion from which lucid analysis was permanently absent. They maintained a desperate, deliberate and well-nurtured duality through which they tried to live outside of the real world, without it, against it. As a *symptom*, maybe Surrealism was important. The most unfortunate thing the Surrealists did was to condemn the abject reality of the inter-war years along with human reality itself – to brand man's potentiality and the degrading destiny of the bourgeoisie with the same mark of infamy.

Their second misfortune was to fall into the hands of someone – Monsieur Breton (André) – who was able to capture, to use and to degrade the purity of those who were drawn to him: he was not only the pope of Surrealism, he was its politician.[26]

Applying all the procedures of traditional political life to the 'management' of the 'Surrealist group' – flattery, divide and rule, attraction, provocation, calumny, exclusion – he was able to lead this clan of young poets as if they formed a party on the fringe of political parties as such. Surrealism's allegedly 'spiritual' discoveries were in fact *political* discoveries, that is to say they were determined according to the needs and perspectives of the group's policies, and to events which were totally external to it.[27] Dadaist anarchism had been born in the 'disorder' which followed the 1918 armistice. In this truly revolutionary period, all that was needed to overthrow this established disorder were thought, organization and the sense of a new order; but the anarchist intellectuals failed to realize this. Then, in the post-war years, at the moment Marxist economists call the period of relative stabilization of capitalism, Monsieur Breton, after having proclaimed: 'Leave every-thing ... Leave your wife ... Set out along the highways ...',[28] had the (political) shrewdness to perceive that there was a general need for a definite doctrine and for a system propped up by logic; the hour had come for a universal call: 'Snobs of the world, unite', as well as for a skilfully organized confusion between 'permanent revolution' and permanent scandal. As the momentary stability of established society continued for a while, the man who had previously adopted the slogan 'art is stupidity' pompously devised the possibility of Surrealist art – of Surrealist poetry, painting, sculpture, cinema. The hour had also come when the outrageous in art could be made socially acceptable and profitable. At the same time Monsieur Breton was able to exploit the persistent confusion between anarchism and Communism, between the 'spiritual' and the social transformation of man. The time had come for sibylline discussions about 'Spiritual Revolution' which offered much-needed support and sustenance to the declining prestige of 'Surrealist thought'.[29] Nowadays if we attempt to examine the content of this 'thought', we will observe that doctrinal Surrealism, which started off with such enormous pretensions – to be a new mysticism, a method of knowledge of the 'interior abyss' – ended up as nothing more than a lot of superstitious nonsense. Its only remaining interest is that it was a symptom. At one and the same time Surrealism marked the absurd paroxysm and the end of the methodical disparagement of real life and the stubborn attack on it which had been initiated by nineteenth-century literature.

Surrealism wanted to deal a death blow to 'directed thought'. It wanted to be 'dictated by thought, in the absence of any control exercised by reason, exempt from any aesthetic or moral concern ...'.[30] It even aimed to wreck 'all the other psychic mechanisms and to substitute itself for them in solving all the principal problems of life ...'.[31] And this enormous pretension (this 'great ambition', this 'overwhelming message', to use the fashionable jargon of twenty years ago, before it was a question of 'commitment' and of 'assuming' reality ...) justified itself in terms of a simple-minded Hegelianism: 'I believe in the future resolution of these two states, dream and reality, which are seemingly so contradictory, into a kind of absolute reality, a surreality ...'[32]

But disillusionment was just around the corner. And just about all that came out of these aspirations to renew thought, knowledge and reality was the theory of the 'modern marvellous':

New myths spring up beneath each step we take. Legend begins where man has lived, where he lives. All that I intend to think about from now on is these despised transformations. Each day the modern sense of existence becomes subtly altered. A mythology ravels and unravels ... How long shall I retain this sense of the marvellous suffusing everyday existence? I see it fade away in every man ... who advances into the world's habits with an increasing ease, who rids himself progressively of the taste and texture of the unwonted, the unthought of ...[33]

It is you, metaphysical entity of places, who lull children to sleep, it is you who people their dreams. These shores of the unknown, sands shivering with anguish or anticipation, are fringed by the very substance of our minds. A single step into the past is enough for me to rediscover this sensation of strangeness which filled me when I was still a creature of pure wonder . . .[34]

The gateway to mystery swings open at the touch of human weakness and we have entered the realm of darkness. One false step, one slurred syllable together reveal a man's thoughts. The disquieting atmosphere of places contains similar locks which cannot be bolted fast against infinity. Wherever the living pursue particularly ambiguous activities, the inanimate may sometimes assume the reflection of their most secret motives: and thus our cities are populated with unrecognized sphinxes . . .[35]

Rereading these Surrealist texts twenty years after they first appeared, it is impossible not to be surprised by their shortcomings both in form and content: an assertive, icy tone which passes from point to point, linking them but never establishing any real connections – an insensitivity, an almost nightmarishly inflexible dependence upon verbal automatism, an obvious disparity between alarming promises and what was actually accomplished.

The Surrealists promised a new world, but they merely delivered 'mysteries of Paris'.[36] They promised a new faith, but did that really mean anything? Oh Literature, what petty crimes are committed in your name!

In their *nouveau merveilleux* there was nothing new – and nothing marvellous. Nothing that had not already appeared in the mental confusion pursued by Baudelaire and Rimbaud. A bit of metaphysics and a few myths in the last stages of decay (no more or no less than in Giraudoux and Claudel); some psychoanalysis, some Bergson-izing (the return to the purity of childhood sensations); an eclecticism, an impenetrable doctrinal confusion, together with a remorseless Parisianism – such are the ingredients that the most cursory analysis will discern in the 'modern marvellous'. On closer inspection, we find a number of original elements as compared with the Baudelaire–Rimbaud period:

(a) In Surrealism, the morbid element (mental confusion) is brought to the fore and 'systematized'. A paranoiac may get to the stage where he 'regards the very images of the external world as unstable and transitory, if not actually suspect ...', and this is a proof of '*the omnipotence of desire*, which has remained since the beginning surrealism's only act of faith'.[37] To suppress any possible complicity with the real world, *duality* is exacerbated until even insanity is seen as acceptable.

(b) The 'new realm of the marvellous' is marvellous no longer. In so far as there ever was a poetry founded on the marvellous, it depended upon myths and religion (naïve myths, myths 'lived out' by simple souls); even then, there was a derivativeness about this metaphysical and moral sphere. With Surrealism (and the text by Aragon quoted above is full of tacit admissions of this), it is no longer really a question of the marvellous, but of the weird, the unexpected and the bizarre, of mere effects of surprise and exoticism.

(c) In fact, this so-called marvellous realm operates only on the level of everyday life. Not above it or outside it, as in the cases of magic, of myth or of the supernatural, where everything is really, and instantly, possible. The marvellous is supposed to turn everyday life inside out, to discover its other, infinitely more interesting side. To shift the sense of what is important in life, to throw it off centre. This explains the pedantically detailed descriptions, and the ridiculous importance Breton attaches to looking for 'Surrealist objects'. It was even proposed that practical Surrealist objects should be produced for ordinary use. For example:

> two solids: one in the shape of a quarter of an orange resting on its rind, the two upper planes forming a sharp ridge, the other solid a sphere split at its base and suspended by a thread over the first. This sphere was therefore mobile and swung over the lower solid so that the latter's ridge was in contact with the split base of the sphere. This contact was not a penetration. Now, everyone who has seen this object function has felt a violent and indefinable emotion, doubtless having some relation with unconscious sexual desires ...[38] [and any impartial psychologist might add: linked with infantile and neurotic desires].

Here, with unshakable naivety, Nadeau the historian/commentator adds that dreams, automatism and the unconscious thus enter 'the realm of everyday life ...' and that 'the Surrealists, acquiring an awareness of their new gifts, believed themselves to be capable, by

launching an infinite number of such objects into the world, of putting
life entirely in the service of the unconscious ...'.[39]

This penetration – inevitable, logically determined – of everyday life
by Surrealism produces the following results:

> Daily life abounds, moreover, in just this sort of small discovery ... I am
> profoundly persuaded that any perception registered in the most in-
> voluntary way – for example, that of a series of words pronounced off-stage
> – bears in itself the solution, symbolic or other, of a problem you have with
> yourself ...
>
> So that, in order to have a woman appear, I have seen myself opening a
> door, shutting it, opening it again – when I had noticed that it was not
> enough to slip a thin blade into a book chosen at random, after having
> postulated that such and such line on the left page or the right should have
> informed me more or less indirectly about her dispositions, confirming her
> immediate arrival or her nonarrival – then starting to displace the objects,
> setting them in strange positions relative to each other, and so on. This
> woman did not always come, but then it seems to me, it helped me to
> understand why she wasn't coming; I seemed to accept her not coming
> more easily. Other days, when the question of absence, of the invincible
> lack, was solved, I used to consult my cards, interrogating them far beyond
> the rules of the game, although according to an invariable personal code,
> precise enough, trying to obtain from them for now and the future a clear
> view of my fortune and my misfortune ... The way of questioning the deck
> that I preferred and still prefer supposed from the beginning that you place
> the cards in a cross, placing in the center what I am asking about: myself
> and her, love, danger, death, mystery; above, what is hovering; on the left,
> what can frighten or harm; on the right, what is certain; below, what has
> been overcome. My impatience at too many evasive answers caused me to
> interpose, rapidly and within the figure, some central object, highly
> personalized, such as a letter or a snapshot, which seemed to me to bring
> better results. This time I alternated two little disturbing characters which I
> had taken in: a mandrake root ...[40]

And so forth. But enough of these old wives' tales. If the inter-war
period was impenetrably closed to any authentic attempts to renew
thought, it was only too open to every conceivable type of spiritual
charlatanism.

Worried at first, then panic-stricken, intellectuals ran headlong
towards false solutions, taking any way out but one which might offer a

real answer or demand a real 'commitment', a real responsibility, a real renewal. For almost twenty years Surrealism has provided amusement for some; for others, shocked by its outrageousness, it has helped to strengthen certain wavering convictions; but now its failure seems complete and incontrovertible. Objectively it can only appear as an ersatz Romanticism, a woeful literary 'fin de siècle'. And if Breton was right in his *First Manifesto* when he linked Surrealism essentially with *defeatism*, this was only half the story, for it was not just a question of temporary political defeatism but of a deep, lasting defeatism in respect of man, of thought, of love and of the totality of the real.

Nevertheless, the analysis of Surrealism allows us to formulate, or rather verify, one of the laws of the human mind: a law which will provide us with one of the guiding ideas for the critique of everyday life, and which will reappear several times in that critique in other forms and supported by other evidence:

The law of the transformation of the irrational

The mysterious, the sacred and the diabolical, magic, ritual, the mystical – at first all of these were lived with intensity. They were part of the real lives of human beings – thoroughly authentic, affective and passionate forces. Then, with the appearance and development of rationality, they were doubly modified, along with their relationship to everyday life.

(a) *Demotion* – Gradually ritual becomes gestural. The diabolical becomes shameful, ugly. Myth becomes legend, tale, story, fable, anecdote, etc.

Finally, *the marvellous and the supernatural fall inevitably to the level of the weird and the bizarre.*

(b) *Internal transformation and displacement* – Everything that once represented an affective, immediate and primitive relationship between man and the world – everything that was serious, deep, cosmic – is displaced and sooner or later gradually enters the domain of play, or art, or just simply becoms amusing or ironic verbalization.[41]

This internal transformation takes place at the same time as the 'demotion' mentioned above. It is inseparable from it. Thus as man develops and becomes rational, the old, primitive irrationality maintains its connections with his everyday life.

We already know (albeit in a way that is still too vague and general, since as yet these questions have not been adequately studied) that toys and games are former magical objects and rituals. Be it children's hoops or dolls, the simple ball or playing cards and chess, they are all 'cosmic' objects which have been demoted (in one sense) and (in another sense) transformed and clothed with a new social meaning. There are good grounds for studying playing cards, for example, not after the fashion of Monsieur Breton, who sinks to the level of old women who use them to tell fortunes, but in terms of their history, in order to determine the source and the nature of the passionate interest they excite in people. So deep is the fascination and so passionate the involvement of human beings in the various games they play that there must surely be a direct connection between playing games and life itself.

It is demonstrable, for example, that games of chance embody the possibility of becoming conscious of, and (in the imagination) dominating a double-sided situation: on the one side, chance and a non-dominated nature (including one's own nature); on the other side, freedom (but an empty freedom, the freedom to take advantage of chance). This situation is in fact *that of everyday life*, corresponding exactly to the residue of weakness, powerlessness and irrationality which the now partially rational human being still harbours. By virtue of their use of former magical objects, games of chance are the social expression and the consciousness of this situation – and in a sense a spontaneous criticism of it.

Let us return to the weird and the bizarre. What are they? The mysterious displaced, transformed (with the marvellous acting as a halfway stage) and demoted. This demotion has turned the mysterious into something *everyday*, at one and the same time familiar yet surprising. When brought into sudden contact with each other, perfectly trivial objects and ordinary words can produce an impression of weirdness and bizarrerie. All it needs is for the familiar routine to be upset – but not too much, for otherwise it will give way to anxiety or, at the very least, expectation. A word of our language pronounced by a foreigner – a creaking door which sounds like someone groaning – an unfamiliar expression which passes fleetingly across a familiar face – and we say: 'How bizarre ...' Abruptly, familiarity is transformed into something new, but nothing too disconcerting or 'upsetting'. An ambiguous mixture of the known and the unknown which confuses thought and meaning without actually revealing the unknown to the mind or the senses, without producing any real enigmas or problems, without ever really being disturbing or worrying, such is the momentary experience of the bizarre. The bizarre is a mild stimulant for the nerves and the mind – particularly recommended as risk-free for cases of nervous fatigue and mental impotence. It is both a stimulant and a tranquillizer. Its only use is as a spice for banality, a cosmetic for insignificance. It is a pseudo-renewal, obtained by artificially deforming things so that they become both reassuring and surprising. (As in so many so-called 'modern' paintings and poems, where although the meaning is quite obvious, well-known objects or ideas are presented in a way which provokes a slight nervous twitch, a feeble jolt from the reassuringly recognizable to the mildly surprising.) The bizarre is a shoddy version of the mysterious from which the mystery has disappeared. Oh, women with strange faces, portraits and poems with weird imagery, peculiar objects, all you prove is that there is no more 'feminine mystery', that mystery has disappeared from our world, that it has degenerated into something public, that it is a game, an art-form, that it has lost its ancient glamour founded on terror and wild hope, that it has become mere journalism, mere advertising, mere fashion, a music-hall turn, an exhibit . . .

It is most certainly impossible for a 'viable' feeling of life to be based upon the impression of the bizarre. Such a feeling can only have its basis in the consciousness of human *power*, that power which surrounds us, upon which we live, and in which we participate in all the acts of our everyday lives – and yet which escapes us in such a way that we are unable to live it, so that nearly all our ideas and feelings still come to us from a time when man was weak in the face of nature.

But it is extremely revealing that an attempt was made to do this, and that a new feeling of everyday life should have been sought through the weird and the bizarre. This attempt, this game for aesthetes, nevertheless provided a certain criticism of our everyday life, but a clumsy one, equivocal, dangerous and thoroughly negative. Considered as a symptom it reveals:

(a) A malfunction, a disorder of the senses and the brain which has become conscious and more or less normal (especially among intellectuals). The physiological functions of the 'modern' man's nervous and cerebral systems seem to have fallen victim to an excessively demanding regime, to a kind of hypertension and exhaustion. He has not yet 'adapted' to the conditions of his life, to the speed of its sequences and rhythms, to the (momentarily) excessive abstraction of the frequently erroneous concepts he has so recently acquired. His nerves and senses have not yet been adequately trained by the urban and technical life he leads. Modern concepts are like a kind of electrical supercharge to his brain (a natural consequence of the extreme complexity of these concepts and of the situations in which we struggle), and, to pursue the metaphor, his nerves and senses are frequently short-circuited. And so the 'modern' intellectual, an extreme example and a complete product of this situation, is no longer able to abstract the concept or idea which is both within things and *different* from them, and to perceive it as on another stage or level of consciousness. In his perception the abstraction and the thing are mixed together, merged, the concept is like the thing's double – distinct, ideal, 'mysterious'. Furthermore, it is a second-rate abstraction, not *a way of knowing*, a *rational* element, but a 'signifying' of things, a symbol, a second thing, a façade. The elements of consciousness, its 'functions' or its 'stages', are at once separated and reunited in a false, confused unity in which their relations, their order and their hierarchy are lost.

For a century now this state of *mental confusion* has been manifesting itself clearly in modern art. It is a state of 'hysteria' (Baudelaire), 'disordering' (Rimbaud), or 'paranoia' (Surrealism) – but it is an incipient state only, and one compensated for by very real considerations; if it presents no real dangers this is precisely because it is accepted, deliberate, exploited aesthetically (whereas for the genuine sufferer such states are involuntary, unconscious or resisted). This state of deliberate semi-neurosis, partly play-acting, often little more than an ambivalent infantilism, allows the 'modern' intellectual to push far from his lips the bitter chalice of an everyday life which *really is* unbearable – and will always be so until it has been transformed, and until new foundations for consciousness are established.

By his attempt to maintain such an incipient neurosis as a reflection of his detachment, the 'typical' intellectual is able to replace the trivial and the familiar with emotions and illusions which he finds more appealing, more bearable: the mysterious, the strange, the bizarre. He 'lives out' these emotions, and the element of play-acting is rarely significant enough to provoke accusations of insincerity.

(b) A perpetual expectation of something extraordinary, an ever-disappointed and ever-rekindled hope, in other words a dissatisfaction which seeps into the humblest details of day-to-day existence.

How can we fail to believe in the marvellous, the strange, the bizarre, when there are people who lead marvellous (or seemingly marvellous) lives full of departures and incessant changes of scenery, lives which we see carefully reflected in the cinema and the theatre and novels?

– when there are technical processes which bring things which are distant and inaccessible to our senses near to us, revealing the astounding shapes of crystals, organs and organisms, nebulae and molecules (so that to our unprepared senses the realest things seem unreal or 'surreal' ...)?

– when we know that there are so many beautiful, idle women in the world whose only aim in life is pleasure and the quest for novel experiences; so that each time the adolescent or the young poet hears a knock on the door, his heart beats faster, and if the telephone rings, he rushes to answer it in the belief that the miracle is about to happen, that at last that beautiful, unique, absolute, mysterious woman (who with a bit of luck may be rich and a virgin to boot) is about to appear ... (for many confirmed idealists betray a very real tendency towards parasitism or pimping ...)?

Everything – life, science, both the ideal and the idea of love, not to mention that arch-sorcerer of the Western world, money – conspires to instil in the sensitive, lucid, cultivated young man with a gift for 'belles-lettres' a feeling of unease and dissatisfaction which can only be assuaged by something strange, bizarre or extraordinary. If we add to this the fact that his nerves and senses require sudden shocks, that his heart needs novel thrills – that in his unbalanced mind each object of thought must be defined through a kind of nervous and sensorial spasm, that a certain laziness or even a revulsion towards work (so clearly, so brutally expressed by Rimbaud and the Surrealists) prevents him from broaching any investigation which might compromise his convictions, and confirms him in his decision to stick with a facile and immediately-saleable re-hash of ancient mysteries – then we will have a more than adequate explanation of the cult of the bizarre and its success.

The strange and the weird were never more than a cheap and contaminated substitute for mystery. Of what value is the bizarreness of *The Songs of Maldoror* when compared with the mystery which animates *The Divine Comedy* – or with the passions kindled in the catacombs by the first Christian ceremonies – or by the Eleusinian mysteries?

For while mystery had its specifically consecrated times and festivals, the attraction of the strange is all-pervading. This myth of the modern world – decaying like all our enchanters[42] and all our myths – has this particular characteristic: the rotting remnants of what once was grandiose, exceptional and solemn, it seeks to penetrate, it can penetrate, it does penetrate our every moment. Woe betide the bewitched adolescent! He is in danger of being lost for ever; he is in danger of no longer belonging to this world; polluted, fanatical, his blood has become tainted. Did he long for a mysterious woman. absolute love, 'ideal' beauty? Real love, real women, real beauty will never be his. (Baudelaire's concept of beauty loses nothing by this; do strong spirits and the drugs healthy people can safely take in small doses lose their virtues simply because we describe them accurately as poisons?) Dante, in love with Beatrice, was a healthy, social, political man; there was nothing morbid about Petrarch and his Laura. But Baudelaire, the man who dominates our culture poetically, who was a dandy, a little buffoon, a Second Empire bourgeois ham – who at the same time denounced the forms his class was imposing upon life – is an important dealer in narcotics; hence his success, for our day-to-day life makes us vulnerable to the thirst for drugs and intoxicants. He did not wish to kill life, to commit treacherous murder on all that is human. For he wrote in his notebooks: 'Even as a child I felt two conflicting sensations in my heart: the horror of life and the ecstacy of life.'[43] He simply wanted to *line* life with another, truer life, the life of the 'soul'. He wanted to live through the mind, giving the real world a lining of enigmas, strangeness, correspondences,[44] with every colour, every sound, every taste and every perfume concealing a host of perceptible and tangible meanings. He was one of the first (but alas! by no means the last) to try to reanimate the old category of mystery, but on the level to which it had declined, on the level of the perceptible and the everyday. So he compromised *this* world and *this* life even more effectively than any of the metaphysicians, theologians and mystics who were seeking 'another life' to replace the everyday; the only thing that interested him, seduced him, fascinated him, was the *lining*. (Only symbols, only the mind, and they alone, can 'fascinate' and 'seduce', for, as opposed to any feelings based upon man's power, they weaken man and then exploit that weakness, drawing him down into a vertiginous chasm of mental confusion.)

Since Baudelaire, the world turned inside out has been deemed better than the world the right way up. Its hinterland is no longer the realm of Platonic Ideas, which at least left life, matter and nature to run along according to their own movements, governing them from on high, from 'Eternity'. Baudelaire's satanism has brought this hinterland into the world like a supplementary 'dimension' (to use today's fashionable pseudo-scientific, confusionist jargon), like a 'spiritual dimension'. In other words, he has put the cat among the pigeons, the maggot in the fruit, disgust in desire, filth in purity; and not as stimulants, but as poisons, all mixed together in an unspeakable confusion.

Under cover of the sublime and the superhuman, all manner of dehumanization is being smuggled in. Under cover of purity and 'pure' beauty, we are being invaded by impurity and ugliness.

The result is that if this strange *duplicity* loses its power to shock the nervous system (a power dubbed 'spiritual' for the nonce), and if things are perceived in themselves and not in terms of their magical lining, then interest, desire, love, become aimless. If it is to seduce and fascinate, the real world must be metamorphosed, transfigured. If it is to be noticed, every object, every living being, must be exaggerated, rendered surprising. For those hearts and minds infected with this scourge, the result is nothing less than a 'spiritual' *inability* to live, to love, to understand any human being who fails to show ambiguous, equivocal or psychopathological characteristics – a fake, a façade. For us the *dualities* of mind and matter, the ideal and the real, the absolute and the relative, the metaphysical and the tangible, the supernatural and the natural, have become a living duplicity, a lining, a façade, a fake, just impotence and lies lived out under the pretence of thought, poetry and art.

Moreover it is clear that in the end, despite the intention to reject it, the real world is accepted, since it is transposed, instead of being transformed by knowledge!

The attack on life led by poetry is just one episode, and literature is only the active-service unit of a much larger army. Like the poets, philosophers are wavering between the familiar, the trivial, the 'inauthentic', and the anguishing, the mysterious – between bourgeois reality and mystical unreality – and are pushing human reality to one side.

'The temperate zones of universal and human life bear no resemblance whatsoever to the polar and equatorial zones ...', writes Chestov, a contemporary 'existentialist' mystic and irrationalist philosopher.[45] This comparison between the soul and the earth, which is intended to discredit man's 'temperate' zones, misses out a rather important fact: the polar and equatorial zones are scarcely fit for habitation, and all civilization has developed in the temperate zones – the zones of everyday life. The mystic metaphor ends up defeating itself.

Another mystic has recently expounded his theory of paroxysmal moments in even crueller terms:

> There are certain instants, minimal in the passing of time, but extremely important in terms of their plenitude, when the mind breaks through the circle in which it had been enclosed, and begins to contradict itself, to have intuitions, flashes of insight, which, try as one may, cannot be denied afterwards – they really happened ... There are masses of times, enormous and stupid, in which nothing happens; and short, marvellous moments in which lots of extraordinary events take place. So far no one has ever come up with anything to prove that truth is in proportion to abstract time, that what lasts for a long time is true and that what only lasts for an instant is false.[46]

We must emphasize that this theory, of mystical and religious origin, but scarcely tenable in its original forms nowadays, has become demoted to the rank of philosophical theory, a 'secular' theory of truth. For our contemporary mystical philosophers, paroxysmal instants have lost their unique, divine, revelatory character. According to them, privileged instants can *be repeated*: Heidegger's anguish, the heady charms described by Sartre,[47] no longer have the 'unique' character of a mystic vision; they fall to the level of common 'existence'; the philosopher can pass from trivial, everyday and 'inauthentic' existence to this moment of revelation by a process which can be analysed and described. And yet the paroxysmal moment dispossesses mundane, everyday existence, annulling it, denying it. *It is the very thing which denies life*: it is the *nothingness* of anguish, of vertigo, of fascination.

Thus metaphysical mystery is being demoted in parallel with poetic mystery. Reduced to the level of everyday life, it appears merely as everyday life turned inside out. Except that the philosophers, who are more lucid – more cynical perhaps – than the poets, proceed in a way which 'unveils' (fashionable vocabulary) the point of the operation. Average life is repudiated; human life is relegated to the rank of the 'enormous and stupid' masses. But there is more, and worse, to come: this life must be 'made nothingness' so that the secret of existence may be revealed, namely nothingness, the nothingness within every man, his 'infinite' ability to free himself from any instant, any moment, any state, any determined situation, in and through nothingness. The underside of life reveals itself to be its nothingness; and the confusion of nothingness and being is to be found at the heart of the confusion between the abstract and the concrete, the symbolic and the real.

The poets now only like beings for the forms in which they can be *expressed* – the existence of human beings, of women, of love, is paralleled by a 'poetic' existence (uncertain, hazy, unreal, because it is essentially verbal); similarly the philosophers only like human beings for what they *mean*: like poetic expression, philosophical 'meaning' is located on the level of real life, within it and yet above it, like a *lining* to its reality, which is the only thing about it which is interesting, attractive, seductive or fascinating. The philosophers go on to emphasize the nastiest aspects of everyday life so that they can clearly demonstrate the negation of this life, the nothingness which liberates, in the world of philosophy.

'Hell is other people', maintains one of Sartre's characters, with metaphysical 'profundity'.[48] But is not the hellish part of us rather this 'other-than-being', this hinterland (or rather, nothingness) which the mystics, the theologians, the poets, the philosophers, have maintained in their consciousness, and in which they obstinately continue to live their visionary lives without realizing the level to which it has been demoted?

But we should not take such 'profound' theories too seriously. Anguish and mystery (the feeling of mystery) cannot be reduced to a theoretical level, it is impossible to theorize them. Genuine anguish, the anguish of a lost child, of a primitive man lost in the jungle, of a being who feels utterly weak and helpless in the face of nature, such anguish escapes us. The feeling of human power (not the will to individual power, but the consciousness of the collective, social power of man over nature) penetrates our every thought and every sensation, albeit indirectly. 'But what about death?' ask the metaphysicians, 'your death – yes, yours, tomorrow, today, in a few minutes? Have you got time to wait until biologists find a way of delaying death (supposing that to be possible)?' Alas, no, I haven't the time. But so what? Do you think that is a reason for me to stop living, loving, being a man and participating in all man's possibilities? Even at this very moment action, work, love, thought, the search for truth and beauty are creating certain realities which transcend the transitory nature of the individual. And the fact that this assertion has become trivial, that it has been put to use too often – sometimes to the worst kind of ends – does not mean that it has stopped being true. On the contrary: let us reaffirm the certainties of human community; let us renew and re-establish these foundations of the human in all their strength and youth. Philosophers, metaphysicians, you are like dogs baying at death! Or rather – excuse me – I should say *pretending* to bay at death. For you death is like a perfect thought which you can recall, repeat and merge with every moment of your lives; and you are inviting us to follow you, to accept this final phantom from the other world, and it really is no more than a phantom. But this 'other', this absence, this 'tragic' feeling of existence, this consciousness of the absurd, I observe it in men who lead very skilful, successful lives; they hold forth on the subject of anguish to fashionable audiences in lecture halls, and it becomes a topic for scholarly essays; people sit in cafés and newspaper offices writing about anguish, cleverly, shrewdly, technically, and with verbal elegance. The floral tributes thrown to death are nothing more than rhetorical flourishes. No matter how profound, how inhumanly existent (or nonexistent!) 'existentialist' metaphysicians may be, they will never stop anguish from becoming demoted and displaced. Brute, primitive anguish is fading from our lives; to rediscover it is to experience a moment of weakness which in no way leads back to the 'authentic' or to 'the depths of the abyss'. Ancient wisdom knew that old age is an evil worse than death. Our metaphysicians, who go on so much about 'the other-than-being' (to use their jargon yet again), have little to say about old age. This is because it is not exciting to think about, there is nothing other-worldly about it. It is simply a sad reality; and yet thinking about it will tell us what we need to overcome, and immediately, within each of us, no matter how young we may be, and in every moment of our everyday lives. In any case we know only too well that old people do not need to make an effort to think about death, such thoughts come naturally and there is nothing positive about them. But if young people feel the need to think about death to stimulate their sense of being alive, if they proclaim their youth arrogantly in the belief that the simple fact that they are young suffuses their lives with truth – and if at the same time their youth becomes blighted by the obsessive thought of death – then one can only pity such premature senility.

Thus philosophy has joined forces with literature in this great conspiracy against man's everyday life. Even in our so-called 'modern' poets' and metaphysicians' most polished verbal and technical games we can find the elements of a certain criticism of everyday life, but in an indirect form, and always based upon the confusion between the real in human terms and the real in capitalist terms.

The true critique of everyday life will have as its prime objective the separation between the human (real and possible) and bourgeois decadence, and will imply a *rehabilitation of everyday life*.

It is not distinguished poets and philosophers who have plumbed contempt for man and his real life to its very depths, but the despicable and in a sense brilliant Louis-Ferdinand Céline.[49] We must reverse this slide into contempt and corruption. To rehabilitate the masses – the masses of instants that philosophers condemn to 'triviality' as well as the peoples that poets relegate to the shadows – are related tasks. Is it not in everyday life that man should fulfil his life as a man? The theory of superhuman moments is inhuman. Is it not in day-to-day life (not the life we lead now but a different one, already attainable) that the truth in a body and a soul must be grasped? If a higher life, the life of the 'spirit', was to be attained in 'another life' – some mystic and magical hidden world – it would be the end of mankind, the proof and proclamation of his failure. Man must be everyday, or he will not be at all. As one of the characters in Jean Cassou's novel *Le Centre du monde* exclaims: 'For that's what's important, don't you see, giving up believing in magic. And there comes a moment in every man's life when he has to, when he's got to throw all the tricks and mumbo-jumbo away for ever.'[50]

Cassou's novel poses a problem. The debate it engages between reason and irrationality grows into a debate between the real and the unreal, between the human and the inhuman, between the mysterious and reality. The title itself is vaguely cabbalistic, redolent of mysteries to come. Where is the Centre of the World? Everywhere, nowhere, within us, within each of us perhaps. Could it be the Secret, the famous secret of existence which we are supposed to look for night and day, even if we have to go to the ends of the earth to find it? But as soon as we begin reading we see a conflict growing between the attractions of magic, the expectation of a magical sense or aspect of life, and the desire, the necessity, of breaking the spell.

And yet the very *charm* of Cassou's book is the child-like magic which from the start transforms simple, everyday beings. A pretty girl becomes 'the Duchess of Montbazon', an old man becomes 'the Old Man of the Mountain'. And the father, the wizard, keeper of the secret and dispenser of good things, what is he really? A former bureaucrat, a poor old man with rheumatism and funny little habits who dies like everyone else, and whose corpse smells bad. Hélène is the magic, mysterious woman, the pure feminine myth sought by Raphaël, who finds her through a chance encounter, only to lose her again in the disappointment of her realness. Raphaël lives in a hermetic and mysterious world, an incomplete being, alone and powerless. Lost in the society he has rejected, he seeks refuge in a magical world where conflict has been eliminated, where everything is reassuring, and resolves his problems by denying that they exist. He comes down to earth again – at the moment of death. Then, as he slides into nothingness, everything he has lived through falls into place according to the perspectives and proportions of the real world. At last he understands, and wants to go on living. Too late. 'How long the night seemed, and yet it did not become fantastic. The fantastic had happened before. Outside, there was the street, not a meadow full of lunar horses. Everything fantastic was in the poor life he had led ...'[51]

Here death no longer appears as the Muse of poets and metaphysicians, the 'great captain' and 'she who gives us life' (Baudelaire), but as the great disillusionment which puts everything back in place. Are we then condemned to hesitate, to waver between self-deception and awareness, between the illusion that confounds us and the reality which in its way is equally confounding?

Jean Cassou's book remains a novel about a defeat, an unresolved duality. It fails to resolve the problem of the marvellous, but poses it with a certain lucidity; it is almost a farewell to magic; such works announce the end of one era and the beginning of a new one.[52] 'Spiritually' we have not yet left the nineteenth century. When the new man has finally killed magic off and buried the rotting corpses of the old 'myths' – when he is on the way towards a coherent unity and consciousness, when he can begin the conquest of his own life, rediscovering or creating *greatness in everyday life* – and when he can begin knowing it and speaking it, then and only then will we be in a new era.

2

The Knowledge of Everyday Life

Therefore, in the contemporary period, art and philosophy have drawn closer to everyday life, but only to *discredit* it, under the pretext of giving it a new resonance.

This action against life resembles the 'right-wing critique' of institutions and things which was rife during the period of superficial freedom and abstract democracy preceding the collapse of 1940; for several decades Barrès, Maurras and their disciples – and many others as well – gnawed away at the structure and substance of democracy like termites, from within, both in thought and action.[1] They criticized its political economy, even appearing to attack capitalism and trusts in the name of precapitalist ideologies and institutions (guilds, the primacy of the spiritual realm, etc.).

The only real critique was and remains the *critique of the left*. Why? Because it alone is based upon *knowledge*.

Mystical or metaphysical criticism of everyday life, be it from poets or philosophers, ends up in a reactionary position, even if and above all when its arguments have *formal* similarities with those of the 'left'. Escape from life or rejection of life, recourse to outmoded or exhausted ways of life, nostalgia for the past or dreams of a superhuman future, these positions are basically identical. This is why extremist, 'far-left' critiques so closely resemble reactionary ones. In France, fortunately, the total, relentless rejection of life and the real world has had neither the time nor the opportunity to reap its harvest of Dead Sea fruits. The total rejection which, according to all available documentary evidence, gave the Hitler Youth movement strength until the very end, allowed it and perhaps still allows it to cope with the collapse of its 'superhuman' dreams by giving that collapse the value of a holocaust. Make the rejection of everyday life – of work, of happiness – a mass phenomenon, a malady of the decaying middle classes, a collective neurosis (where in France it was merely an individual phenomenon), and you end up with the Hitlerian 'mystique'.

At the same time as art, literature and philosophy were attacking everyday life so relentlessly, without discriminating between its two sides (the bourgeois and the human), the world of knowledge was also moving closer to it, but in order to study it as seriously as possible. Important discoveries were made in several scientific fields through the study of humble, everyday and (at first glance) insignificant objects. Let us recall the following passage, one of the most extraordinary Marc Bloch ever wrote, and a curiously moving one, even if one does not accept all the conclusions.

> Nevertheless, in France, three main types of agrarian civilization may be distinguished which are all closely linked at once to natural conditions and to human history. First, a poor terrain which had been only half-heartedly, and for a long time intermittently, exploited, and the greater part of which – up until the nineteenth century – remained unchanged: a system of enclosures. Then two more intensive types of farming, both in principle involving the collective control of ploughing, which, given the extent of cultivation, was the only way to maintain the proper balance between arable and pasture necessary if everyone was to survive – consequently neither was enclosed. The first of these, which we may cal 'Northern', invented the plough and is characterized by the particularly strong cohesion between its communities; it can be recognized by the generally elongated shape of its fields, which are grouped in parallel strips ... Finally, the second of these open types, which for the sake of convenience but with some reservations may be called 'Southern', combines a continued use of the swing plough and – in the Midi proper, at least – two-yearly rotation of crops, with noticeably less community spirit in the exploitation of the land and agrarian life itself. There is nothing to stop us thinking that these sharp contrasts between ways of organizing and thinking in the old rural societies did not have profound repercussions for the evolution of the country overall.[2]

How many times have we all 'strolled' through the French countryside without knowing how to decipher the human landscape before our eyes! We look with the eyes of unskilled aesthetes who confuse natural facts with human facts, who observe the product of human actions – the face that a hundred centuries of working the soil have given to our land – as though it were the sea or the sky, where the wake of man's passage quickly fades away. We do not know how to see this reality, so near and so vast, these forms creative labour has produced. City dwellers getting away from it all, intellectuals at a loose end, we wander through the French countryside simply for something to do, we look but we are unable to see. We are caught in a hybrid compromise between aesthetic spectacle and knowledge. When the flight of a bird catches our attention, or the mooing of a cow, or a shepherd boy singing, we think we are being very clever and very concrete. But we are unable to seize the human facts. We fail to see them where they are, namely in humble, familiar, everyday objects: the shape of fields, of ploughs. Our search for the human takes us too far, too 'deep', we seek it in the clouds or in mysteries, whereas it is waiting for us, besieging us on all sides. We will not find it in myths – although human facts carry with them a long and magnificent procession of legends, tales and songs, poems and dances. All we need do is simply to open our eyes, to leave the dark world of metaphysics and the false depths of the 'inner life' behind, and we will discover the immense human wealth that the humblest facts of everyday life contain. 'The familiar is not necessarily the known', said Hegel. Let us go farther and say that it is in the most familiar things that the unknown – not the mysterious – is at its richest, and that this rich content of life is still beyond our empty, darkling consciousness, inhabited as it is by impostors, and gorged with the forms of Pure Reason, with myths and their illusory poetry.

We have become too sensible for these myths, which imply naïvety; we no longer believe in mysteries, but pretend to believe in them; and there is nothing so tiresome as the false naïvety, the false stupidity of certain poets who in other respects have all the tactics, the tricks of the trade, the technical subtleties of literature at their fingertips (Claudel, Pierre Emmanuel, etc.).[3] But we are not sensible enough to get beyond abstract, formal, metaphysical reason in our lives and in our consciousness of them. Thus we are caught in a state of uncertain transition between old and new Reason; and our consciousness is still only a 'private' consciousness (individual and isolated, becoming universal only in its abstract form, thought – deprived of real contact with the real and of any consciousness of its practical and everyday character). We perceive everyday life only in its familiar, trivial, inauthentic guises. How can we avoid the temptation to turn our backs on it?

Like the magnificent fruit and the beautiful creatures of temptation – which crumble to ashes should we touch them – myths, 'pure' poetry, mysteries, await us with open arms.

Who would have thought it possible a century ago that the first hesitant words of infants or the blushes of adolescents – or the shape of houses – could become the objects of serious scientific study? In so far as the science of man exists, it finds its material in the 'trivial', the everyday. And it is the science of man – knowledge – which has blazed the trail for our consciousness. At all times and in all circumstances our consciousness is tempted to believe in its own self-sufficiency, its own self-awareness, its ability to possess itself and its objects. Now and again real knowledge teaches it some hard lessons in modesty; and for the foreseeable future such lessons will continue to be necessary, since our consciousness always has its own ways of interpreting the results knowledge itself produces; it always feels the need to believe that science must deal with sublime, mysterious things – when it is quite simply a matter of those first words of the child or the shape of that field (or even, for the most up-to-date physicist, the blue colour of the sky or the 'trivial' impact of two bodies upon each other).

Before we go any farther, one particular ambiguity must be eliminated. In their arguments and reflections the historians of the old school always made sure they introduced painstakingly detailed and often repellently trivial descriptions of everyday life at a given period, of royal illnesses and love affairs, of life in the medieval castle or of the seventeenth-century 'peasant interior'. Such details have no relation whatsoever with the idea we are likely to develop of a knowledge of everyday life. They only appear to do so; and they are merely a mask for whimsical interpretations of history. It is quite possible to move from a 'realistic' description of the peasant at work, or of a worker's oil-stained blue overalls, to a fanciful theory about peasant life or the destiny of the working class. And such sleight of hand is the easiest thing in the world; it is how many philosophical or political tricksters work, substituting the concrete (the apparently concrete, and conse-quently false, deceptive and mendacious) by an abstraction (conse-quently a pointless abstraction), and relying solely on well-turned but unconnected and intellectually stagnant phrases.

Knowledge and genuine thought pass methodically from the individual scale to the social and national scale (by a process of thought comparable to the mathematical integration of very small elements). Thus they succeed in establishing a scientific notion of the social whole – and in particular a scientific theory of *social labour*. In this way tools, and the way workmen handle them – be they peasants, craftsmen or factory workers – appear like elements, moments in the totality of labour; and we know that this totality of labour has modified and transformed the face of the world. In this context the nation ceases to be an abstraction, a 'moral person' (Renan), or a (national or racist) myth. We have learned how to perceive the face of our nation on the earth, in the landscape, slowly shaped by centuries of work, of patient, humble gestures. The result of these gestures, their totality, is what contains greatness.

Of course, details retain their brutal reality; this wheelbarrow is still creaky and cumbersome, this peasant's life is still harsh and that worker's life is still dull and joyless. Things have not been transfigured, and we do not get carried away by mystical joy. And yet our conscious-ness of these things becomes transformed and loses its triviality, its banality, since in each thing we see more than itself – something else *which is there* in everyday objects, not an abstract lining but something enfolded within which hitherto we have been unable to see. In fact if the harshness of peasant life and the squalor of the farmyard, or the sadness of life in a proletarian neighbourhood, appear intolerable, they seem even more so once we become aware of the magnificent, grandiose character of the works they have produced by their labour. Our awareness of this contradiction becomes more acute, and we find ourselves faced necessarily with a new imperative: the practical, effective transformation of things as they are.

Guided often unconsciously by these perspectives, the genuinely modern historian has abandoned those lofty spheres in which kings, generals and princes of the Church used to parade in their stately robes, uttering nothing but historical statements. Now the historian helps us to enter historical reality by showing us for example how the former kings of France turned themselves into large feudal landowners and established the solid foundations on which their 'grand policy' was built by buying fiefs and increasing their ownership of land. Unglamorous facts were actually the more important ones, and for us historians they are more revealing than sensational events. Here the shift from 'significant' facts to the sum total of everyday events corresponds exactly to the shift from appearance to reality – an operation which is as important for science as is the shift from individual elements to the totality. Only this certainty that we are moving from glamorous appearances to the essence saves us from the illusory perspectives with which individuals and groups have viewed themselves throughout their history, allowing us to see the beginnings of a science, rather than a bookish rehearsal of out-moded masquerades.[4]

The great scenes on the stage of history have never been 'representations' in the psychological and philosophical meaning of the word, as naïve people still believe; they were not the work of naïve people, expressing themselves 'with complete sincerity' and eager to speak the truth. They were more like theatrical 'performances' (and let us not forget the profound link that has always existed between theatre, acting and life itself); historical scenes have always been cleverly and cunningly 'staged' by certain men who were aiming for specific results. They were acts. Every word, every gesture constitutes an act, and acts must be understood according to their purpose, their results, and not merely in terms of the person speaking and acting, as though he could somehow express or 'externalize' his reality and sincerity. More exactly, words and gestures express an *action*, and not simply some ready-made 'internal reality'. When men speak they move forward along their line of action in a force field of possibilities. You need only watch a child to realize that whatever it says is intended to influence you, to obtain a specific result from you, and must therefore be understood in terms of yourself, the moment in time and the intention; it is the very essence of childhood: a weak being seeking to get results from stronger beings whom he sees as being terrible, grandiose, powerful ... and ridiculous.

A keener awareness of everyday life will replace the myths of 'thought' and 'sincerity' – and deliberate, proven 'lies' – with the richer, more complex idea of *thought-action*. Since words and gestures produce direct results, they must be harnessed not to pure 'internal consciousness' but to consciousness in movement, active, directed towards specific goals. Whether spontaneously or deliberately, we always get results by rapidly summing up the situation and the person we wish to influence. The effects we use will always have their share of play-acting and artistry, persuasion, seduction, oratorical display, intimidation, histrionics. It is not a question of that ready-made characteristic of sincere people, 'sincerity', on the one hand, and of 'lying' (planned and plotted by 'liars') on the other. In everyday life or in the full glare of the theatre footlights, human beings always behave like *mystifiers*, who manage to 'play a role' precisely by exaggerating their own import-ance. Sometimes the acting is crude, sometimes extremely subtle; and moreover the actor becomes committed, compromised; it is a serious business. The parts must be acted out until the end; they are not pure roles, which an actor can give up when he is tired or when he feels he is acting badly. They extend reality, and are equally as real; acting explores what is possible; in the abstract, play-acting does not exclude sincerity; on the contrary, it implies it, while at the same time adding something extra – something real: the knowledge of a situation, an action, a result to be obtained.

It is precisely in this way that everyday life resembles theatre – and that theatre is able to resume, condense and 'represent' life for real spectators.

If he fails to examine history in the light of everyday life, the historian is falling naïvely and of necessity into a trap laid for simpletons. There he is among the onlookers, open-mouthed, a minor intellectual too awe-struck to approach – on paper, that is – the great men of this world. Scenes were staged (with more than enough sincerity) with glory and prestige in view; the naïve historian is taken in, just as contemporaries were. He has no awareness, no irony, no craftsmanship. He is erudite to the *n*th degree, and yet he is without substance, weight, human consciousness. He is content to churn out the same old historical scenarios event by event. And the anecdotes pile up before him; he is all but ready to start believing in the divine nature of kings.

While taking care not to deny the importance of the leading players, more profound historical study takes the whole into account: specta-tors, situations, the canvas of the immense *commedia dell'arte*. Once the historian and the explorer of human reality realize they have been fooled, and begin consciously linking history and the knowledge of mankind with life – everyday life – in the past and in the present, they will have left their naïvety behind. Such historians denounce appearances, those appearances which use reality in a way that enables the 'great men of this world' cleverly to nurture their prestige and present their own reality to its best advantage – and hence to perpetuate that reality.

Thus bit by bit there is a growing conviction that *in one sense* lavish institutions and grandiose ideas were façades – theatrical costumes.

On the almost stagnant waters of everyday life there have been mirages, phosphorescent ripples. These illusions were not without results, since to achieve results was their very *raison d'être*. And yet, where is genuine reality to be found? Where do the genuine changes take place? In the unmysterious depths of everyday life! History, psychology and the science of mankind must become a study of everyday life.

Here and there, bit by bit, though sadly sporadic, fragmented and without an overall strategy, this conviction is dawning in the work of certain historians (Marc Bloch) – certain geographers (Demangeon) – certain psychologists. No one so far has attempted a synthesis.

3

Marxism as Critical Knowledge of

Everyday Life

> Our age is, in especial degree, the age of criticism, and to criticism everything must submit. Religion through its sanctity, and law-giving through its majesty, may seek to exempt themselves from it. But they then awaken suspicion, and cannot claim the sincere respect which reason accords only to that which has been able to sustain the test of free and open examination.[1]

But after this magnificent declaration of the rights of Human Reason, Kant failed to grasp the essential. He was content to criticize 'Pure Reason'; thus he remained on that level. Only at certain moments and in certain places does his critique rise to the level of a *critique of man.* Wishing to eliminate dogmatisms, theologies and metaphysical systems in favour of a rational order, he failed to discover the human foundations upon which the speculative aberrations he was attacking are founded. This is why after Kant metaphysical explanations enjoyed a new lease of life; his critical tempest turned out to be just a storm in a teacup, a squall which uprooted some weeds only to bring forth others.

Why do some men go on pursuing a 'hidden world' with so conscious and so emotional a determination? They call themselves sincere; they have reduced their innate tendency to posture to a minimum (for it is a function of the philosophical and scientific mind to do so). But we can argue that, despite all their sincerity, their speculations still contain elements of intellectual play; and that the simple idea that the secret of the universe should reveal itself to them, and to them alone, implies an exaggeration of their own importance so extreme as to border on the burlesque, requiring hypocrisy, play-acting, even clowning. But just for the moment let us put to one side the consideration of *metaphysical* thought as dramatic posturing and hypocrisy. Let us just say that they are sincere.

Over there I can hear someone crying out to God – but why? He is the son of a merchant, of a parvenu. He is rich, he can live off his private income and dedicate himself to happiness, love, seduction, art. But the truth is that he is incurably bored. And yet he is very gifted, witty, even brilliant; he loves life, and at the same time hates it: 'All existence makes me anxious, from the smallest gnat to the mysteries of the incarnation; all life is a plague to me, most of all myself.' His thought and his intelligence merely serve to make him anxious about everything. He hates himself, and yet thinks more of himself than of anything else in the world: 'Basically only one quality exists, the individual, that is the axis of everything.' He is walled up within himself, trapped in the framework of his life like the bourgeois with a private income, the intellectual, the literary hack he is. But he values the very things which are destroying him, because he exists through them alone. He possesses everything it is possible to possess: money, property, leisure, talent, thought. And yet he possesses nothing, and knows it, and says it: 'I believe I am brave enough to doubt everything, to fight against everything; but I am not brave enough to recognize nothing, to possess nothing.'

He does not even possess his body, his flesh, his desires. His upbringing has killed everything inside him. We should realize that this man's father was not a run-of-the-mill shopkeeper. One lonely, hungry, painful evening, when still a young shepherd watching his flocks on the barren heath beside the sea, he cursed his God; and judged himself accursed and damned. Subsequently, thanks to his dourness and austere inflexibility, he managed to save money and to rise in the social hierarchy. But he carried within himself the consciousness of his sin – of his nothingness. Late in life (through humility, through shyness . . .) he married (and terrorized) his servant. Sometimes he would take his son into an unlit room and talk to him in passionate terms about the world, ships, ports, faraway countries. At the same time he taught him to fear Sin, to recognize Sin within himself. This unfortunate son admits that 'if a child was told that it was a sin to break his leg, how anguished his life would be. And he would be all the more likely to break it.'

And so this young man suffocates in the narrow framework of his life and consciousness. He cries out for – what? Something different, something Possible. What of his thoughts? They bring him no deliverance, no future possibilities. Quite the opposite, they enable him to 'leap over life'. Although he falls in love, he is unable to sustain it. He leaves his fiancée, and spends the rest of his life regretting it, calling on God to bring her back, to bring his lost life back – like old Faust calling on the Devil. He believes in God, his hopes are in God. His faith 'struggles like one possessed' against the suffocation of everyday life. Only through madness, regret and the transposition of his despair into literature does he remain a man, or go beyond the suffocating limits of his life. He is a believer; no, he is a non-believer. He has hopes; no, he has no hopes. 'What is faith? A rope from which we dangle, unless we use it to hang ourselves with', and again: 'Faith is a category which is only to be found in distress', and 'my doubt is terrifying'. He hates sin, and yet all his literary skills gravitate around eroticism and an impotent lusting after sin and 'the secret of sinning'. His intense inner life is rotting away, lit by the phosphorescence of its own decay. He claims to place his own drama, his own case, at the centre of philosophy and religion – to found faith, all faith, on an anguish resembling his own. He claims that in his own internal microcosm he is behaving 'in the most macrocosmic manner', but writes: 'How awful when history becomes eclipsed by the morbid ruminations of our petty tales.' And wanting to base faith on anguish, on the cry for deliverance from subjective anguish, he acknowledges the dual, ambiguous, equivocal character of his anguish: 'Anguish is the desire for what we most dread ... it is an alien power which takes hold of the individual, who neither can nor wants to free himself, for he is afraid, but that very fear is a desire.'

The conflict between everyday life as it is – as it has been made by the bourgeoisie – and the life which a human being actually demands, begs for, cries out for with all his strength, that is the conflict which harrowed Søren Kierkegaard.[2] He resolved it in his own way – very badly. In psychology – although psychologists are not always able to discern the deep, historical, social and human sources of conflict within the individual – the term for an inner conflict which has been badly resolved is 'anxiety neurosis'. But the notion of a morbid condition does not fully explain the situation of someone like Kierkegaard. We must understand that his faith, and his appeal to the world beyond, are based on the demands of his earthly being; that his madness is based upon his reality and his rationality. Whenever he attempts to stop being a slave to necessity, and to revolt against reality as 'robust champion', he is making a protest against life as it is in existing society, and that is the reality he rejects. And if on the ideological level Kierkegaard's philosophy has functioned as a reactionary philosophy (in his appeal to the absurd, to the irrational, to faith without knowledge), when we see his work as a whole and in the context of the hopeless 'existence' he led we realize that it nevertheless offers an implacable criticism of bourgeois life: dissatisfied, suffocated, the individual feels as though he is dying before he has lived, and is forced into the insane situation of pleading for a 'repetition' of the life he has never had. Imprisoned by a necessity he cannot understand, and desperately doubting the power of reason which fails to bring him *another life* (a different life) but which seems instead to approve and justify that necessity, he appeals to the absurd. He even gives up expecting any world beyond, but makes do with asking for a 'repetition' of his life, a chance to start again.

Theological faith is dead, metaphysical reason is dead. And yet they live on, they take on new life – insanely, absurdly – because the situation and the human conflicts from which they were born have not been resolved. Now these conflicts are not in the realm of thought alone, but *in everyday life.* The works of Baudelaire, like Dostoevsky's or Rimbaud's, may take on a revolutionary meaning – provided that they are understood and situated by knowledge, by social criticism of men and ideas. This is also true of Kierkegaard's works, as long as they are understood and situated within a general critique of everyday life. Taken in themselves, in isolation, these works provoke absurd, illusory feelings; situated in the overall context of the human problems of our time, their character changes. This 'revision' of meanings and 'values', as brought about by knowledge, will surprise only those whose thoughts are petrified in an attitude of contemplation towards men and their works.

Rational criticism, when carried through to its logical conclusion, will deal not only with 'Pure Reason' but also with life in all its impurity. From an intellectual heaven where the ghosts of former gods battle on, critical thought will descend into everyday life. Criticism of ideas will not be abandoned, far from it: taken up on another level, it will become deeper, since it will have become criticism of men and actions.

In 'pure' ideas, as in the great ceremonies of royal courts, we can perceive a certain amount of ceremoniousness, etiquette, deliberate and pretentious grandness – of play-acting – which no longer fools us. Louis XIV's divine prestige may have disappeared, but this only enhances our appreciation of its expert staging, grandiose spectacle and delightful entertainments, so splendidly set among the halberds, muskets and canons. As with Louis XIV, so it is with Bossuet and his *Discourse on Universal History*;[3] but have no fear, we may appreciate its high style, construction and pace all the more now that we are no longer intimidated and that we can see it for what it really is – a display, a work of art! We do not have to believe in gods and 'pure' ideas in order to appreciate the true 'worth' of the spectacle they afford. Quite the contrary, it is when we stop believing in them that they take on a 'pure' aesthetic significance, and in general it is when our belief in gods and ideas starts to waver (when they can still move us, but not overwhelmingly so) that they become subject matter for great art. Religious dread, religious hope, divine 'presence', fear inspired by myths when myth is accepted as a part of life, all these preclude aesthetic considerations. Here the law of the displacement of the irrational[4] finds a new application.

'Pure' ideas have real meaning, as Marx and Engels so profoundly understood. As historians, they refused to be idle onlookers of history. As philosophers, they stopped being mere flies on the wall so far as politics was concerned. They were the first to perceive how thought is linked to *action*. They were able to get to the very roots of ideas, to the fundamental questions. With Marx and Engels philosophical thought at its most coherent and most methodical comes down to the level of life and penetrates it, reveals it. By refusing to leave the real world for the exile of a world beyond – by becoming the consciousness and the critique of mankind, of men and of human conditions – Critical Reason, the Critical Reason of Descartes and Kant, becomes concrete, active and constructive.

A modern proletarian is not first and foremost a man with a ready-made human soul or nature of which he is in full 'spiritual' possession, a man who leads a proletarian life simply because of an unfortunate conjunction of circumstances. His opinions and feelings as a worker are not something that the hazards of fate have superimposed upon an already acquired, 'deep' human essence, something external to it, and produced by questionable influences and theories. No. First of all he lives the daily life of a proletarian; and if he becomes humanized, it is because he has succeeded – by luck or by will-power – in transcending proletarian life.

But here the problem gets a little more complex. The proletarian 'condition' has a dual aspect – more precisely, it implies a dialectical movement. On the one hand it tends to overwhelm and crush the (individual) proletarian under the weight of the toil, the institutions and the ideas which are indeed intended to crush him. But at the same time, and in another respect, because of his incessant (everyday) contact with the real and with nature through work, the proletarian is endowed with fundamental health and a sense of reality which other social groups lose in so far as they become detached from practical creative activity. The petty bourgeois and the bourgeois, the intellectuals and the specialists – they all degenerate, decay and wither. Considered collectively as an oppressed class, the proletariat is as 'deprived' of consciousness and culture as it is of wealth, power and happiness. But this deprivation proves to be of a quite different kind to that which devastates the 'private consciousness', the 'private' life of the bourgeois or petty-bourgeois individual. The latter is not aware, or is only partly aware, of being deprived. He tends to become withdrawn and to conflate his 'deprivation' and his property, for the two go together: he thinks he owns his self, his ideas, his life, his family, his country, just as he owns his material 'assets'. The deprivation of the working class is rich in possibilities. For the individual proletarian to become conscious of the proletariat as a class, of its social reality, and thus of society as a whole, of its action, and therefore of its political future, is to have already superseded the proletarian condition. It is to have achieved a great and true thought: that of the social and human totality, of creative labour. On the other hand, the petty bourgeois and bourgeois who discover self-consciousness, but fail to reject the self (as they would if they came over to Marxism) become remote from this great truth; they stop being able to see man, society and human labour in their totality. Rather than superseding deprivation they withdraw into a 'private consciousness'; unless, that is, they are sufficiently aware and lucid to create a political machine designed to extend their control – and their spiritual and human poverty.

To put it another way, from the human point of view the 'proletarian condition' and the 'bourgeois condition' are fundamentally different.

The proletarian qua *proletarian can become a new man.* If he does so, it is not through the intervention of some unspecified freedom which would permit him to liberate himself from his condition. Such metaphysical freedom is nothing more than a survival from the former 'human nature' common to all men. It is *through knowledge* that the proletarian liberates himself and begins *actively superseding* his condition. Moreover in this effort to attain knowledge and awareness, he is forced to assimilate complex *theories (economic, social, political . . .)*, i.e. to integrate the loftiest findings of science and culture into his own consciousness.

On the other hand the petty bourgeois and bourgeois, *as such*, are barred access to the human.

For them to become humanized, they must break with themselves, reject themselves, an endeavour which on an individual level is frequently real and pathetic ... We should understand men in a human way, even if they are incomplete; conditions are not confined within precise, geometrically defined boundaries, but are the result of a multitude of obstinate and ever-repeated (everyday) causes. Attempts to escape from the bourgeois condition are not particularly rare; on the other hand, the failure of such attempts is virtually inevitable, precisely because it is not so much a question of *supersession* but of a complete *break.* (Among intellectuals, this notion of supersession is frequently false and harmful: when they *supersede themselves as petty-bourgeois or bourgeois intellectuals,* they are often merely continuing in the same direction and following their own inclinations in the belief that they are 'superseding themselves'. So far from gaining a new consciousness, they are merely making the old one worse. There is nothing more unbearable than the intellectual who believes himself to be free and human, while in his every action, gesture, word and thought he shows that he has never stepped beyond bourgeois consciousness.) In any event, a man's consciousness, his condition, his possibilities, do not depend upon a relation with some timeless Reason, a permanent human nature, a ready-made essence or some indeterminate freedom. His consciousness depends upon his real life, his everyday life. The 'meaning' of a life is not to be found in anything other than that life itself. It is within it, and there is nothing beyond that. 'Meaning' cannot spill over from being; it is the direction, the movement of being, and nothing more. The 'meaning' of a proletarian's life is to be found in that life itself: in its despair, or conversely in its movement *towards freedom*, if the proletarian participates in the life of the proletariat, and if that life itself involves continuous, day-to-day action (trade-union, political ...).

The method of Marx and Engels consists precisely in a search for the link which exists between what men think, desire, say and believe for themselves and what they are, what they do. This link always exists. It can be explored in two directions. On the one hand, the historian or the man of action can proceed from ideas to men, from consciousness to being – i.e. towards practical, everyday reality – bringing the two into confrontation and thereby achieving *criticism of ideas by action and realities*. That is the direction which Marx and Engels nearly always followed in everything they wrote; and it is the direction which critical and constructive method must follow initially if it is to take a demonstrable shape and achieve results.

But it is equally possible to follow this link in another direction, taking real life as the point of departure in an investigation of how the ideas which express it and the forms of consciousness which reflect it emerge. The link, or rather the network of links between the two poles will prove to be complex. It must be unravelled, the thread must be carefully followed. In this way we can arrive at a *criticism of life by ideas* which in a sense extends and completes the first procedure.

Let us return to our earlier example. As soon as we stop being taken in by the spectacle of the royal court of Louis XIV, we can start looking for the social, political and economic realities which that spectacle concealed. We first move from ideologies – appearances, but somehow real, pretences, but effective ones – to the more concrete (and thus more human) underlying realities. Then, by moving in the opposite, complementary direction we will at first seek to grasp and to re-constitute the real life of that period, and to rediscover how the men who led that life could subscribe to certain forms of consciousness, certain prestigious ideologies, and find them valid despite their remoteness from their real lives. The contrast between ideas and life, the complex relationship between them, will then entail not just criticism of ideas by life but also, and more specifically, criticism of life by ideas (criticism of the real life of seventeenth-century peasants, craftsmen, country squires or bourgeois by reference to the 'represent-ations' of the world and of themselves that they found acceptable). What does the fact that they accepted the divine right of kings without too much opposition tell us about their real lives? Why did all the pomp which was part and parcel of royal power prove so effective? What did this effectiveness correspond to in men's lives? How did those illusions which were formulated into ideas by official spokesmen take shape in the depths of the social sediments and 'strata', in the heart of the 'masses'? How and why did they accept them? In this instance criticism of life consists in studying the margin which separates what men are from what they think they are, what they live from what they think. It re-examines the notion of *mystification* more deeply. Most ideol-ogies have been mystifications in so far as they have succeeded at certain periods in making men accept certain illusions, certain appearances, and in introducing those appearances into real life and making them effective there. We must first denounce mystifications, and then proceed to a study of how they could have begun, of how they were able to impose themselves, and of how ideological *transposition* can operate in men's consciousness; for ideologies and mystifications are based upon real life, yet at the same time they disguise or transpose that real life. A complete understanding of mystification presupposes that the link between ideas and the real has been followed in both directions, thus incorporating criticism of life by its own consciousness of itself.[5]

When a proletarian believes that he is simply a 'citizen' comparable to every other citizen, or that he is destined to work because it is written for all eternity that every man 'must earn his bread with the sweat of his brow', he is being *mystified*. But how, and why? Because for him, his work is a laborious,exhausting burden *in real terms*, and – under certain pressures – if he does not understand (or *know*) that work can and must become something else, he may well interpret it as a fatality of the human condition or as his own personal misfortune. But the belief in the political and legal equality of the individual, which is an illusory belief for any proletarian who takes it at face value, becomes trans-formed into an admirable means of action as soon as he begins insisting that democracy stop being a legal and political fiction. The study of mystifications reveals their ambiguity – an ambiguity which at first makes them acceptable but which subsequently makes it possible to supersede them. In mystification appearance and reality are confused, inextricably bound up together. But on the one hand, mystifications rebound upon the mystifiers themselves, notably when consciousness penetrates them by superseding them (and supersedes them by penetrating them), while on the other hand, they teach us something about the lives of the people who accept them. Appearance and reality here are not separated like oil and water in a vessel, but rather amalgamated like water and wine. To separate them, we must *analyse* them in the most 'classic' sense of the word: the elements of the mixture must be isolated.

In the first instance Marxism may be defined as the scientific knowledge of the proletariat: it is the 'science of the proletariat'. This expression must be understood in two ways: Marxism studies the proletariat, its life, its reality, its social function, its historical situation. At the same time, this science comes from the proletariat and expresses its historical reality and its social and political ascension.

Scientific knowledge of this social reality, of this *class*, implies knowledge of society and of the history of human consciousness in their totality. The one leads to the other; it is the only methodologically possible starting point. Of course, when a science develops it goes a considerable way beyond the point from which it began, while continuing to incorporate it. And the analysis of the proletariat, of its *practical, historical and social* reality, implies and involves the assimilation of the deepest and most subtle methods elaborated over the centuries by human thought in the course of its investigations and trial-and-error experiments (I refer, of course, to the dialectical method). Thus the problem of the proletariat encompasses all the problems of thought, of culture, of the human.

To study the proletariat scientifically is to begin tearing away the veil of ideologies by which the bourgeoisie has attempted to explain history to itself and to explain – to make acceptable – the proletarian situation to the proletariat. These ideologies tend to *deprive* the proletariat (as individuals and as a class) of consciousness, of the *new consciousness* it can attain and which is the proletariat's own achievement. These ideologies share a common characteristic. Whether it is a question of religion, of the theory of 'human nature' and 'pure' Reason, of the allegedly historical themes of the Human Spirit and immanent justice, or of the great 'Ideas which shape the world', they are all *idealist and metaphysical.* They are masks which shield men from their *real lives* (which in turn poses the question: how and why do men accept them? what does the repeated complicity with the forces which crush them implied by this acceptance consist of?).

Marxism describes and analyses *the everyday life of society* and indicates the means by which it can be transformed. It describes and analyses *the everyday lives of workers* themselves: separated from their tools, connected to the material conditions of their labour solely by the 'contract' which binds them to an employer, sold like commodities on the labour market in the (legal and ideological) guise of the 'free' labour contract, etc.

The real, everyday life of the worker is that of a commodity endowed, unhappily for him, with life, activity, muscles – and with a consciousness which the concerted pressure of his Masters seeks to reduce to a minimum or to divert into inoffensive channels (let it be said that this pressure is very often involuntary – for we should avoid falling into the proletarian myth of the sadistic bourgeois, rotten to the marrow, consciously and strategically mendacious, a myth which in point of fact only the Fascists made into a reality).

Thus Marxism, as a whole, really is a critical knowledge of everyday life.

It is not satisfied with merely uncovering and criticizing this real, practical life in the minutiae of social life. By a process of rational integration it is able to pass from the individual to the social – from the level of the individual to the level of society and of the nation. And vice versa.

This penetration of dialectical method into individual, everyday life is so unfamiliar that it is absolutely necessary at this point to offer a summary of Marxism considered as a critique of everyday life.

(a) *Critique of individuality* (Central theme: the 'private' consciousness)

The very things that make a man a social and human being, and not simply a biological creature that is born, grows up and dies steeped in natural life – namely his work, his social activity, his place and situation in the social whole – are the things that also limit him and confine him according to *the way labour is currently organized.*

Durkheim maintains that the division of labour is the foundation for individualization. Marxists reply that the fragmentation of labour provides only a *negative* foundation for individuality; in this world of production, individuals have an effective self-consciousness, but of a kind which makes them lead inward-looking lives, centred upon their particular skill and specialization. As regards the rest of social and human life, they are conscious of it only in so far as they reject it, despise it or transpose it to a level of unreality. They tend towards *individualism.* Now if human individuality must consist in a specific relationship between single beings and the universal – reason, society, culture, the world – then there can be no question here of real individuality, but merely of an abstract, empty, negative *form* of individualism. This form, with its minimal content, is what may be called the 'private consciousness'. It is a self-consciousness, but limited, restricted, negative and formal. Separated from the conditions in which it could flourish or even exist, it believes itself to be self-sufficient, and aspires to be so. It is in the process of degenerating. And the expression currently in use to designate the everyday life of individuals in this social structure – *private life* – sums this up perfectly.[6] When an individual life is shaped by individualistic tendencies, it is literally a life of 'privation', a life 'deprived': deprived of reality, of links with the world – a life for which everything human is alien. It is a life split into contradictory or separate poles: work and rest, public life and personal life, public occasions and intimate situations, chance and inner secrets, luck and fate, ideal and reality, the marvellous and the everyday. Instead of expanding, of conquering the world, this consciousness shrinks in upon itself. And the more it shrinks, the more it seems to be 'its own'. Crass and complacent, the individual settles down amid his familiar surroundings. Consciousness, thought, ideas, feelings, all are seen as 'property' on a par with 'his' furniture, 'his' wife and 'his' children, 'his' assets and 'his' money. In this way the narrowest, most barren, most solitary aspects of life are taken (and with such crude sincerity) for what is most human.

Thus everyone 'is' what he is and nothing more. We will find descriptions of these genera of bourgeois society, including not only usurers, gangsters and social climbers, but also all those fixed 'beings' who are determined solely by their function and established in their private lives, in *The Human Comedy*,[7] where Balzac offers probing accounts of this dual nature of bourgeois life, which was forming and consolidating during his lifetime but which holds no surprises for us: on the one hand, formal individualization (or as classic philosophy would put it, a greater subjectivity), thus an enhanced consciousness in increased isolation; on the other hand, an 'objectification', beings who are more 'involved' in their own physicality, weightier, thicker, more opaque. This dual character is beautifully reflected in Balzac's work, in its very style: so weighty, compared with the lightness of the eighteenth century, and so lucid. This dual character also corresponds to the dual character of bourgeois society: progressive in terms of technology, thought, consciousness – but otherwise retrogressive. And finally it corresponds to the dual character of capital: a brutal objective *reality* which eludes human will and drags it along towards a predestined fate for as long as human thought and action, straining towards another order, cannot reverse it – and yet at the same time an abstraction, an *unreality*, a complex of signs and concepts.

Before Balzac, in that epic of human consciousness in the ascendant which bears the name *The Phenomenology of Spirit*, Hegel had ironically described 'abstract animals', specialists, experts, imprisoned in a narrow field of practice or thought.

And nowadays we are still struggling with this deep – in other words *everyday* – contradiction: what makes each of us a human being also turns that human being into something inhuman. More biological than truly human, this organization smothers the individual, dividing him and stunting his development at the very moment it is striving to create him as a human individual. It is just one of the many painful contradictions our era is experiencing, and which we must resolve if we are to move forward. These contradictions are at the same time a measure of the greatness, the richness and the suffering of the age in which we live. We are all familiar with the drama of youth destroyed by this arrested state of the human being, as also with that drama of more mature, more conscious years, acted out within the asphyxiating strait-jacket of fragmented activities.

How can this organization be superseded? By practical and theoretical participation in work and in the knowledge of work, in the social and human totality. If the world is to be transformed, this is one of the fundamental problems.

We must supersede the 'private consciousness'.

(b) *Critique of mystifications*
(Central theme: the 'mystified' consciousness)

We should note that the proletarian does not escape the dangers of the 'private consciousness' completely. Agreed, his work is always collective, and this tends to reinforce his awareness of social activity and society as a whole.

However, the tasks of workers in workshops or even in factories are generally fragmented. The most tangibly collective work – assembly-line work – is also the most exhausting. Human contacts tend to be established after work, outside the factory, in cafés, sports teams, etc. Thus the forms in which these contacts are established are precisely those of the individualistic bourgeoisie (family, press, cinema, etc.).

Although the material conditions of modern production tend to form a social and human consciousness whose first stage is class consciousness, there is nothing inevitable about this formation. It is not *spontaneous*. (The theory of proletarian spontaneity came from intellectuals who had 'studied' the proletariat!) Consciousness must be gained over and over again through action and struggle as well as through organizations whose role is to penetrate everyday life and to introduce a new, more elevated element (from unions to sports and 'cultural' organizations ...).

In life there are no absolute boundaries. The proletariat no more has a ready-made essence, soul or consciousness (clearly separate from 'bourgeois' realities) than does humanity taken as a whole. Hence the role of *knowledge* as both action and theory.

And so the bourgeoisie can exert permanent, and to a certain extent successful, pressures upon the proletariat – an influence which tends to split it up into individuals.[8] Individualism is not simply a theory, but also a fact and a class weapon. It is not simply through its ideas and its conception of the world that the bourgeoisie exerts this influence. Admittedly, its theoretical individualism, its 'social atomism', are by no means ineffectual, but the way it actually organizes everyday life, leisure, family life, etc., is infinitely more important.

Paradoxically – or apparently so – the bourgeoisie is a class of individualists. Its theory of social atomism tends to represent society as a collection of juxtaposed atoms, breaking the social body down into separate elements – fictitious, dead, inert elements: 'pure' individuals.

This representation is nothing more than an ideology, i.e. a means of action, an efficient illusion – and the consciousness of the average bourgeois, and above all of the petty bourgeois, is taken in by it. Not so the governmental, political and police arms of the bourgeoisie; on the political level, the bourgeoisie understands perfectly about masses and classes. Those who effectively 'represent' the bourgeoisie are kept very well informed, thanks to that class's political practice and Machiavellianism – thanks, in other words, in the absence of guidance from general philosophy, to the police.

Moreover, this 'representation' in no way stops the most individualistic social groups from having been or actually being classes, or masses, objectively, historically and socially. There is a remarkable image in Nietzsche which expresses this paradoxical situation well. Typically the middle classes are individualistic social groups made up of 'human sand'. Each grain is quite distinct and separable. And taken together they form a mass – indeed the heaviest and most impenetrable of masses. A sandbag can stop bullets!

What is comical about this is that each grain of human sand thinks itself to be not only distinct, but infinitely original. But nothing is more like a grain of sand than another grain of sand. Bourgeois individualism implies the dreary, ludicrous repetition of individuals who are curiously similar in their way of being themselves and of keeping themselves to themselves, in their speech, their gestures, their everyday habits (meal times, rest times, entertainments, fashions, ideas, expressions).

Any objective anthropology or scientific description of the contemporary man will have to begin with this obvious paradox – which constitutes the *comical mystery* of bourgeois life ...

In the modern world, mystifying ideologies presuppose and imply the *private consciousness.*

The individual who is deprived of human reality is also deprived of truth. He is separated from his concrete human and social reality, deprived of a consciousness of the practical, historical and social whole (even though, nowadays, given modern social structure, science and techniques, such a consciousness is both possible and necessary).

Turned back upon himself, secure within some imaginary inner fortress, he is the plaything of every hallucination, every spontaneous or deliberate ideological illusion. The 'thinker', self-taught or not,

concocts his own little personal philosophy; the 'non-thinker' interprets what he reads in books (or preferably in newspapers) as best he
can; and then one day individualism begins to collapse (and not as a
result of a crisis of ideas or 'world views', but because of a *material* crisis,
both economic and political), and these erstwhile individualists rush
headlong to form a crowd, a horde, urged on by the most insane, most
loathsome, most ferocious 'ideas', leaving the last vestige of human
reason behind, caught up in a collective mental fever: and we have
Fascism, the Fascist 'masses' and Fascist 'organization'.

The private consciousness and the mystified consciousness go hand
in hand, reinforcing each other and becoming increasingly entrenched
as a result of instabilities which have their origins in real life, and not in
'pure' ideas.

(c) *Critique of money*
(Central theme: fetishism and economic alienation)

There is a sentimental rhetoric, corresponding to the 'spiritual state' of
the petty bourgeois who hates and envies people who are richer than
he is, which readily waxes emotional about deserving paupers and
unhappy millionaires alike, and which rails against money. The best
things in life are free! And with women particularly in mind: she was
poor, but she was honest! etc. These melodramatic and moral motifs
are part of the everyday lives of poor people. Verbal propaganda of the
rich, they make up the greater part of the average person's ideological
baggage. Disguised as an indictment of money, they justify wealth by
reducing it to a mere accident of the human condition (in itself moral
or metaphysical). They give consolation to the poor and full satisfaction
to people who are threatened by poverty but who nevertheless hope
with all their 'soul' to become rich. These motifs have been raised to
the dignity of philosophical and lyrical themes in the work of that
demented petty bourgeois, Péguy.[9] Moreover, as proverbs which seem
to contain eternal truths, they have penetrated the consciousness of the
people, where they act as corollaries to the capitalist axiom: 'There will
always be rich and there will always be poor.' Their aim is to
consolidate, to crystallize those absurd concepts 'wealth' and 'poverty',
to present them as opposites, to incarnate them in individuals,
enclosing them so effectively within these sentimental and moral

categories that the most violent statement against 'the rich' will in no respect go beyond the parameters of capitalist ideology.

The result is a curious one. Today, for the Marxist, the first task in this area must be a *rehabilitation of wealth*. Wealth is neither an evil nor a curse. Wealth, like power, is part of man's greatness and of the beauty of life. The solution to man's problems is to be found not by sharing out weakness, poverty and mediocrity – but by seeking power and wealth; they alone have permitted and conditioned everything magnificent and brilliant that has ever been in culture, in civilization, in life – from palaces and stately homes and cathedrals to those slowly nurtured works of art whose creation used to demand and still demands long periods of leisure, silence, peace of mind and physical security.

And yet (and this is the essential point) the parameters of power and wealth are in the process of changing. It is impossible to go any further towards *individual* wealth. Today, wealth is becoming *social*; in fact, it has always been social; and within the framework of capitalist economy, under the guise of the individual acquisition of wealth, it was indeed society as a whole which was developing and to a certain extent progressing. Today this social wealth can develop no further within the framework of individual appropriation (of capitalist private property); it clearly needs reorganizing. But the aim is not to combat wealth with a view to achieving a general mediocrity, an 'equality' of mediocrity. The aim is still wealth: wealth that becomes progressively universalized, socialized wealth. This progressive expansion can only be achieved by degrees, by stages, by a series of measures suited to the complex, concrete, unpredictable circumstances of economic and political life.

Thus the Marxist finds himself impelled to criticize those *myths* of capitalist democracy which are still so widespread (though much less effective than their extension might suggest): the myth that wealth is immaterial or intrinsically bad, and the myth of egalitarianism (both obviously bound up with the myth of the 'private' individual, always identical to himself whatever the conditions or circumstances may be . . .).

Once this has been achieved, it becomes apparent that the Marxist critique of money is incomparably more radical than any moralizing rhetoric can be. And here, once again, it goes to the heart of the question.

Under capitalist regimes, 'to exist' and 'to have' are identical. 'The man who has nothing is nothing.'[10] And this situation is not a theoretical one, an abstract 'category' in a philosophy of existence; it is an 'absolutely desperate' reality; the man who has nothing finds himself 'separated from existence in general' and a fortiori from human existence; he is separated from that 'world of objects', i.e. the real world, without which no human existence is possible.

Spiritualism and idealism maintain that the loftiest situation for man is that of a spirit or a soul independent from the 'world of objects'. This situation is experienced, ironically, by the man who has nothing: 'Not having is the most despairing *spiritualism*, a complete unreality of the human being, a complete reality of the dishumanized being, a very positive having, a having of hunger, of cold, of disease, of crime, of debasement, of hebetude, of all inhumanity and abnormity.'[11]

Doubtless this is the 'profound' reason why spiritualism calls on people who have nothing at least to 'possess' their souls: this abstraction expresses their state of non-possession perfectly. Moreover it appears that objects are not simply important in so far as they are goods, but also as a shell for man's objective being, 'the *existence of man for other men*, his *human relation to other men*, the *social behaviour of man to man*'.[12] In this way, by arguing that non-possession is superior to possession, idealism situates 'profound' human reality – more profound than wealth – within the absence of real human relations, in other words within the loneliness and emptiness of abstraction.

Opposing this argument for non-possession is the argument which considers possession as an essential. If we accept the principle that the possession of objects constitutes the basis of human reality, it will lead us immediately to demand *equal possession for all*. This is exactly the principle of Proudhon's egalitarianism and petty-bourgeois socialism. The most cursory examination of this principle will reveal that it never goes beyond bourgeois ideology or the categories of bourgeois political economy; on the contrary, it places the category, the concept of 'possession', at the highest level. Thus it becomes involved in empty recriminations and moralizing, ineffectual anti-capitalist postures.

And how easy it is for bourgeois thinkers to demonstrate that this apology for ready-made equality of possession for all individuals is nothing more than an apology for boredom, uniformity, humdrum, day-to-day greyness! It really is petty-bourgeois mediocrity raised to the level of supreme truth and socialist 'ideal'!

But is this not precisely the same idealism that some people today[13] are proposing to restore in order to 'complete' Marxism and to take up the defence of the 'human being' against both capitalism and Marxist materialism? Is it not the hidden principle of the 'humanist socialism' with which they are trying to challenge Marxist humanism – which is Marxist not because Marxists have their own definition of man but because Marxist (dialectical materialist) method alone allows for the study of human reality and the creation of the new man who today is *possible* and implied in the *movement* of human reality?

According to Marxism, the relation between man and object is not the same as a relation of possession. It is incomparably broader. What is important is not that I have possession (be it capitalist or egalitarian) of an object, but that I can enjoy it in the human, total meaning of the word; that I can have the most complex, the 'richest' relationships of joy or happiness with the 'object' – which can be a thing or a living being or a human being or a social reality. Moreover it is by means of this object, within, in and through it, that I enter into a complex network of human relations.

Apropos of love, the term 'to possess' (e.g. to possess a woman) brings with it a long procession of feelings, aspirations, prejudices, myths and 'paroxysmal moments'. Still too frequently the myth of possession is countered by the myth of non-possession, according to which love is just a function, an inessential activity which does not involve the human being in his totality; so that promiscuity, infidelity, the absence of jealousy, become signs of freedom, of the new love, of the emancipated 'feminine personality'. This myth of non-possession remains firmly within the abstract category of the 'private' individual, allegedly endowed with an 'inner being' that is inaccessible and indifferent to (external) activities. The dialectical truth may be formulated roughly as follows: a man's (or a woman's) relationship will be richer, more human, more complex, more joyful (but also possibly more deeply painful) with someone who is free than with someone who allows him or herself to be 'possessed'. At last relationships will be humanized, and in the process will do away with those zones of indifference perpetuated as much by myths of possession as by myths of non-possession (either of accomplished and complete possession or of the inadmissibility of possession). By bringing together two complex free beings these physiological, psychological, 'spiritual' relationships will go infinitely farther than the merely sexual, although the sexual will be by no means marginalized. Their *tendency*, therefore, will be to enter everyday life; to allow their presence to impregnate the other human relations (social activities, thought, etc.), which henceforth will be accomplished through them, but not without them. The (humanized) object for me makes me into a (humanized) object for it; I thus enter the sphere where my human possibilities are totally, objectively realized. The object then will have accomplished the totality of its functions as an object.

Whereas Proudhon declares that 'possession is a social function',[14] the Marxist theory of the object expressly supersedes this kind of 'socialism' and moves in the direction of concrete, total humanism, affirming with Marx that 'what is "interesting" in a function, however, is not to "exclude" the other person, but to affirm and to realise the forces of my own being',[15] which is possible only by the other person, with the other person and in the other person.

In the social domain, capitalist theory and practice end up producing a mass of individuals deprived of any rights over objects of social importance such as large factories, large businesses, works of art, the spaces in which rest and leisure take on superior value and meaning (mountains, the sea, the air, etc.).

On the other hand, the 'socialist' apology for possession as a 'social function' creates some very strange illusions. For example, it might lead one to compare large social buildings – gigantic factories, palatial public edifices – with the pyramids of Egypt, for which the Pharaohs sacrificed innumerable slaves. The proletariat will appear to be making a decisive step towards freedom whenever it 'shares in the profits' of a business, or becomes a shareholder, or has a vote in the nomination of a management committee, etc. The possession of a minuscule square inch of property will be seen as a liberation of the individual – and of the sum total of individuals, the proletariat, the people.

In the first place this kind of 'socialism' omits an essential distinction, the distinction between consumer goods and the (social) means of production.

Consumer goods, the objects linked to my everyday life – this pen, this glass, these clothes, etc. – are obviously 'mine' and should stay so. The question is not one of taking 'my' objects away from me, but on the contrary of giving me more of them. Only a few cranks, inspired by ascetic, monastic Communism rather than by scientific socialism, have gone so far as to criticize the principle of the *individual* appropriation of consumer goods. It is moreover evident that the motto of phalansterian Communism, 'what is mine is thine', neither eradicates nor supersedes the 'thine' or the 'mine', but on the contrary generalizes them as fundamental categories of everyday life.

What is more, the relation I have with the objects which are immediately 'mine' is not a *legal*, 'private'-property relation. I can break them, give them away, sell them, without drawing up a legal contract. The relation is therefore an immediate one, part of everyday life, and does not have to be altered when the economic, social and legal parameters of the social structure based on 'private' property are modified. But it is precisely this relation that egalitarian socialism tends to generalize into a legal category. This merely serves to reveal how far it lags behind the way the practicalities of life are organized even in bourgeois society; it takes us back to the days when slaves could only dream of being able to say of the most ordinary of objects: 'it's mine'.

The important thing is not that I should have the impression of possessing a minuscule interest in socially important concerns (the means of production) but that these concerns should strive objectively to increase social wealth, to make wealth universal.

The important thing is not that I should become the owner of a little plot of land in the mountains, but that the mountains be open to me – for climbing or for winter sports. The same applies for the sea and the air, regions of the world where the notion of 'private' possession becomes more or less meaningless, but whose appeal and attraction to the 'free' individual is all the more powerful because of that.

In this way and in this way alone the world becomes mine, my estate, because I am a man. In this way and this way alone is the world the future of (social) man.

Only in this way can the 'private' individual, the individualistic model of man, be superseded, and concrete and truly free individuality attained.

The movement of self-realization of the human proceeds from the subject (desires, aspirations, ideas) to objects, to the world – and equally from the object to the subject (liberation from any external determinism, from any destiny which has not been understood and controlled). In philosophical terms, this realization may be described equally as a deeper *subjectivization* – a more lucid awareness – and as an *objectification*, a world of material, controlled objects.

Subjectivization and objectification go hand in hand, inseparably.

The big disadvantage of traditional terminology is that there is one major aspect of the problem of man it fails to emphasize. No amount of theorizing will permit us to attain the total man, or even to define him. Humanized at last, this 'essence' of man, who up until now did not exist and who cannot exist in advance, is made real through action and in practice, i.e. *in everyday life*.

Theorizing has its part to play. If we are to define not so much the human, but the direction in which action must go, we need to call upon knowledge and science. And not just one science, but all of them. Man is not just economic, or biological, or physio-chemical, etc. And yet he is all of this. This is what makes him the total man. From each science, from each partial method of research, total humanism borrows elements for analysis and orientation (in varying proportions according to the moments and the problems ...). The most extensive method of all, the dialectic, is the only one capable of organizing the 'synthesis' of all these elements and of extracting from them *the idea of man*, which, rather than acting as a substitute for real achievement, as idealism does, actually provokes realizing action, strengthening it and guiding it forward.

A human being only is (only exists) through what he *has*; but the present form of 'having', the possession of money, is merely an inferior, narrow, limited one.

Conversely, a human being only completely has what he *is*. This is why 'to be' a social being, or a thinker, or a poet, etc., and to participate in human reality, *to be* as extensive a fragment as possible of that reality rather than to contemplate it, conceive it or control it from outside, is problematic.

On this point, money is a particularly untrustworthy master. Let us imagine a man with a certain amount of potential, a 'personality' as they say, devoting his activities and his talents to getting rich and succeeding (with a bit of 'luck' and above all *an absolute single-mindedness*, almost anyone, even an idiot, can manage to earn money), upon which he buys some paintings by Picasso or Matisse, some luxury editions of Valéry and the complete works of Monsieur Gide. As we all know, in a society where everything is for sale, and where consciousness is merely a commodity which costs just a little less than any other commodity, because it is in plentiful supply, money can buy anything. Thus our parvenu has everything at his fingertips: beauty, art, knowledge ... But he could have been a poet, or a painter, or a scientist, someone who would create beauty and knowledge. 'Everything which you are unable to do, your money can do for you.'[16] In the still-dehumanized life of bourgeois society, money symbolizes this tearing away of man from himself; it is more than the symbol of *alienation*, it is the alienation of man itself, his 'alienated essence'. In the capitalist human being it represents all the time devoted not to living (through creative labour or through leisure), but to saving or 'speculating' (in the financial sense of the word) instead. In the creative *belle époque* of ascendant capitalism, the bourgeois 'deprived' himself in order to accumulate capital, to build up his business concerns. At this stage, money had its ethic, its religion: asceticism, economy. It taught 'abnegation'; and thus it spoke to the bourgeois of the seventeenth century, and thus it speaks to the petty bourgeois even today:

> The less you eat, drink, buy books, go to the theatre, go dancing, go drinking, think, love, theorize, sing, paint, fence, etc., the more you *save* and the greater will become that treasure which neither moths nor maggots can consume – your *capital*. The less you *are* ... the more you *have*.[17]

The finance capitalist of the decadent period – the degenerate son of a family rich for generations or the parvenu made rich through speculation – speaks as follows:

> The stronger the power of my money, the stronger am I. The properties of money are my, the possessor's, properties and essential powers ... I am ugly, but I can buy the *most beautiful* woman. As an individual, I am *lame*, but money procures me twenty-four legs ... Through money I can have anything the human heart desires.[18]

To the proletarian money speaks a different language. Ceaselessly, at every moment of his everyday life, it whispers these threats:

> *You need me, and you'll have to swap your own self to get me. You've got to sell yourself. I am your life and the meaning of your life. You're nothing but a thing, a coarse,*

natural object like any other, a commodity among commodities. And what you're swapping for these objects you call coins is your time for activity and living. But in any case it's better for you to imagine that you're expiating original sin or sharing in the misfortunes of the human condition . . .

Although deprivation and alienation are different for the proletarian and the non-proletarian, one thing unites them: money, the human being's alienated essence. This alienation is constant, i.e. practical and everyday.

(d) *Critique of needs*
(Central theme: psychological and moral alienation)

The more needs a human being has, the more he exists. The more powers and aptitudes he is able to exercise, the more he is free.

In this field, (bourgeois) political economy creates a single need: the need for money. In the hands of the individual, money is the only power which gives him contact with the alien, hostile world of objects. The vaster this world of objects becomes, the greater the need for money. And it is thus that 'the *quantity* of money becomes more and more its sole *important* property'.[19] Every being becomes reduced to this abstraction: market value; man himself becomes reduced to this abstraction. Money, man's alienated essence, the projection beyond himself of his activities and his needs, is only a *quantitative* essence. And there is nothing to determine or limit it qualitatively. For this reason, functioning outside of men and yet produced by them, an 'automatic fetish', money becomes inflated out of all proportion, as does the fundamental need (in capitalist regimes) which bears witness to its presence in men's hearts. And every other need is adjusted and revised according to the need for money. As a set of desires, the human being is not developed and cultivated for himself, but so that the demands of this theological monster may be satisfied. The need for money is an expression of the needs of money.

On the one hand, therefore, every effort is made to create fictitious, artificial, imaginary needs. Instead of expressing and satisfying real desires, and of transforming 'crude need into human need',[20] the capitalist producer inverts the course of things. He starts with the object which is the simplest or the most lucrative to produce, and endeavours – mainly through advertising – to create a need for it.

Satirically, Marx has demonstrated the 'idealist' character of this operation, which begins with the external, abstract concept of the object in order to stimulate a desire for it. This idealism culminates in fantasy, whims, the bizarre (as in the decadent aesthetic, for example!). Like the eunuch who panders to his rich master's every desire, or the priest who exploits every imperfection, every weak spot in the human heart and mind in order to preach about heaven, the producer becomes the pimp for the individual and his own self: he 'places himself at the disposal of his neighbour's most depraved fancies, panders to his needs, excites unhealthy appetites in him, and pounces on every weakness, so that he can then demand the money for his labour of love.'[21]

But at the same time, for all those unable to pay, needs die, degenerate, become more simple. As a result the worker stops feeling the simplest needs, which are also the most difficult needs for workers to satisfy: the need for space, for fresh air and freedom, for solitude or contemplation. Man the proletarian

> reverts once more to living in a cave, but the cave is now polluted by the mephitic and pestilential breath of civilization. Moreover, the worker has no more than a precarious right to live in it, for it is for him an alien power that can be daily withdrawn and from which, should he fail to pay, he can be evicted at any time. He actually has to *pay* for this mortuary.[22]

So man sinks even lower than an animal. Needs and feelings no longer exist in a human form; they no longer even exist in a dehumanized form, therefore 'not even in animal form'. Not only does man cease to have human needs, but he loses his animal needs: to move about, to have contacts with beings of the same species ...

It is a state of affairs that the bourgeois economist finds eminently satisfactory; it means that all is well in the capitalist economy. Money reigns; everyone serves it in their particular way, according to the position they hold in 'human nature': the bourgeois worship it in a refined, even artistic, way, while the workers' homage is humble and austere.

The human being's many needs and desires have their foundation in biological life, in instincts; subsequently social life transforms them, giving this biological content a new form. On the one hand needs are *satisfied by society*; on the other, as history unfolds, society *modifies* them both in form and in content.

Thus as soon as the objects it perceives stop being crude objects immersed in nature and become social objects, 'the eye has become a *human* eye'.[23]

What psychologists call 'perception' or the 'perceptible world' is in reality the product of human action on the historical and social level. The activity which gives the external world and its 'phenomena' shape is not a 'mental' activity, theoretical and formal, but a practical, concrete one. Practical tools, not simple concepts, are the means by which social man has shaped the perceptible world. As regards the processes of knowledge by means of which we understand this 'world', torn as it is from the immensity of nature and rendered coherent and human, they are not 'a priori categories', or subjective 'intentions'; they are our senses. But our senses have been transformed by action. Capable of understanding and organizing certain wholes, certain forms, the human eye is more than just the natural organ of vision of a superior vertebrate, of a lone figure lost in the natural world, of a primitive man or a child.

Thus the 'world' is man's mirror because man makes it: it is the task of his practical, everyday life to do so. But it is not his 'mirror' in a passive way. In this his work man perceives and becomes conscious of his own self. If what he makes comes from him, he in turn comes from what he makes; it is made by him, but it is in these works and by these works that he has made himself.

Thus it is that our senses, organs, vital needs, instincts and feelings have been permeated with consciousness, with human reason, since they too have been shaped by social life.

The creation of these human feelings, along with the appropriation of objective reality (the constitution of a human 'world'), constitute *the fulfilment of human reality.*

And it is in everyday life, and through everyday life, that humaniza- tion is accomplished. Every moment of inspiration, of genius or of heroism must serve – and even despite itself, does serve – everyday man. Should any other claims be made for such moments, they must fall into the realm of 'alienation', where man is torn apart. Great things have been attempted in the name of 'alienation'; they have failed or have been subsumed, but in unpredictable ways everyday man and the everyday world have benefited from them. It is in this fact, which idealism uses to prove the inevitable failure of all 'greatness', that we must on the contrary see the forming of true greatness, the greatness of human life.

(e) *Critique of work*
(Central theme: the alienation of the worker and of man)

The relation of every humble, everyday gesture to the social complex, like the relation of each individual to the whole, cannot be compared to that of the part to the sum total or of the element to a 'synthesis', using the term in its usual vague sense. Mathematical integration would be a better way of explaining the transfer from one scale of greatness to another, implying as it does a qualitative leap without the sense that the 'differential' element (the gesture, the individual) and the totality are radically heterogeneous.

Within the parameters of private property, this relation of the 'differential' element to the whole is both disguised and distorted. In fact, the worker works for the social whole; his activity is a part of 'social labour' and contributes to the historical heritage of the society (nation) to which he belongs. But he does not know it. He thinks he is working 'for the boss'. And he is indeed working 'for the boss': he provides him with a profit. In this way the portion of the social value of his labour which does not come back to him in the form of wages is retained by the boss (surplus-value). The only *direct* relations the worker has are with the boss. He is ignorant of the overall or total phenomena involved. He does not know that the totality of surplus-value goes to the bosses as a group or capitalist 'class'. He does not know (at least, not spontaneously) that the sum total of wages go to the proletarian 'class'; he is even more ignorant of the fact that the way the sum total is distributed – surplus-value, wages, products, rates of profit, purchasing power, etc. – obeys certain laws.

Integration takes place beyond the will of individuals, outside of their 'private' consciousness. The individual capitalist is just as ignorant of the laws of capitalism as the individual proletarian. As an individual, a capitalist may be intelligent or stupid, good or vicious, active or inert. He does not know that his essential reality is that of a member of a class. Here again, his essence is outside of him. In good faith, the individual – be he bourgeois or proletarian – can deny the existence of social classes since objective social reality functions beyond his own 'subjectivity', beyond his own 'private' consciousness.

The direct, immediate relation between the wage-earner and the boss is therefore a rigged, ambiguous, formal relation which conceals a hidden content.

The wage-earner's relations with society as a whole pass via the employer, through the mediation of money and wages. But in everyday life the deep, objective relation is disguised by direct, immediate relations, apparently real – until knowledge begins to penetrate the real.

Here, therefore, *everyday life functions within certain appearances* which are not so much the products of mystifying ideologies, as contributions to the conditions needed for any mystifying ideology to operate.

The social whole is essentially constituted by the total activity of society – by work and by the various activities of society considered in its totality.

But within the parameters of 'private' property, labour is 'alienated'. The alienation of labour is many-sided. The wage-earner works for the employer and the proletarian class works for the capitalist class; but that is *only one aspect of alienation,* the easiest aspect to understand – above all for those who stand to gain from it! – and the one which will help to elucidate the others.

Alienated labour has lost its social essence. Though its essence is indeed social, labour assumes the appearance and the reality of an individual task. Moreover, as it is social labour, it takes the form of a buying and a selling of labour-power.

The individual ceases to feel at one with the social conditions of his activity. Not only do the tools of his trade loom up before him like an alien, threatening reality – since they do not belong to him (either as an individual, as in a craft, or as a member of a collectivity, as in socialism) – but also he becomes separated, disassociated from his own self, in his real, everyday life. On the one hand he is a human individual; on the other, he is 'labour-power', labour time which is up for sale like a commodity, a thing. For the worker, participation in the creative activity of the social whole takes the form of an external necessity: the necessity of 'earning a living', and it is thus that, for the individual, social labour takes on the appearance of a penalty, a mysterious punishment. The necessity of having to work weighs down on him from without as though he were an object. It turns him into an object, dragging him into a mechanism he knows nothing about. The wage-earner sells his labour-power like a thing – and becomes a thing, a base object. 'Man himself, viewed merely as the physical existence of labour-power, is a natural object, a thing, although a living, conscious thing, and labour is the physical manifestation (*dingliche Aüsserung*) of that power.'[24]

The human being – ceasing to be human – is turned into a tool to be used by other tools (the means of production), a thing to be used by another thing (money), and an object to be used by a class, a mass of individuals who are themselves 'deprived' of reality and truth (the capitalists). And his labour, which ought to humanize him, becomes something done under duress instead of being a vital and human need, since it is itself nothing more than a means (of 'earning a living') rather than a contribution to man's essence, freely imparted.

The wage-earner is confronted with the use of his labour-power 'as *something alien*'.[25] Not only is his labour-power bought from him, but it is also used in combination with other people's work (the technical division of labour) of which he has no knowledge; and no one really understands this division of labour; occasionally experts and specialists in the area might know about it *at the level of their own firms* (but it is well known that in France the level of design and planning is less efficient and productive than it could be); such experts know nothing about the division of labour *at the level of society*; only a *plan* for social labour could demonstrate how it functions and control it. Therefore, for every individual, worker or expert, the division of labour is imposed from without, like an objective process, with the result that each man's activity is turned back against him as a hostile force which subjugates him instead of being subjugated by him.

In this way a dehumanized, brutally objective power holds sway over all social life; according to its differing aspects, we have named it: money, fragmented division of labour, market, capital, mystification and deprivation, etc. 'This fixation of social activity, this consolidation of what we ourselves produce into an objective power above all, growing out of our control, thwarting our expectations, bringing to naught our calculations, is one of the chief factors in historical development up till now.'[26]

It is always changing shape, now appearing as the objective laws of political economy, now as the destiny of politicians, now as the State, or as the market, as historical fatality, as ideologies.

Only man and his activity exist. And yet everything happens as though men had to deal with external powers which oppress them from outside and drag them along. Human reality – what men themselves have made – eludes not only their will but also their consciousness. They do not know that they are alone, and that the 'world' is their work. (Here we are using the word 'world' to signify the coherent, organized, humanized world, not pure, brute *nature*.)

There is a name for this fixing of human activity within an alien reality which is at one and the same time crudely material and yet abstract: *alienation*.

Just as the creative activity of the human world is not theoretical but practical, a constant, everyday activity rather than an exceptional one, so too *alienation is constant and everyday*.

Alienation is not a theory, an idea or an abstraction – it is rather that the theories, the ideas or the 'pure' abstractions which induce man to obliterate his living existence in favour of absolute truth, and to define himself by a theory or reduce himself to abstractions, are part of human alienation.

Alienation appears in day-to-day life, the life of the proletarian and even of the petty bourgeois and the capitalist (the difference being that capitalists collaborate with alienation's dehumanizing power).

In every attitude which tears every man away from what he is and what he can do – in art, in the moral sphere, in religion – criticism will reveal alienation.

Certain gestures, certain words, certain actions, seem to come from an 'alien being', in the general, human sense of the term: it is not 'me', a man, who has spoken, but 'him', the artificial being, presumptuous, angel or devil, superman or criminal, created within me to stop me from being myself and from following the lines of force whereby action achieves *more reality*.

Appearance and reality intertwine. Appearances graft themselves onto reality, encompassing it, replacing it. For people who have been unable to overcome alienation, the 'alienated' world – social appear-

ances, the theories and abstractions which express these appearances –
seems the only reality. Thus any criticism of life which fails to take the
clear and distinct notion of human alienation as its starting point will
be a criticism not of life, but of this pseudo-reality. Blinkered by
alienation, confined to its perspective, such a critique will take as its
object the 'reality' of the existing social structure, rejecting it wholesale
as it yearns for 'something else': a spiritual life, the surreal, the
superhuman, an ideal or metaphysical world. This kind of criticism
will therefore move more and more towards alienation, reinforcing it in
the process.

Genuine criticism, by contrast, will expose an *unreality* in the 'reality'
of the bourgeoisie, a system of phenomena which have already been
refuted by life and thought, a group of appearances which seem real
but which consciousness has overcome or is in the process of over-
coming.

Genuine criticism will then reveal the human reality beneath this
general unreality, the human 'world' which takes shape within us and
around us: in what we see, what we do, in humble objects and
(apparently) humble and profound feelings. A human world which has
been torn away from us, disassociated and dispersed by alienation, but
which still constitutes the irreducible core of appearances.

The notion of *alienation* is destined to become the central notion of
philosophy (seen as criticism of life and the foundation for a concrete
humanism) as well as of *literature* (seen as the expression of life in
movement).

It is a key notion. It replaces out-moded ideological 'centres of
interest' by a new interest in individual and social man. It enables us to
discover how man (every man) gives in to illusions in which he thinks
he can discover and possess his own self, and the self-inflicted anguish
which ensues; or how he struggles to bring to light his 'core' of human
reality. It enables us to follow this struggle through history: to see how
appearances fade or become strengthened, and how truly human
reality seeks to go beyond appearances and discover a reality 'other'
than the one we live and yet which will still be that reality, brought to
light at last in all its truth, and reinstated as the keystone of the very
edifice beneath which it has been entombed.

The drama of human alienation is much more profound and
enthralling than any of the phony cosmic dramas or divine scenarios

which man is supposed to act out in this world.

The drama of alienation is dialectical. Through the manifold forms of his labour, man has made himself real by realizing a human world. He is inseparable from this 'other' self, his creation, his mirror, his statue – more: his body. The totality of objects and human products taken together form an integral part of human reality. On this level, objects are not simply means or implements; by producing them, men are working to create the human; they think they are moulding an object, a series of objects – and it is man himself they are creating.

But in this dialectical relation of man to himself (the relation between the human world and human consciousness), a new element emerges to confuse the situation and halt its development.

As he strives to control nature and create his world, man conjures himself up a new nature. Certain of man's products function in relation to human reality like some impenetrable nature, undominated, oppressing his consciousness and will from without. Of course, this can only be an appearance; products of human activity cannot have the same characteristics as brute, material things. And yet this appearance too is a reality: commodities, money, capital, the State, legal, economic and political institutions, ideologies – all function as though they were realities external to man. In a sense, they are realities, with their own laws. And yet, they are purely human products ...

Thus the human being develops through this 'other' self, half-fact, half-fiction, which becomes intimately involved with the 'human world' in its process of formation.

Analysis must therefore distinguish between the real 'human world' on the one hand, the totality of human works and their reciprocal action upon man, and, on the other, the unreality of *alienation.*

But this unreality appears to be infinitely more real than anything authentically human. And this appearance contributes to alienation; it becomes real, and as a result a great abstract 'idea' or a certain form of the State seems infinitely more important than a humble, everyday feeling or a work born of man's hands.

Thus the real is taken for the unreal, and vice versa. Moreover this illusion has a real, solid basis, for it is not a theoretical illusion; it is a practical illusion, with its basis in everyday life and in the way everyday life is organized. This real and this unreal are not speculative categories but categories of life, of practical activity – historical and even tragic categories. If the human is the fundamental reality of history, the inhuman is reduced to an appearance, a manifestation of man's becoming. And yet how well we know the terrible reality of the inhuman! Only a concrete dialectic which demonstrates the unity of essence and appearance, of the real and the unreal – a unity in the process of becoming, in which the two poles merge and act one upon the other – is capable of giving a meaning to the 'human' and the 'inhuman' in history.

Man attains his own reality, creates himself through, within and by means of his opposite, his alienation: the inhuman. It is through the inhuman that he has slowly built the human world.

This humble, everyday, human world has been taken as a crude façade for certain sublime realities. We know today that these 'higher realities' were simply the manifestation, the appearance, of man's attempt to create his own reality in everyday life – but possessing the monstrous power, peculiar to alienation, of absorbing human reality, of crushing it and throwing it off centre, so to speak.

Now it has reached its moment of highest intensity, the conflict between what is apparent and what is real is about to be resolved through a progress in consciousness and activity. Alienation, now made conscious, and thus rejected as mere appearance and super-seded, will give way to an authentic human reality, stripped of its façade, and liberated.

(f) *Critique of freedom*
(Central theme: man's power over nature and over his own nature)

What does freedom consist in?

According to Article 6 of the 1793 Constitution: 'Liberty is the power which belongs to man to do anything that does not harm the rights of others'; and the Declaration of the Rights of Man of 1791 maintains that: 'Liberty consists in being able to do anything which does not harm others.'

Quoting these texts[27] gives Marx the opportunity of directing his irony against the idols of the bourgeoisie.

The limits within which each individual can move *without* harming others are determined by law, just as the boundary between two fields is determined by a stake. The liberty we are here dealing with is that of man as an isolated monad who is withdrawn into himself ... But the right of man to freedom is not based on the association of man with man but rather on the separation of man from man. It is the *right* of this separation, the right of the *restricted* individual, restricted to himself.[28]

It is therefore the right of the 'private' individual, and in its practical application consists essentially of the right to 'private' property (Article 16 of the 1793 Constitution).

So this bourgeois definition of freedom has something narrow and sordid about it. Yet its partisans see it as noble and profound; it protects the rights of 'individual conscience', of 'inner freedom', of the 'personality'. And it is not entirely false, in so far as the way the lives of individuals have been organized has allowed certain privileged people to develop an intellectually rigorous or morally sincere 'conscience'. But when we consider the sum total of results, the sum total of 'private lives' formed and established within the parameters of this bourgeois freedom, it is easy to see that its nobility and profundity are part and parcel of the process of mystification.

Even at best, freedom defined in this way is totally negative. One must never do anything for fear of encroaching upon one's neighbour, even if he needs help! When it attempts to be active and 'positive', this freedom becomes the art of twisting the (moral or legal) law, of interfering cunningly in other people's lives and property. But since by definition intermonadic relations cannot be organized and work to all intents and purposes haphazardly, any positive attempts to be free become nothing more than the skilful exploitation of chance in relations founded on money (markets, sales, inheritances, etc.) and the skilful use of money according to the whim of the 'free' individual.

The Marxist definition of freedom is concrete and dialectical.

The realm of freedom is established progressively by '*the development of human powers as an end in itself*'.[29]

The definition of freedom thus begins with the *power* man increasingly has over nature (and over his own nature, over his self and the products of his activity). It is not a ready-made freedom; it cannot be defined metaphysically by an 'all or nothing': absolute freedom or absolute necessity. It is won progressively by social man. For *power*, or, more exactly, *the sum total of powers* which constitute freedom belong to human beings grouped together in a society, and not to the isolated individual.

In the first place, then, freedom must be won; it is arrived at through a process of becoming: there are therefore *degrees of freedom*. (In the same way, to take a comparison from a political problem which is not unconnected with the general problem of freedom, there are *degrees* of democracy, more democracy, less democracy, a development in democracy ...)

In the second place, the freedom of the individual is founded upon that of his social group (his nation, his class). There can be no freedom for the individual in a subservient nation or class. Only in a free society will the individual be free to realize his full potential.

In the third place, there are *freedoms* (political and human, both on the social and the individual level) rather than 'freedom' in general. All freedoms imply the exercise of *effective* power. Freedom of expression, effective participation in the running of the social whole, these are political freedoms. The (complementary) rights to work and to leisure – the possibility of attaining the highest consciousness and development of the self through culture – contribute to *concrete* individual freedom. All power is liberating; thus, to take a very simple example, someone who can swim or run is attaining a higher level of freedom: he is free in relation to a material environment which he controls instead of being controlled by it. 'Spiritually' and materially, the free individual is a totality of powers, i.e. of concrete possibilities. Freedom reduced to so-called freedom of 'opinion', or to the open-ended possibilities of adventure or flight of fancy, is one of the illusions of the 'private' consciousness – mystifications accepted by the 'subject' who has been separated from the natural and human 'object'.

Nevertheless the notion of freedom in general retains a meaning. Dialectically it even takes on a new meaning, higher and more profound. It designates the *unity* of the different aspects of freedom, of the various freedoms. There can be no concrete freedom for the individual without social, economic and political freedoms. The power which will liberate is not the power which certain men have wielded over other human beings, but the power which man, considered as a whole, wields over nature.

There is no metaphysical dilemma of the order: 'Either absolute determinism – or else absolute freedom. All or nothing!' The universe is not an indifferent, immovable mass, an immediately available 'world' which unfolds according to inexorable 'Laws'. Such a vision, which deprives man of the world, has a name which situates it in the history of thought and which demonstrates how much and by what means we have superseded it: it is called 'mechanism'. This vision served a purpose by lending support to science, as a transitional stage, at the very moment when action founded upon science was demonstrating how erroneous an interpretation it was. The 'laws of nature' do not forbid effective action, they are its foundation. If we get rid of mechanism, we get rid of the inevitability of destiny. The way opens up for the conquest of the world. *The world is man's future.*

So long as man did not understand the laws of nature and history, they weighed him down; because he did not understand them, they inevitably seemed to be governed by a 'mysterious', oppressive, blind necessity.

Knowledge and action extend the 'dominated sector' of nature and man, taking this necessity over and transforming it into powers, i.e. freedoms: man dominates nature and his own social nature by 'understanding' them. Necessity is blind only in so far as it is not understood.

In the realm of necessity, human needs became degraded. They represented 'the sad necessities of everyday life'. People had to eat, drink, find clothes ... and so they had to work. But people whose only reason for working is to keep body and soul together have neither the time nor the inclination for anything else. So they just keep on working, and their lives are spent just staying alive. This, in a nutshell, has been the philosophy of everyday life – and it still is.

And yet, every human need, conceived of as the relation between a human being and the 'world', can become a power, in other words a freedom, a source of joy or happiness. But needs have to be rescued from the realm of blind necessity, or at least its ascendancy must be progressively reduced.

'Man appropriates his integral essence in an integral way, as a total man.'[30] This 'essence' is not a metaphysical essence, but a set of needs and organs which become social, human, rational, as a result of the power of social man over nature (and over his own nature). Whether we are concerned with the eye or genitals, with rational consciousness or physical activity, it is always a question of the 'appropriation of *human* reality' of the 'approach to the object',[31] and this is what 'the *confirmation of human reality*'[32] consists in. On the one hand, man's 'essence' is factual: his body, his biological reality. But on the other hand, seen as practical activity which appropriates these biological realities and transforms them into freedoms and powers, the 'essence' of the human cannot be defined as a ready-made nature; it creates itself, through action, through knowledge – and through social becoming.

One particular aspect of art demonstrates this transformation well. In a painting, the human eye has found its 'appropriate object'; the human eye has formed and transformed itself first through practical and then through aesthetic activity, and by knowledge: it has become something other than a mere organ; for the painter at least, through this work which has been freed from all external constraints, truly prefiguring the realm of freedom, and producing the work of art, the eye partakes of that 'joy that man gives to himself'.[33] (Of course, such a sketchy analysis scarcely scratches the surface of the problem of art ...)

It is perfectly obvious that the realm of 'private' property forms part of the realm of blind necessity. Every human activity which is controlled by this narrow and limited entity will devote itself to perpetuating it. In bourgeois ideology, it appears as an *inner part* of the individual, one of his fundamental 'rights', something his freedom is founded on. In fact, and consonant with the dialectical principle according to which what appears to be most internal is in fact most external, analysis shows that it is really an external, oppressive entity. When they are linked to this institution, 'individual' feelings and needs cannot attain a humanized level. '[An] object is only *ours* when we have it ... Therefore *all* the physical and intellectual senses have been replaced by the simple estrangement of *all* these senses – the sense of *having*.'[34] Moreover Marx transforms this observation about human poverty into something hopeful, for he adds: 'So that it might give birth to its inner wealth, human nature had to be reduced to this absolute poverty.'[35]

The realm of blind necessity is retreating before the combined onslaught of knowledge and action. Liberated from sordid necessity, needs per se are becoming suffused with reason, social life, joy and happiness. Moreover people are having to spend less time working in order to satisfy these needs; in the past only the subjection of the masses allowed the upper classes that freedom which is to be found beyond the sphere of material production. In our era, especially in our era, the condition which restricted creative leisure and 'spiritual' activities to the oppressors has disappeared. It is a complex dialectic: needs are becoming more extensive, more numerous, but because the productive forces are broadening, this extension of needs *may* imply their humanization, a reduction in the number of hours worked to satisfy immediate needs, a reduction of the time spent at work generally, a universalization both of wealth and of leisure. If, in a sense, the realm of natural necessity is growing more extensive, since the needs of modern man *are tending towards* a greater complexity than those of primitive man, then the realm of freedom will only become greater and more profoundly rooted in nature as a result.

Nevertheless, first and foremost:

(a) 'The associated producers must ... govern the human metabolism with nature in a rational way, bringing it under their collective control instead of being dominated by it as a blind power.'[36]

(b) The material and moral parameters of practical (everyday) life, which are determined by private property, must be transformed.

(c) Through activities devoted to satisfying and controlling immediate necessities, there must be a growth in the sphere of '*the true realm of freedom, the development of human powers, as an end in itself,* [which] *begins beyond it, though it can only flourish with this realm of necessity as its basis*'.[37] This sphere, this 'spiritual' domain of man, consists in the first place in a social and rational organization of free leisure. As Marx asserts in *Capital*: 'The reduction of the working day is the basic requisite.'[38]

4

The Development of Marxist Thought

But in that case, one may say, Marxism *already* offers a complete critical knowledge of everyday life!

No.

The significance of the work of Marx and Engels is still far from being clearly elucidated.

Two obstacles have hindered a deeper elaboration of Marxist thought. Some take Marx's and Engels's texts *literally* – seeing each text in isolation, without link, without unity – rather than attempting to grasp and extend the evolution of the thought they contain. In this way certain Marxists have lost sight of its dynamic, living character. Although they are conversant with the texts, such theoreticians have become bogged down in literal exegeses which add nothing to Marxist thought (even though they are preferable, admittedly, to the flights of fancy of people who write or talk about Marxism without knowing anything about it); this is a doctrine about thought in movement and about movement in things, and they immobilize it. They are thus incapable of reconstructing the work of Marx and Engels in the integrality of its meaning.

On the other hand, attempts to develop Marxism 'freely' have too often involved deliberate modifications of its most solidly established foundations.

The genuine line of development of Marxist thought avoids both these dead-ends: literal dogmatism and the allegedly 'free' revision of first principles.

Dialectical materialism develops as a method of thinking which is neither empty nor formally separable from its object (an academic and scholastic way of conceiving method); instead it elaborates both itself and its content at the same time.

Before Marxist *humanism* could be fully reinstated, there were some fairly widespread errors which had to be refuted.

Marx and Engels began their work with philosophical research; then moved on to economics and political action.

Some – philosophers rather than economists – have concentrated exclusively upon the philosophical works. Conversely, others see Marx's economic works as eclipsing his philosophical works. In fact for a long time there was a widely held but fallacious theory that Marx's economics and politics had eliminated his philosophy. The fact that economic science and political action had *superseded* speculative philosophy fostered the false conclusion that Marx had abandoned any conception of the philosophical world.

This narrow, one-sided position was based on a traditional mistranslation. In the economic and political works of Marx and Engels, philosophy appears *aufgehoben*.[1] But there is no verb in French which translates this Hegelian term exactly; it means *at the same time* to abolish something (as it was) and to raise it to a higher level. From the first French translator of Hegel (Véra) onwards, the dialectical term *aufheben* has been repeatedly translated and traduced by the word 'supprimer'. The word 'dépasser', which is used nowadays, while nearer in meaning, still falls short of rendering the *double movement* Hegel's verb signifies; it fails to show clearly that the reality which has been *aufgehoben*, the dialectical *moment* which has been 'superseded' as such, takes on in the process of being 'superseded' a new reality, higher, more profound. Thus the philosophy must be rediscovered in the economy and the politics, and not as an 'eliminated' stage, but on the contrary as a moment and an essential element, which indeed only acquires *its full importance* in the higher reality.

Gradually the certainty has been reached that the *dialectical method* is an essential element of scientific sociology – indeed of all scientific thought.

But there is still more progress to be made. It still remains to be demonstrated clearly that this dialectical method is not one that is 'formally' separated from philosophical research and then subsequently applied to economic or social data. The dialectical method contains and implies a scientific, philosophical and human content. Thus philosophy ceases to be speculative and systematic; on the one hand it opens itself up to science, and on the other to the totality of human reality. Not only does it become 'committed' (a vague, abstract term), but it also becomes rationally (dialectically) articulated with the sciences and with the *movement* of scientific thought, with the human and with the *movement* of human reality, in other words with the action which transforms this reality, with the knowledge of its laws (i.e., precisely, its movement) as starting point.

We are still dealing with philosophy and with an *overall* conception of man and the world, but in a *renewed* sense: concrete, dynamic philosophy, linked to practical action as well as to knowledge – and thus implying the effort to 'supersede' all the limitations of life and thought, to organize a 'whole', to bring to the fore the idea of *the total man*.

In this way Marxism – a philosophy and a method, a humanism, an economic science, a political science – can be reconstructed in all its integrality. In this way and this way alone have certain major notions which had to be rediscovered and brought to light become apparent in Marx's works: the notion of *alienation*, of *fetishism* and of *mystification*.[2]

This preparatory work was absolutely vital if the methodical study of human reality was to continue, and if certain equally vital questions concerning concrete humanism were to be tackled.

The first principles and fundamental ideas which enable us to formulate and resolve these problems effectively are implicit in the work of Marx and Engels, provided this work is taken as a whole and understood in terms of its basic tendency. It is nevertheless true that the ideas in question are not dealt with comprehensively in the classic texts of Marxism, and that therefore they need not only clarifying but also developing.

Thus Marxism develops as a living whole (in economic, political and also *philosophical* research), without, however, ever emerging either as an 'orthodoxy' or scholasticism or, alternatively, as a shapeless eclecticism.

Where economy and philosophy meet lies the theory of *fetishism*.

Money, currency, commodities, capital, are nothing more than relations between human beings (between 'individual', qualitative human tasks). And yet these relations take on the appearance and the form of *things* external to human beings. The appearance becomes reality; because men believe that these 'fetishes' exist outside of themselves they really do function like objective things. Human activities are swept along and torn from their own reality and consciousness, and become subservient to these things. Humanly speaking, someone who thinks only of getting rich is living his life subjected to a thing, namely money. But more than this, the proletarian, whose life is used as a means for the accumulation of capital, is thrown to the mercy of an external power.

On the one hand, therefore, the economist observes *facts*; using *induction* and *deduction*, i.e. the procedures proper to the experimental sciences, he establishes laws to explain these facts – the law of value, of prices, of money, etc. The (dialectical) analysis of reality enables him to grasp the moments and the stages, the contradictions, the movement of this economic and social reality. It appears to be, and in one sense *is*, a reality independent of human consciousness and human will, developing according to a *natural and objective* process.

But in another sense, nothing else exists but human consciousness and human will. Only, they are 'alienated' – and alienated not merely in the domain of ideas or intuitions, but also in the domain of *practical* life. The theory of *economic fetishism* is fundamental because it enables us to understand the shift from human activities (individual, qualitative tasks) to economic 'things'; it also enables us to understand why economic and social truth is not immediate, how and why all the questions in this domain are veiled with a *social mystery*, namely, because economic 'things', fetishes, envelop and *disguise* the human relations which constitute them. When we handle money we forget, we no longer realize, that it is merely 'crystallized' labour, and that it represents human labour and nothing else; a deadly illusion endows it with an external existence ...

The theory of fetishism demonstrates the *economic, everyday* basis of the *philosophical* theories of mystification and alienation. We say of goods that are sold, that they are 'alienated'. We say of someone enslaved, that he has *alienated* his freedom. In its most extreme sense, the word designates the situation of people who have become estranged from themselves through mental illness. More generally, at certain stages of its development, human activity spawns relations which masquerade as *things*. Now these things and the way they function are beyond the grasp of action or consciousness, and permit interpretations, bizarre hypotheses and pseudo-explanations which are as remote from reality and truth as they could possibly be: ideologies ...

And that is precisely what human *alienation* consists in – man torn from his self, from nature, from his own nature, from his consciousness, dragged down and dehumanized by his own social products. This explains how there can be such a thing as a *social mystery*. Society becomes a mechanism and an organism which ceases to be comprehensible to the very people who participate in it and who maintain it through their labour. Men are what they do, and think according to what they are. And yet they are ignorant of what they do and what they are. Their own works and their own reality are beyond their grasp.

Man has been unable to avoid this alienation. It has imposed itself in everyday life, in social relations more complex than the immediate relations of kinship and primitive economy. Man has developed and has raised himself above the animal and biological condition of his lowly beginnings via socio-economic fetishism and self-alienation. No other way has been open to him. *The human has been formed through dehumanization* – dialectically. The division between the human and its self was – and remains – as deep, as tragic, as necessary as the division between man and nature. The one is the corollary of the other. Man, a being of nature, forever united inseparably with nature, struggles against it. He dominates it and imagines he can separate himself from it, through abstraction, through self-consciousness – something only attained by painful effort. Thus it is through the (theological and metaphysical) alienation which has allowed man to believe himself outside of nature and the world, through *idealism* itself, that we have successfully dominated nature. It is in contradiction and painful division, in the struggle against nature and against his own self, that man becomes what he *can* become.

Now the time of *rediscovered, recognized unity* is beginning, but at a higher level. Once more man recognizes himself as a being in nature, but now possessed of power and a consciousness which the immense and painful effort has afforded. Division, alienation – fetishism, mystification, deprivation – the formation of the total man, these *philosophical* ideas make up an organic, living whole. Man, his thought and his reality have developed *dialectically*. Dialectical method, the expression of all real processes, controls, organizes and illuminates this complex of ideas and confers on it the rigour of concrete logic.

Moreover, fetishism is *equally* a *scientific theory*, resulting from an analysis of data, from a series of inductions and deductions in the domain of economic science.

Thus Marxism cannot be reduced to being simply a *prise de conscience* of the world. When Marxists maintain that they are philosophers *as well*, what they mean is that they are not *only* philosophers, but something more: intellectuals on the one hand, men of action on the other. And this is where they part company with those philosophers who perpetuate the old tradition of metaphysical speculation. Marxism cannot be compared to a 'description' of the modern world, to a 'phenomenology of economic essences'. Without the work of the natural and social sciences, without the 'demystifying' influence of action, consciousness (the philosopher's) would come to an abrupt halt and become ensnared in alienation and mystification. Consciousness cannot free itself from existing illusions by its own strength alone; it will either atrophy in antiquated interpretations of the social structures inherited from the past, or else construct new 'ideological' interpretations.

Man is an infinitely complex being and his knowledge entails a multitude of aspects, investigations, techniques – all organically linked by dialectical method.

In the days when people wrote studies about 'human nature', moralists used to moan that there was not much left to say. Later, in the days of romantic idealism, this lament was repeated ad nauseam and transformed into a poetic dirge: we were born too late into a world too old. By proclaiming that man's youth is to be found in the future, dialectical materialism is also revealing the complexity of human reality, its richness. It renews and recreates interest in the human – and first and foremost by reintegrating the humbler reality of everyday life into thought and consciousness.

How could Marxism, which opens up a new horizon to consciousness and action, limit consciousness and tell it: 'Stop, there's nothing more to say!'? The founders of Marxism drew up the general guidelines for the criticism of life, but how could they possibly have completed that criticism? Marxism must move the knowledge of human reality forward, and this is what it is doing. Research and action reveal the human, and enrich it at the same time. Each new stage reveals new aspects of life – which we find increasingly complex, increasingly rich in the 'spiritual' sense of the word.

Dialectical method excludes the possibility that there can be nothing more to say about the human or about any domain of human activity. On the contrary, it supposes that the *knowledge* of man and his *realization* are mutually inseparable and constitute a total process. To penetrate ever more deeply into the content of life, to seize it in its shifting reality, to be ever more lucid about the lessons it has to teach us – this is the essential precept of research.

Lenin's analysis of historical situations has demonstrated the complexity of their elements and their interactions. For the trans-formation of the world to become possible, there must first be an *objective* crisis, a disassociation of the economic and the social structures (under the impetus of forces of production, caught between the mode of production and those legal relations which they are destined to shatter). This objective element is not enough. For a 'revolutionary crisis' to occur, however, a *subjective* element is equally necessary: revolutionary theory, upon which the action of a party, a class – as large and as well-informed a fraction of the social whole as possible – will be founded. But in the last resort the revolutionary solution to economic and social contradictions will only become possible when the human masses *are no longer able or willing to live as before*. Therefore Lenin calls upon everyone who wants to think like a man of action and to act like a man of thought to be open to what life can teach, and above all to look at everyday life. There is no such thing as the spontaneity of the masses, and theory by itself is not enough. And yet it is the awkward, tentative, spasmodic efforts of the human masses to free themselves from oppression – and the theory which understands, studies and illuminates mass movements – which quicken the idea of revolution. 'Unity of theory and practice' – this tenet dominates and sums up living Marxism. And it is in life that this unity is achieved and perpetuated, that this idea comes to maturity, that the union between its various elements – practical and theoretical, objective and subjective – is realized. None of these elements can be defined or can work effectively if separated from the others. The spontaneity of the masses is just an illusion, a myth created by people who expect 'history' to achieve its ends and to accomplish its task aided only by providence. Theory and knowledge outside of action are in themselves mere abstractions, and the myth of the 'vanguard' and the 'active minority' is no less harmful than the myth that the 'masses' can set themselves in motion spontaneously. Individuals and 'private' consciousnesses can only become a creative force through a theory and an action which unites them as a totality, an active mass, a lever for thought to lift the world with. Individual and mass are two opposing terms, but, like thought and action, they are bound together. And once more it is practical, everyday life which demands this unity, and develops it. It is in life – and in the light of previous knowledge and experience – that forms of organization and effective ideas are to be found. Only thus does the dialectic stop being an anti-dialectical abstraction to become the movement which unites opposing aspects and elements. It is no coincidence that Marxists repeat the word 'concrete' so frequently. Adversaries of Marxism refer ironically to the exaggerated and excessive use of the word (Malraux, for example, apropos of the Communist Pradas in *Days of Hope*); but talk of the 'concrete' is only truly ridiculous when it becomes an abstraction itself, an automatism. (Which in fact is what happens when people who believe they are acting and thinking dialectically stop looking at everyday life, stop learning from it, stop searching for its deeper significance. This is treachery, self-betrayal: in their mouths the dialectic reverts to being just so much metaphysical waffle; they become congealed in their own mystical speechifying about movement and history; they talk about the 'concrete', but they end up being more abstract than anyone!)

In the zone of clarity which precedes and follows action (or to put it more dialectically, *thought-action*), the theoretical themes of alienation, mystification, fetishism and deprivation spring suddenly to life. I see 'concretely' how human beings are mystified, hoodwinked, annihilated, confused; when I fight this many-sided alienation practically, I am better able to perceive how certain acts, certain words, split me from my self to feed the vampire of the non-human – that 'substance' which is, precisely, nothing, because from the point of view of the human, it is 'other', the negation of the human, the human cast to the winds and into the valley of death.

'Alienation' – I know it is there whenever I sing a love song or recite a poem, whenever I handle a banknote or enter a shop, whenever I glance at a poster or read a newspaper. At the very moment the human is defined as 'having possessions' I know it is there, dispossessing the human. I thus grasp how alienation substitutes a false greatness for the real weaknesses of man, and a false weakness for his true greatness.

Bombastic language, abstractions, deductions, every devilish device to vaporize man's will and man's thoughts – all vouchsafe me a glimpse of alienation in action.

This is not to say that I am able to separate what is human from the inhuman simply by thinking about it. The task is much more difficult, the division within the self and the waste of self are too deep-seated. If I have learned to think or to love, it is in and through the words, gestures, expressions and songs of thirty centuries of human alienation. How can I come to grips with my self, or how can we retrieve our selves once more? If I stay on my guard and strip myself of everything suspect, I am left naked, dry as dust, reduced to 'existing' like someone who refuses to be hoodwinked by anything; and what will become of me and my wariness? Nothing. Alienation is an ordeal that our era must undergo, there is no means of escaping it. Only later will future human beings, freed from alienation, know and see clearly what was dehumanized and what was worthwhile about the times we live in.

We are still learning to think via metaphysical, abstract – alienated – forms of thought. The danger of dogmatic, speculative, systematic and abstract attitudes lies ever in wait for us. How long will it take to create a *dialectical consciousness*, as long as our consciousness still feels it necessary to rise above its own self – in the metaphysical way – in order to think dialectically? It is impossible to fix a date; it may need generations before the dialectic can penetrate life by means of a regenerated culture.

And as for love – which for nearly all of us oscillates between coarse biological need and the fine abstractions of passion's rhetoric – what is there to say?

And so our entire life is caught up in alienation, and will only be restored to itself slowly, through an immense effort of thought (consciousness) and action (creation).

The word 'commitment' (commitment to the world – committed thought, etc.) has had its day. As a philosophical slogan, it had a certain meaning. The abstract intellectual, moving about in unreality, felt the need to 'commit' himself to life, to action. He ended up with action for action's sake – commitment for the sake of commitment! As great a folly as art for art's sake, or thought for thought's sake; a new alienation: the ludicrous situation of the 'thinker' who wants to commit himself and suddenly realizes that he was *already* committed in the first place!

Today it is much more a question of becoming *decommitted* from a singularly ambiguous, confused and equivocal era – from a many-faceted alienation. We need to gain control. 'Committed' people are up to their eyes in the mire, the nauseating quagmire of the time they live in, and they will never pull themselves free, never reclaim that time, and eventually will even cease understanding it. They are still grappling with the hoary problem of the intellectual who decides to 'leave his ivory tower' ... (ah! how many times have we heard that old tale!). This intellectual 'gets involved' with life, wanders through the world, and discovers that thought is not everything. So, making an extra effort, he flirts with action, going on about 'commitment' amid applause and self-congratulation; but deep within him there is an unresolved contradiction: he wants to remain *available* while *appearing to be committed.* So he cheats, goes into reverse, starts play-acting. One step forward and two steps back!

Most of the 'important intellectuals' of the inter-war years were actors in this hackneyed old drama ...

But there were some who, less arrogantly and without cheating, really did become 'committed', and who nowadays are faced with the opposite problem: to *decommit* themselves, not from action, not from militant thought, but from all the limited and immediate ways the times we live in are perceived; then, taking the lessons of action into account, *to take control of our era by grasping it in its totality* ...

Action and action alone can guide critical thinking, because it detects deception – and because it is deception which deflects us from action. Many people might be tempted to see this guiding role in the investigation of life and human reality as falling to literature, for literature's importance is today much exaggerated. But literature itself needs to be confronted with life, to be thought out and criticized in the name of human reality, and enriched by action. Only the establishment of action's unassailable primacy, though it will certainly contribute much to literature, can assign its real place – which is neither first nor last.

Literature does not deserve to be held in excessively high esteem, but nor does it deserve the fate of being degraded by resentful, disappointed people. The idolatry of literature can only end in disappointment. Whatever its 'function' may be – testimony or aesthetic pleasure, or something else again – it has only one. It is puerile to expect the practice of literature, taken in itself, to throw any decisive light on life and human reality. Literature cannot bring us salvation, because it needs to be saved itself. Immobilized in the clichés of poetic Byzantinism or the *roman noir*, it too needs new men who will state simply and without bias what was hateful or disgusting about our era, what was good, joyful and sturdy, and by what means human beings managed to go on loving life and hoping for the future.

Action and action alone can bring this healthiness and this elementary equilibrium, this ability to grasp life in its varied aspects, without being deliberately gloomy or abstractly optimistic. Action alone can supersede the aesthetic or theoretic attitudes which allow people to see in the real only what they want to see: degradation, humiliation, stupidity, or conversely joy and greatness left, right and centre – either looking at life on the black side or through rose-tinted glasses.

Action as defined by Marxism – the transformation of the world by a political party which strives to guide the great human masses and carry them along in its path – has as its aim a new *type of human being*. This new man thinks, but on the level of the real, on an equal footing with the real. He thus has no need to *come out of* his own thoughts in order to belong to reality and 'commit' himself. Neither anguished like the self-centred intellectual, nor self-satisfied like the bourgeois, he can avoid this old dilemma (anguish or thoughtless self-satisfaction) because what he loves about the real today and about life at the present moment are the *possibilities* they offer, and not simply the *fait accompli* which can be easily grasped and which can only disappoint. Once he sees human beings as moving towards the future, and once he loves this movement, then this new man can leave the old attitudes of sentimental humanism and callous contempt behind; he can be demanding without being inhuman, because he wants man to show his full potential at long last. Thus today only a new man such as this can find the *appropriate level* for talking precisely about things (which does not exclude violence, indignation, or anger, far from it; for there is no longer any question of being impersonal, neutral, abstractly 'objective'; and the old dichotomies of objectivity and passion, impartiality and action, will also have been superseded and resolved ...). He alone will be able to *extricate himself from immediate reality, without, for all that, forgetting the real in general.*

Every ideology is an 'expression' of its time; but in fact the term has no predetermined meaning; in hindsight a critically minded reader will realize that a novel, a play or a book of poetry was an 'expression' of its times – one possible 'expression' among others. There can be all manner of spaces and distances, transpositions and metamorphoses, standing between reality and the ways reality is expressed, so much so that very differing works of art can equally and quite justifiably be regarded as 'expressing' the same moment in time (Balzac and Stendhal, for example). Here again the distance between what is expressed and the means of expression itself must be bridged by a double-edged line of thought: on the one hand, by explaining each work in the light of real life; and on the other by seeking to discover what we can learn about that life as it was, in the literary work which has 'expressed' it.

It is rather odd that our era, an era of contradictions if ever there was one, has been 'expressed' by works which swarm with weak and shapeless characters without conflicts, without fixed contours. For, to judge by the resounding success of such books as Céline's *Journey to the End of the Night* or Sartre's *Roads to Freedom*, they must indeed be significant. Must we conclude that there is a disjunction between literature and real life here, that books like these work solely in terms of conventions, or that there is something deeply erroneous about them? To a certain extent, yes, they are wrong, they do hold back, distort or ignore reality. But there is more to it than that. In an era when unbearable conflicts and contradictions *strive* to make themselves political and to resolve themselves on the political plane, everything in 'ideological life' finds itself in the business of camouflaging them (no coincidences here!); these contradictions are thus concealed, watered down, denied expression; their depth and their meaning are resolutely ignored. The origins of this tendency are to be found in the tactics of the ruling class, of the bourgeoisie, which is propped up by metaphysical systems or existing religions. It is succcessful because its accomplices are legion (it is so much easier and nicer not to feel beset by contradictions!), and it ends up producing spineless, shapeless literature. Simultaneously cause and effect, this literature *expresses* the situation and expresses it well.

Only action brings a clear awareness of how false this situation is. Action alone reinstates the conflicts and the sharp-edged contradictions in all their truth and violence. It gives us back the 'world' in all its truth. Thus action alone will enable literature to become renewed by giving it something it cannot attain unaided: a living awareness of human reality and its movement ...

Old metaphysical reason deliberately excluded *the irrational* from its definitions and its sphere of influence. As a result it ignored individuality, instincts, passion, practical action and imagination: the living being in his entirety. Abstract Reason could thus approach the irrational only by such indirect and rather ineffectual means as the moralizing sermon. It was always possible, of course, to suppress the irrational (by 'repressing' it), and to condemn it from on high in the name of metaphysical truth.

But we know now that this 'irrationality' was the human, the entire living being. We know that, philosophically and humanly speaking, the irrational has rebelled, that because it was considered 'absurd', it has deliberately made its rebellion an absurd one, and that it has raised the flag of the absurd as a challenge to reason. And this is one aspect of the crisis of modern man and modern culture: they are split between abstract reason on the one hand and an absurdity which wants and believes itself to be 'vital' on the other, torn between two opposites which seem locked forever in a painful and apparently unresolvable confrontation.

Dialectical Reason (Marxism) answers the question by approaching it from another angle. For dialectical thought, it is not and never can be a question of some self-sufficient 'irrationality' doomed to eternal rejection by an equally changeless Rationality. The irrational can only be relative, momentary: it is whatever has not been subsumed, organized and categorized by active Reason.

More precisely, we must distinguish between two aspects of the irrational:

(a) The 'irrational' as such, in other words the sum total of the magical creations, ideological interpretations and fictions about the world that human weakness has produced. This irrational is 'nothing' since in truth it is 'other' to man, his alienation. It is 'nothing' in itself, although on the human level it has been appallingly active. In Chapter 1 we demonstrated the important law according to which this irrationality evolves: after a series of transformations and displacements it installs itself under a new form in the life of rational man. And it is in life and through everyday life that this displacement and transformation of the irrational take place.

(b) So far from constituting something irrational beyond the control of reason, the entirety of the human being's needs and instincts – his 'passions', vital activities – are the very basis and the content of Dialectical Reason. These vital activities are already involved in the processes by which they become the needs and the capabilities of a 'being of nature' with the ability to understand and control that nature – i.e. a rational being. In so far as they are part of man's practical activities, they form the first step in his struggle to control nature; they are thus very much a part of a dialectical process, and therefore rational, and even instrumental in the creation of concrete Reason.

And yet this process is a process of becoming, a process yet to be brought to completion. Human needs and activities do not contain 'a certain amount' of ready-made dialectical reason, which would in any case be meaningless. It therefore rests with methodically worked-out rational thought (dialectical thought) to get to know this rich *human raw material* – and to win recognition from it in turn. It must study and organize this material, and thus contribute to the process whereby men's lives produce living reason, and become rational.

Without being irremediably opaque and irreducible to reason, 'human raw material' is a given. It is a mixture of the *irrationality* generated by alienation (which is far from being completely elucidated and categorized) and the *potential rationality* of instincts, needs and activity of all kinds.

This human material is a fact of everyday life. To pursue the analysis of everyday life and distinguish as far as possible between its various elements, critical knowledge and action must work together.

Although according to this definition 'human raw material' offers no opacity, no absolute resistance to knowledge and action – since this is precisely where their content and their base of operations are located – it is nevertheless *ambiguous*. If on the one hand everyday life reveals the forces which work for and against man, on the other hand it has always been possible to erect the *immediate* as a barrier to wider and more far-reaching ways of seeing. It is in the name of the immediate (immediate demands, immediate needs, etc.) that people have opposed and continued to oppose wider visions, wider solutions to their problems. The immediate – the given human raw material of everyday life – at one and the same time reveals and disguises the deepest of realities, both implying them and concealing them. Thus the task facing active, constructive, critical thought becomes clear: to penetrate ever deeper into human raw material, into the immediate which is a fact of everyday life, and to resolve their ambiguities. Here is a major problem which Marxists know well: to find a link between the immediate and the solutions Marxism proposes, so giving the immediate a positive function as practical and historical intermediary between theory and reality. This is an essential problem for action, but it is equally so for humanist philosophy: to link the *idea* of the human to the human *as it is*. The problem is always a new one, its terms of reference are constantly changing; merely to formulate it requires an ever-watchful lucidity and a method that is both rigorous and flexible.

Let us try to look more closely at certain characteristics of given 'human raw material'.

There is an *average general standard*, specific to every region, to every country, to every moment of life and civilization. This standard of living is both a historical and a practical fact. It is based upon the technical characteristics of the economy (the level of material development, the social power of production) but also upon the extent to which the working masses can resist the pressure exerted by their adversaries.

In the theory of wages, this average standard of living helps to determine the 'lowest living wage' acceptable at any given moment, in other words to determine the *value of labour power* as sold on the market; like any other commodity, labour power is bought by capitalists, 'honestly', for what it is worth, in other words according to the socially necessary labour time required to produce and reproduce it. This labour time is determined by a practical and historical factor: the average standard of living, which as we know is higher in certain states of North America than it is in France, and higher in France than it is in Japan ... The average standard of living is explained by historical factors. (If it is higher in certain parts of the United States, a major reason is that from the start economic development has never been hindered by a pre-existing feudal and medieval economy; but this does not mean that it can avoid *colliding with the internal limits of capitalism*.) But in any event, no matter how precise the economic determinants may be (the value of labour power, wages, etc.), they cannot be used simply as some kind of algebraic calculation. They have a basis in practical, everyday life. What is in question, what must be defended and even improved, is the standard of living, at a given moment, in a given situation. And in this sense again, the study of life and of 'human raw material' is the great precept of dialectical method.

At the same time as a material standard of living there is an intellectual or 'cultural' standard of living. In a given civilization and among a given people there are a certain number of ideas which have been eliminated, superseded, rendered obsolete; and a certain number which are accepted as 'self-evident'. Thus, many people still take occultism, spiritualism, vegetarianism, a particular moral code or the Christian religion seriously; but nobody takes the Greek gods seriously any more. Those people who support a religion, or a moral code, or even a philosophy, demand that their belief be shown the respect owed to all 'sincere' opinions. But anyone who believed in Apollo or Venus would be regarded quite simply as a madman. Such a belief would seem to be completely out of touch with life. It is worth remarking, however, that it has never been proven that Apollo or Venus do not exist; it has simply 'become impossible' to believe in them. Why? The question is worth answering, not least because in our culture, in our 'humanities', Apollo and Venus are forever cropping up, much more frequently than Jehovah, or Christ, or astral bodies!

When an artist wishes to make himself understood, or to express certain feelings, he may still write plays about Apollo or Venus, or paint them, or sculpt them; but nobody or virtually nobody ever presents his ideas or his feelings by means of the Christian god, or the ectoplasmic spirits, which so many people believe in, and which moreover are taken so seriously.

What do these facts mean as far as our culture is concerned? That our art is not serious? Or that we do not address the things we take most seriously when we want to express our most serious ideas? In any event, this is one of the symptoms – a very minor one – of a paradoxical situation and a problem which can only be resolved by examining the ideas implied in our present standards of life and civilization more closely.

This standard of civilization is characterized by the extremely disparate and heterogeneous elements which help to compose it. In its structure, capitalist society brings with it all kinds of outdated forms which it raises to a 'modern level', being unable to eliminate them.

Thus in France itself we find every type of economic structure, from a quasi-primitive pastoral economy (in the Pyrenees, for example), and an almost patriarchal agrarian economy (the small peasantry to be found in many regions), up to the most modern techniques of large industry.[3] In the same way, and as a corollary, there are overlapping and intersecting ideas in our culture and our consciousness which correspond factually and historically to different stages of civilization: from agrarian myths and peasant superstitions to recently acquired scientific concepts. Our 'average standard' is made up of this inextricable tangle. Even in its apparent and pretentious 'modernity' (and what in fact does this 'modernity' consist of?) our culture drags in its wake a great, disparate patchwork which has nothing 'modern' about it ...[4]

'Social milieux' are not separated into watertight compartments. Juxtaposed, without rigorous boundaries, the reciprocal influences between them – a 'spiritual' osmosis – is never-ending. This juxtaposition of socio-economic forms and human types from different ages and different stages in the embryology of the total man produces a curious situation. Seen from this perspective our era looks like a freak with a hypertrophic human brain, the body of an invertebrate and the cells of a protozoan. Or again one might compare it to a folly built to the specifications of some insanely eclectic architect in which Doric columns support Gothic vaulting or reinforced concrete slabs (effects like this are not unusual in the buildings which have sprung forth from the impoverished imagination of the bourgeoisie; and such eclectic imbecility is even less unusual in the ideological constructions of our era!).

Of course, the complex economic, social, legal and political relations which this situation produces are not of direct interest in the critique of everyday life. What it must concern itself with are the overall consequences for life and for the consciousness of life. Given the confusion of facts, actions and the practical conditions of consciousness, how could consciousness itself be anything but extremely confused? (And among the consequences of this confusion we must include the fact that although many individuals receive their ideas and their feelings via the influence of a social formation other than the one they immediately belong to, they nevertheless go on believing in the independence of ideas, feelings and consciousness!) This confusion reflects a fundamental disorder. There is nothing to arrange or organize the elements of life, culture and consciousness, composed as they are of a mixture of styles, types of life, and enthusiasms of very differing origins and meaning. There are certain sophisticated intellectuals who have all the verbal techniques, the entire bag of tricks of bourgeois thought at their fingertips, of whom it can be said: 'They are peasants' (Claudel, for example), or else: 'They are craftsmen' (Péguy). The one ferries the other: the verbal techniques of the era of advanced literary styles are merely a vehicle for agrarian myths or the craft ethic; and vice versa.

There can never be any question of denying anything that exists the right to exist. It is the movement within whatever exists which trans- forms the world, past, present or future, and not theories about what should be rejected and what should be preserved. The essential thing here is to denounce confusion with all its baggage of bad faith, guilty conscience, ideological duplicity, trickery and trumpery. Now this confusion is *lived* – in other words it intervenes in life and in the consciousness of life. It explains how that ideological representative of the most backward peasants and their myths, Monsieur Jean Giono, has managed to be so popular, even with the younger generation in industrial towns, even with mechanics. But it has paved the way for many more paradoxes and sophistries ... Here is a simple example: one can consider that in the West, and in advanced countries, a certain knowledge of the world and even of biological reality has become part of the average consciousness, of 'normal' culture (to use the very equivocal and confused term employed by sociologists ...). Various rather vague notions about health, sport, heredity, have been 'vulgar- ized', as they say, and in this way an 'average' stock of knowledge has been formed (although it is unequally distributed between the various groups and classes). In this way more-or-less scientific notions about heredity have merged in the 'average' consciousness with old models of peasant origin, and old group and class prejudices. This 'vulgarization' of science at its most modern has paved the way, in certain countries at least, for the propagation of a scientifically false theory – racism – which has all-too-easily permeated the masses.

If it is indeed true that the beginning and the end of all knowledge is practical activity, then one may well ask oneself how it can be that during our era of high technology and advanced scientific knowledge the practical lives of human beings can still be so blind and so indecisive. How does such an obvious contrast between a science proud of its triumphs and the humiliation and uncertainty of human lives come about? If all power originates in action, where do life's weaknesses and uncertainties – and its triviality – come from? How can practical, everyday life form the basis of human thought, power and splendour, when it is apparently so impoverished, so lowly, so blind, that we still feel the need to dress it up in illusions, decorations, lavish costumes, or at the very least in weird and bizarre disguises, before we can accept it?

The analysis of the organic and ideological confusion of our era offers an initial answer to these questions. And admittedly this diversity contributes to the richness of our consciousness and our culture. Still we must grasp it, define it, categorize its elements, for what we have inherited from past and superseded eras is precisely a shapeless and *irrational* mass of notions and feelings, a 'rich' but hitherto inextricable muddle.

Only a vast inventory of the elements of our culture – in other words of our consciousness of life – will enable us to see clearly.

This endeavour cannot be undertaken – it cannot even be conceived – with any method other than the Marxist dialectic. It can have meaning only in and through dialectical materialism. The philosophers, theologians, sociologists and literary hacks all *accept* the ideas and feelings that are passed on to them, and on that level. Their criticisms are abstract and timeless. They are unable to situate the elements of our consciousness in historical time, by linking them to successive social formations, to fashions and ways of life. They can describe, but they cannot understand, much less judge and criticize effectively. Only Marxist *social* criticism is capable of uncovering the genesis of 'representations' and feelings; it reveals their conditions, their practical functions, the way they work, and analyses the relative proportions of appearance and reality – the amount of 'play-acting' and the amount of 'human' – that they have contained in the past and that they contain today. It can make links between each 'representation', each symbol, each myth, each concept, and a specific human era.

It can trace the interactions of the social 'milieux' and in this way understand our composite and heterogeneous consciousness of life.

'Consciousness of life' – can those words be right? Are we conscious of our own lives? The words which spring to our lips, the ideas and images at our disposal, are they of a kind to allow us a *true* conscious-ness of our lives? ... No! Our lives are still unrealized, and our consciousness is false. It is not only our consciousness which is false: it is only false because our lives are still alienated. False representations bring with them a false consciousness of what an unrealized life is; in other words they do not bring an awareness of the non-realization (of the degree of non-realization) of human life: they present it as either realized (which leads to vulgar or moral satisfaction) or unrealizable (which leads to anguish or the desire for a different life).

More precisely, nowadays, *we do not know how we live.* And at the end of our lives, we scarcely know how we have lived them. And how bitter this unhappy consciousness is ...

While we are trying to live, at the moment we are living, religion, morality, literature and familiar words impose upon us an official image of ourselves. The individual's 'private' consciousness is comple-mented by a 'public' consciousness; they interact and support one another. The 'private' consciousness refers across to the 'public' consciousness and vice versa; the one is meaningless without the other.[5] The one is as real – and as unreal – as the other. For the 'private' individual, the public consciousness contains the most basic social elements that individualism can adapt to; and at the same time it is laden with deceptive words, mystifying ideas and images. In the 'public' consciousness the 'private' consciousness finds justifications, ready-made explanations, compensations. Individual life oscillates between the one and the other. The famous dialogue between the 'I' and Ego is simply that between the private and the public in the same individual. And in this divided, riven, torn consciousness the questions posed by one fragment are answered by the other. Together, the fragments take on the appearance of a self-sufficient whole. When the private man is secretly worried, his public consciousness assures him that there is no need to be, that everything is fine, that really he is happy – or, conversely, that owing to totally external circumstances, nothing can be done, that he will be unhappy throughout eternity. It eliminates the very need to ask questions. The private man never really asks himself 'how he lives', for he thinks he knows it in advance: he thinks that he owns life like just one more possession; he believes that happiness can be held in the hand, the pounds, shillings and pence of that great capital asset, life.

The critique of everyday life will propose the undertaking of a vast survey, to be called: *How we live.*

(a) We could begin this survey by attempting to reconstruct the real life of a number of individuals (comparing their real lives with their consciousness of them, their interpretations of them), using a variety of research techniques.

How were these 'private' individuals formed? Under what influences? How did they choose their path in life, their profession? How did they get married? How and why did they have children? How and why did they act in such and such a situation in their lives? ...

A survey of this kind would be fairly difficult to carry out (although some newspapers and reviews have already collected and published confidential information of the most intimate kind, if only for publicity purposes), but it would shed much unexpected light upon individual lives in our age. It would be fascinating to compare the results with religious, moral, political and philosophical ideas which are still in circulation – and especially with the individualism which is even more widespread in behaviour than it is in theory.

Methodically carried out, this survey would at long last supplant the ramblings of philosophers or novelists (including those who get emotional about 'beings' and harshly lucid about 'existence') with solidly established 'human truths'. In all likelihood it would help to shift our centres of interest, revealing the part played by alienation, fictions, chance and fate in the real life and death of men.

The documentation we have collected so far (some of which will be published in the *Critique of Everyday Life*) demonstrates the existence in today's social life of some largely unknown sectors – and all the more so inasmuch as the dominant ideologies suggest 'ideas' which appear to explain and schematize them.[6]

(b) This survey should not be limited to a certain number of individual lives taken in their totality, but should examine the details of everyday life as minutely as possible – for example, a day in the life of an individual, any day, no matter how trivial.

A trivial day in our lives – what do we make of it? It is likely that the survey would reveal that taken socially (examined in the light of the hidden social side of individual triviality) this trivial day would have nothing trivial about it at all. During a day at work or a holiday, we each enter into relations with a certain number of social 'things' whose nature we do not understand, but which we support by our active participation; without realizing it we are caught up in a certain number of social mechanisms.

One question we can ask ourselves, for example, is how the average man in his ordinary, day-to-day life, relates to the large corporations. Where does he encounter them? How does he perceive them and imagine them? Theory reveals a complex structure here – in what ways does he move within it? And how does this structure appear to him from morning till night?

(c) Taken more broadly and more generally, this survey of everyday life would become a survey of French life and specifically French forms of life – as compared with the specific forms of other nations.

How have the different 'milieux' of the French nation organized their everyday life?

How do these different social groups use their money, how do they organize their budget?[7] How do they spend their time, what are their leisure activities? In what forms do they act out their sociability, their solitude, their family life, their love life, their culture?

Going on the as-yet incomplete documentation we have collected, it would appear that genuine revelations may be expected.

The survey would reveal how the Frenchman has long been one of the most *exploited* members of the capitalist universe, and how the bourgeoisie which has exploited him has been one of the shrewdest – alternating between deceit and brutality, and always very 'modern', very much in touch with all the tactics of the class struggle (particularly and precisely when it indiscriminately uses either the nation or the individual to deny that the struggle exists . . .).

Using precise cases and examples, the survey would demonstrate how this deceitful pressure results in the debasement both of the social structure (agriculture or industry) and of individual, everyday life.

It would thus contribute towards dispelling certain harmful myths (for example, the economic myth of France's 'natural' wealth – the cultural and spiritual myths of the inherent lucidity and spontaneous moderation of French thought . . .) by demonstrating concretely *what is true* and *what is false* about them . . .

It would also contribute towards the critique of a number of illusions which are particularly disastrous for France. Is it not surprising and fascinating that at the harshest, most oppressive moment of high capitalism so many of the French should have believed and should go on believing that they are free, and that in the name of their freedom a certain (and apparently large) number of them are still rushing headlong into slavery? What can be the meaning of the stubborn and persistent success of this mystification? What can examining the lives of 'private' individuals teach us about it, and what can it teach us about the real lives of these individuals?

In the name of freedom and individuality, we are told, the French have been 'abandoned' (just think of the situation of French youth!). This extraordinary observation was made by Drieu la Rochelle, and the conclusions he attempted to draw from it, were equally extra-ordinary; we know what became of him.[8] The fact is that the 'private' individual suffers from the kind of 'spiritual' abandonment which makes it easy for the whole gamut of phony 'spiritual' powers to tout their false solutions and vow to rid consciousness and life of their sickness ...

It will probably never be possible to complete this picture of French life. But it would take but a few polls to counter the gloomy aspects of the situation, and to reveal the healthy, restorative side of our national life, its real possibilities and genuinely creative elements.

On a completely different level, the study of everyday life would dispel several literary and philosophical myths whose spuriousness is one decadent tendency among many. For example, the myth of *human solitude*. There is ample evidence to show that for the vast majority of human beings, immersed as they are in natural life or undifferentiated social life, being alone is a need, and something to be achieved. For the peasant, merged with the life of natural things, of animals, of the earth, of the village, as for the worker who lives with his family in cramped accommodation and who is even more unfamiliar with freedom to move around than he is with freedom to use his own time, there is no solitude in the 'deep' and 'metaphysical' meaning of the word. Peasants and the workers can be alone: by accident or by chance, through illness, through inability to express themselves, etc., but they are not truly solitary. On the contrary, a worker who lives with his wife and children in one or two rooms feels the need to reflect, to be alone with himself for a while in order to think or to read. He rarely experiences the joys of solitude. For him the need to be alone is already progress, something gained. It is the most 'private' individuals –

intellectuals, individualists, separated by abstraction and bourgeois scholasticism from any relationship or social life – who have invented solitude. Instead of seeing it as the time and the chance to develop a deeper awareness of human relations, they have transformed it – following the usual metaphysical pattern – into an absolute. And then they have used their poetry, their novels or their philosophy to moan and to wallow in self-pity. At the limits of the 'private' consciousness and in the human nothingness of their 'existence', they have rebelled – in vain – against the metaphysical alienation which their own attitude towards life helps to maintain ... For them, the fiction of solitude becomes reality. For them 'alone'!

(d) The critique of everyday life has a contribution to make to *the art of living*.

This art, as new, as unknown as happiness itself, has been pre-figured – in the context of an individualism and dilettantism which was limited even then and has been moribund every since – by several writers, including Stendhal.

It is a domain in which everything remains to be said. In the future the art of living will become a genuine art, based like all art upon the vital need to expand, and also on a certain number of techniques and areas of knowledge, but which will go beyond its own conditions in an attempt to see itself not just as a means but as an end. The art of living presupposes that the human being sees his own life – the development and intensification of his life – not as a means towards 'another' end, but as an end in itself. It presupposes that life as a whole – everyday life – should become a work of art and 'the joy that man gives to himself'.[9]

As with every genuine art, this will not be reducible to a few cheap formulas, a few gadgets to help us organize our time, our comfort, or our pleasure more efficiently. Recipes and techniques for increasing happiness and pleasure are part of the baggage of bourgeois wisdom – a shallow wisdom which will never bring satisfaction. The genuine art of living implies a human reality, both individual and social, incomparably broader than this.

The art of living implies the end of alienation – and will contribute towards it.

From one point of view life strikes us like some immense anthill, swarming with obscure, blind, anonymous beings and actions – and from another we see it shining with the splendour and glamour which certain individuals and certain actions confer on it. We must not avoid the fact that the latter view is produced by the former, and 'expresses' it – that the contrast between the two is only momentary – and that up until now everyday life has been 'alienated' in such a way that its own reality has been torn from it, placed outside it and even turned against it.

In any event, this contrast cannot go on permanently deceiving us, its drama (with the condemnation of life as its theme) cannot be an absolute one. It is merely a passing contradiction, a problem ...

This problem, which is none other than the problem of man, can only be posed and then resolved by dialectical method. Should we admit for one moment that it is otherwise, and that the plebeian substance of day-to-day living and the higher moments of life are forever separated, and that the two cannot be grasped as a unity and made to become a part of life – then it will be the human that we are condemning.

5

Notes Written One Sunday in the French

Countryside

Some fairly precise documents exist which allow us to travel back in our minds to the origins of our civilization – not to prehistory nor to the so-called 'primitive' era, but to a more recent age, the dawn of Greek civilization, for example, or Roman, or medieval.

We can imagine villages and rural landscapes which scarcely differ from those we can see in modern Greece, Southern Italy or even in certain parts of the South of France. Let us conjure up this country life which in more ways than one has continued into the present day ...

In Greece countryfolk had their festivals and religious ceremonies; the dates for these festivals were fixed by the country calendar. It seems that the religious season par excellence was winter, which in our rural areas is still the time for late-night gatherings. In the Classical period which followed the Archaic period, some of the most important festivals in Greece were still celebrated at the beginning of winter, or at the end: the Pyanespis, in autumn; the Anthesteria, when spring came; the Thalysis, a festival for the local goddess in which all the inhabitants of the village participated, lying on swaths of reeds and vine leaves and eating the θαγὺσιος, bread made from the new corn.

These country festivals consisted essentially of a large meal; the peasants feasted, lying on the ιστιϐάδες or swaths, and in specific places: near woods, mountains, springs, rivers.

Everyone brought a contribution to the communal meal. Each village constituted a community: a large family of people linked by blood, a way of life, and also by a practical discipline and a fairly strict collective organization of work (dates when tasks were performed, etc.). About the system of property we know nothing very precise or very certain, but we can be sure that at the beginning it had not yet disassociated the peasant community.

The neighbouring villages in each canton came to the main festivals – as they do to this day in the fairs and 'votive festivals' still celebrated in French rural areas.

During the feasts there was much merry-making: dancing, masquerades in which boys and girls changed clothes or dressed up in animal skins or masks – simultaneous marriages for an entire new generation – races and other sports, beauty contests, mock tournaments; exchanging comical taunts and insults, neighbouring and rival communities, men and women, associated but competing guilds, would try to outdo each other. The festivities would end in scuffles and orgies.

Peasant celebrations tightened social links and at the same time gave rein to all the desires which had been pent up by collective discipline and the necessities of everyday work. In celebrating, each member of the community went beyond himself, so to speak, and in one fell swoop drew all that was energetic, pleasurable and possible from nature, food, social life and his own body and mind.

Festival differed from everyday life only in the explosion of forces which had been slowly accumulated in and via everyday life itself.

We must imagine rough peasants, full of joviality and vitality, and fairly poor. For these celebrations they make great 'sacrifices', in the practical sense of the word; in one day they devour all the provisions and stocks it has taken them months to accumulate. Generously, they welcome guests and strangers. It is the day of excess. Anything goes. This exuberance, this enormous orgy of eating and drinking – with no limits, no rules – is not without a deep sense of foreboding. Should a disaster happen, too harsh a winter or too dry a summer, a storm or an epidemic, then the community will regret this feast day when it devoured its own substance and denied its own conditions. How can the need for exaltation on both an individual and collective level, the need for a few hours of complete, intense living, be reconciled with foreboding and fear? Men know how weak they still are when confronted with nature! How can this contradiction be borne? Festival is a risk, a wager on the future. What is there to be won, and what to lose?

In those days when human beings lived so to speak on the level of nature and natural life, in its elemental violence, its uncomplicated freshness and also its ignorance, they imagined nature via their own preoccupations, fears and desires; conversely and simultaneously they still defined and understood their basic humanity through the phenomena of nature, animals and plants, the heavens or the bowels of the earth.

Already witches and magicians existed, with spells, rituals and gestures which were intended precisely to console weak humanity with the illusion of having direct power over nature – nature so familiar and yet so terrifying.

Rural communities associated nature specifically with human joyfulness. Nature was peopled with 'mysterious' powers, powers that were human and close, yet at the same time fantastic, distant and dangerous, distinct but at the same time merged in a recondite unity.[1] If festivals were successfully held, it was felt to be because nature and its powers had been good, favourable, regular, bringing rain and sunshine, heat and cold, the seasons and their allotted tasks, according to their expected, favourable cycle (birds, coming and going with the seasons, appeared as magic and prophetic signs of this order). Thus when the community gathered to carry out this simple action of eating and drinking, the event was attended by a sense of magnificence which intensified the feeling of joy. By celebrating, the community was welcoming Nature and was rejoicing in its gifts; more than this, it was associating Nature with the human community, binding the two together. The regular place given in the country calendar to festivals and specific tasks represented the regularity of human actions – their punctual accomplishment – and appeared to guarantee and assure the regularity of the seasons. Very soon, if not from the start, peasant festivals became eminently important; they represented not only joy, communion, participation in Dionysiac life, but also a cooperation with the natural order. Simultaneous marriages 'represented' the fertility of nature while at the same time ensuring it and fixing it firmly, as if to shape and tie down the future in advance (in this way certain polyvalent rituals had a magical aspect, a symbolic aspect and an aspect of play; in the primitive stages the latter was subordinated, but later it came to the fore, displacing the irrational aspects of the action; the seesaw, for example, was at one and the same time a game bringing the sexes together, a fertility ritual and a symbolic action ...).

So the 'sacrifices' which everyone had to make for the festival – gifts, contributions from each family and each household – appeared as a down-payment for the future. To refuse to participate would have been to set oneself apart from the community – and to risk interrupting the normal, fertile course of nature and human life. It would have been to invite bad luck, starting with the magic curses of the people who collected the contributions. To this day in the French countryside, during certain festivals children or young people or poor people still exercise the last remaining privileges of the old peasant communities by going from house to house collecting (money, eggs, flour, sugar ...) for the feast; anyone who refuses is cursed ritually according to traditional formulas: drought for their land, sickness for their flocks ...

The Greek word: συμβάλλεσθαι, which gives us that word so characteristic of our religions and ideologies, 'symbol', means initially 'to pay one's share', hence: to participate in the magic action, in the effectiveness of the ritual.

It would be perfectly clear to the members of the rural community that the larger the gift, the more effective it would be; festivals were a way of assuring the future, and the more active the participation in them, the larger the amount of blessings in return, the greater the prestige, the influence, the power. Thus through their gifts to the community, the wealthy (once private property had become differentiated) could make their wealth accepted, and were able to consolidate it. The very fact that they gained social prestige enabled them to become even wealthier. Landowners became both powerful and blessed – and hated. They controlled the good fortune and the power of the community. At this point the object of study for the sociologist seems to shift: we move from the level of magic to the level of the 'social mystery' (i.e. religion); from man's relationship to nature to the formation of differentiated, divided human society, where all community is fictitious ...

So originally the human order and the natural order seemed interwoven, joined by a 'mysterious' link (but which for those simple peasants seemed the most immediate, the most natural thing in their world). If the peasant tradition was strict to the point of routine, it was only because all change threatens 'order'. Also, human activity tends to become codified practice, so that festivals, and even the gestures and speech of everyday life, became ritualized. Perhaps this sums up how magic developed, or even how it was born, and how solemn and sacred gestures became generalized, taking their elements from day-to-day life, but transposing them to the level of an imaginary effectiveness. In such conditions the festive meal became a sacred meal in a holy place, a cosmic and efficacious action. The union of the sexes also became a magical act which challenged nature in its entirety, which could be blessed or blighted, prefiguring problems or happiness to come. And the gift, the offering, the contribution to the celebration, became a 'sacrifice' in the mystic sense of the word: an insurance for the future, an exchange of favours with obscure forces, future benefits secured by means of present hardship.

The association of Nature with man means first and foremost the Earth. In the magic and the religions which have been part of the becoming of Western civilization, the Earth is represented humanly and sexually: Mother Earth, wounded and harrowed by the plough, and fertilized – like a woman – by man. Moreover, at once frightening and fruitful, the Earth receives the dead and grows fat with their corpses.

It would appear that the ancient peasant communities were fairly quick to achieve a relatively stable balance, which, as rural history (a recent science which is still in the process of formation) has demonstrated, had strict conditions and surprisingly subtle elements: a balance between pastures, forests and arable land; a balance between the animal and human populations; a balance in the organization of tasks between 'individual' activities and collective disciplines; a balance between the sharing-out of land and the structure of property. In our own history, in our Middle Ages, the sociological historian finds the same process once again, the same balance, which is shattered (as it seems to have been in Antiquity) by the formation of a rural aristocracy followed by a rural bourgeoisie. This natural and human balance, achieved and preserved by a peasant wisdom, by a set of techniques and a spontaneous skill which astounds the historian, appeared to be the supreme good, divine, marvellous, fragile. It was precisely in order to maintain this balance that the peasant community clung firmly to its own traditions and reinforced the role of magic and ritual.

To preserve this 'order', the peasant order – for every class, every social formation has its order and its idea of order – man cooperated with nature; he maintained and regulated its energies, both by his real work and by the (fictitious) effectiveness of his magic. But from the very moment they became prosperous, communities were faced with a serious danger. They needed children to renew the community generation by generation, children who would be initiated into its tasks and its secrets, receiving and passing on the communal heritage. Too many or too few births would endanger the balance: too many mouths to feed, or not enough arms to plough the land, and famine would engulf the community. By virtue of illusion which ethnographers discover in many places, the deep cause of which – in other words the *practical* cause – seems as far as our present knowledge can tell to be very simple and everywhere the same, and number of 'souls' was part of the 'order' as conceived by these peasants. Births and deaths were governed by the cosmic law, and remained regular so long as that law remained undisturbed. The number of human beings was determined by nature. Thus every birth was a reincarnation: a soul was taken from the group's available stock, and came back to life. 'Souls' were immortal, even if their existence beyond the living group remained shadowy and vague. (This notion of the soul 'overdetermines' even more ancient representations including perhaps that of the double, of that 'other' which is still a human being).

And it is the Earth 'who bears and fosters all living things and receives from men libation to quicken her seed anew'[2] who supplies the souls. Following one of their most ancient traditions, the Athenians of the Classical Era still scattered seeds on newly-closed tombs – just as we bring flowers. In the Earth, their temporary home – mother and tomb – the dead continued to participate in the order of things, in the regularity of the seasons and of human activities. Strange phantoms, they went on moving and living as they made their preparations to be born again. They were still part of the order; and they could disturb it. By dint of honours, of funereal rites – which guaranteed order and were a part of order – by dint of libations and sacrifices, the community sought the favour of its dead. And in these offerings, the fruits of the earth – wine, foliage, flowers, or wheatcakes – played an essential role.

The rural community was therefore also community with the dead, and festivals for the dead found a place amidst the festivals for the living. In man's state of weakness in the face of nature, disquiet appeared alongside joy, ever more defined, ever stronger, until it became anxiety, and anxiety too had its funeral festivals and its celebrations. And the wealthy, land-owning families, which were such a burden on the community, always tried to justify themselves by appealing to the past – to real or fictitious ancestors, heroes, dragon-killers, founders or pseudo-founders of cities, inventors of new techniques. Funeral festivals became the privileged festivals of dead kings and heroes. Dionysiac joy gave way to terror. Human life was torn apart as it embarked upon its harsh and inevitable journey into alienation.

Certainly, right from the start, festivals contrasted violently with everyday life, *but they were not separate from it.* They were like everyday life, but more intense; and the moments of that life – the practical community, food, the relation with nature – in other words, work – were reunited, amplified, magnified in the festival. Man, still immersed in an immediate natural life, lived, mimed, sang, danced his relation with nature and the cosmic order as his elementary and confused thoughts 'represented' it. On the same level as nature, man was also on the same level as himself, his thoughts, the forms of beauty, wisdom, madness, frenzy and tranquillity which were available to him. In his reality, he lived and achieved all his potential. Feeling no deep conflict with himself, he could give himself up – in that magnificent state of balance which was the peasant community – to his own spontaneous vitality. No aspect of himself, of his energy, his instinct, was left unused. Perhaps he was basic and elementary, but at least he lived without being fundamentally 'repressed'; and maybe he sometimes died appeased.

The 'pure' nature that some writers applaud is in fact this peasant life at a highly evolved stage, and in point of fact at only very rare moments and places in history has it achieved a successful, happy, balanced form. In most cases, the continuation of a nomadic, bellicose way of life, or poor soil, or a bad climate, or, furthermore, and especially, social crises and the rapid formation of brutally dominant castes, have dragged social life down dead ends, nearly always precipitating its decline.

The balance of the community was threatened on two fronts:

– in nature, by all manner of catastrophes, and even more by the fear produced when acts were no longer ritualized and performed in order to maintain and celebrate life, but merely for the sake of their sacred form and for the sake of the magical power that that form was supposed to exert;

– in social life, through ever more differentiation and inequality.

The simultaneous emergence of families isolated from the community, of 'private' property outside of the collective systems, and of the power which certain families and certain individuals wielded over the community, destroyed that community from within. The crisis of the community, its dislocation, the distress of most of its members, went hand in hand with technical progress and social differentiation. It is hard for us to imagine the astonishment with which the members of old communities must have greeted these social changes which were happening around them and which they were unable to comprehend. Let us not forget that by the gifts and 'sacrifices' they made in proportion to their wealth and influence, the chiefs became increasingly powerful while at the same time still appearing to be the embodiment of the community's own power. Those who were breaking up the community seemed to be strengthening its 'deep' reality; they were enslaving the community while appearing to be its servants – and in a sense they were serving it, in that they defended it, that they stood for technical progress, and that they alone had access to ideas, thought, wisdom, prudence, a sense of responsibility, of potentially rational foresight. The social process was now masked by its own conditions. How was it possible not to attribute it to 'mysterious' causes, external to everyday life: to original sins, supernatural punishments, an incomprehensible 'destiny'? The developing social mystery – the reality which escaped men's consciousness, although they were its authors and actors – was destined to become a religious mystery; and religion now superimposed itself upon magic, but without destroying it. Chiefs and kings contrived to receive the blessing of the communities they oppressed (i.e. the blessing of its gods); in a curious but perennial mixture of illusion and reality, they maintained both the cosmic order, by virtue of their magical functions, and the human order, by virtue of their political functions.

(But in these quiet little towns and villages which sit at the junctions of ancient tracks that have criss-crossed the French countryside for thousands of years, how does one become a public figure, someone respected, such as a town or regional councillor, or a member of parliament, nowadays? If there are no urban centres nearby and if the workers' parties have no influence, then even today it is only via the

Church, charitable organizations, the commune, sports societies or the fire department that a parvenu manages to become accepted and to consolidate his support and his influence. And this is achieved without any 'politics' – i.e. by the oldest of all political processes, which is just as unconscious now as it has been for centuries. It is taken for granted that unless there is some extraordinary accident such as a natural upheaval (a war or a crisis), the prosperity of public figures and the prosperity of the community go hand in hand; the one produces the other; everyone in the village or the canton benefits: through gifts, charitable donations, and because the important peasant or tradesman 'makes work' for the poor. These men are blessed – by the gods and by their fellow man. They have their own pew in church. People bless them in public but hate them in private. They are the object of a thousand repressed and 'private' grievances ...)

Therefore, in ancient rural communities, according to all the available documents, a certain human fulfilment was to be found – albeit mingled with disquiet and the seeds of all the agonies to come. That fulfilment has since disappeared. It has been lost in two senses. First, rituals and symbols and their interpretation as elaborated by the religious imagination have tended to dispossess human actions of their living substance in favour of 'meanings'. Secondly, social life has improved, but has changed its structure in the process; from being on a horizontal level, so to speak, on the level of natural life and the 'world', it has become pyramidal, with chiefs, kings, a State, ideas, abstractions, at its apex. Symbols have become more and more abstract; in its own way, like money, but on the political level, the State is also in a sense a *realized abstraction*, endowed with effective power which is ever more real. At first rituals conjured up the confused 'powers' of nature, the 'hidden side' of things and human beings, then mythical heroes, then increasingly elaborate gods; later, however, they came to centre on a 'spiritual' power, i.e. a realized abstraction, the God of the universal religions. At the same time, the theories justifying the power of political chiefs and kings have become more and more abstract. And at the same time too, century after century, genuine knowledge and thought, implying logical abstraction (science), have appeared to be progressing and advancing in line with ideologies – whereas these are two different and possibly incompatible levels of human consciousness.

The result for our rural areas has been a deprivation of everyday life on a vast scale, by religion, by abstraction, by the life of the 'mind', by distant and 'mysterious' political life ... Bit by bit everything which formerly contributed to the elementary splendour of everyday life, its innocent, native grandeur, has been stripped from it and made to appear as something beyond its own self. Progress has been *real, and in certain aspects immense*, but it has been dearly paid.

And yet it is still there, this innocent life, so very near, but impoverished and humiliated, both strong and pathetic, creative but threatened, producing the future but beset with foreboding about all the imponderables that future has in store.

It is still there, not unchanged, but degraded rather, humiliated, while in other respects, and proportionally, science and consciousness have progressed. Take for example an ordinary village in France ... The network of roads and paths, fences and hedgerows, encloses a land which is by no means unworkable, a docile, easy land which rises and falls almost imperceptibly as if with the breath of the distant mountains. Scattered farms and then, around the church and the graveyard, a few houses grouped together, the village. A green land; meadows, their brooks full with autumn rain.

The village still huddles closely around its dead. The living still bring their floral tributes to the dear departed; many people believe that it is the right thing to do to put cheap and nasty metal-and-glass mementoes on the graves; ritual has become hideously commercialized; the graceful tributes of fruits of the earth which sustained the life of the dead, linking them with the living and preparing for their return to life, have been replaced by a 'sacrifice' of money which is made once and for all – a way of settling one's conscience concerning the dead person, of making him permanently harmless. It is true that some people may think that what they inherit from the dead is somehow a settling of accounts, but they too can have pangs of conscience. Some visit the graves of the dead. ('I'm just off to say hello to my poor departed husband', said Mme X as she made her way jauntily to the graveyard where her spouse lay 'at rest'.) These are people who apparently believe that the dear departed are simultaneously and at one and the same time in heaven (or hell) and here, under these stones and this ground, under these artificial flowers. In this consecrated fold, they experience the feeling of a 'living' presence – instead of the terrifying reality, the horror of death. Their cold breast is flooded with a cruel, sweet emotion. Many of them believe in ghosts, in phantoms, in 'spirits'; yet instead of preparing the return of their dead to the light of day and the community with love, terror and respect, they simply relegate them to oblivion. Fresh corpses get visited; the others, the old ones, lie forgotten as in a communal grave. The myth of the community and its dead goes on, but demoted, weakened, deprived of warmth, linked to vague, abstract affirmations about 'souls' which can never be translated into tangible acts ...

The winter solstice is still an important date; but the great solar myth of the god who is reborn to fill the Earth with new and burning life has become just a sentimental, vaguely charming series of images – a little family portrait. What remains of ritual and myth? A date, a vague impression of birth, of hope, of grandiose drama – the idea of an all-powerful god who is nevertheless mysteriously destined to be born and to die; and then theological abstractions, sublimations relegated inaccessibly to the background; and then those childish but touching pictures – the animals, the manger, the Wise Men and their star, inseparably linked to the cosmic, human infant ...

Every time spring arrives, processions intended to confirm the regularity of the season and the fertility of the fields go round the village, winding drearily along through the paths between the fields. Drearily, plunged in an immense boredom which is like an ultimate sacrifice: people 'give up' the time, put up with the inconvenience. All the Dionysiac joy has gone out of this ritual, which is known arrogantly as 'Rogation Days'. It is a request for fine weather and a rich harvest. Actually, nobody believes that prayers can be really effective, but many still believe that not to attend or to stop the ritual completely would be bad luck. Prudently they take precautions. The negative side of the traditional ritual has completely annihilated the positive one, which was joy in human community.

In this same village, in the same springtime, pious hands still hang garlands on sacred trees and, occasionally, on the roadside crosses which have long dispossessed old Hecate of her domain ...

And when war comes, and drought, the peasants bemoan their fate, saying: 'Everything's gone haywire.' They see cosmic order and human order as inextricably linked, as in the original agrarian myth ... And they do not easily understand the specifically human means by which order (a coherent, rational order) can be re-established ...[3]

The mystical notion of 'sacrifice' lives on more or less everywhere; if anyone tried to forget it, there would be wars and social dramas to revitalize it. But age has not favoured it; and now sacrifices are only vaguely felt to be 'sacred'. Parents make 'sacrifices' to bring up their children; people also 'sacrifice' part of the present for the future, by saving from their earnings and 'investing' them, or by taking out 'insurance'. Meanwhile they continue preparing for the future by negotiating with the supernatural – donations, charity, offerings of personal suffering, of merits achieved in the eyes of men and gods – for a repayment proportional to the hardship involved . . .[4]

There is one special little item which every well-off and god-fearing family budgets for: charity. By private gifts and public donations the god-fearing can relieve their consciences of any residual qualms they might feel, and can also justify themselves to other people. They are contributing to the permanence of their order, while at the same time reducing poor people's resentment – and making their lot a little easier. 'Sacrifice' has several meanings and several aims, some conscious, others unconscious, some selfish, others altruistic (and collectors and apologists for charity will quote one or other of these aims as circumstances demand . . .).

It is well known that wars are a punishment for people's sinfulness, indolence and cruelty. And so is defeat. (This Christian mystique – originally a peasant mythology – was made official under the Vichy regime.) The poor should make sacrifices by working a lot, and the rich by giving a little. What are sacrifices? 'Spiritual' investments! Their worth is a function of the effort they cost, i.e. the amount of hardship people are prepared to put up with in their fear of the future. Unfortunately statistics concerning the amounts charities receive are never made public. What material they would provide for the study of everyday life across the classes and social groups! It is very possible that both in cash and in kind, the poor give more than the rich. Their uncertainties, their fears for the future – and their generosity too – are they not greater? Moreover, anyone who has nothing to give, or is unwilling to give, can always placate the mysterious powers by offering up their wishes, their sufferings, their hearts and their minds . . .

The uncertainties peasants feel about nature become superimposed – as religion was superimposed upon magic – by the disquiet of several other social groups about human, economic and political circumstances. Ignorance of the laws of sociology, the inability to act without dependence on political lies and strategies, along with a sort of direct contamination from myths and rituals, fosters and perpetuates the idea of fate and predestination; masses of individuals (each believing himself to be free and lucid), entire groups react to human circumstances in the same way that countryfolk responded to the circumstances of nature; they accept wars and crises as inevitable, pleading with their gods to bring these calamities to an end, thanking or cursing the heavenly powers that be.

And in life itself, in everyday life, ancient gestures, rituals as old as time itself, continue unchanged – except for the fact that this life has been stripped of its beauty. Only the dust of words remains, dead gestures. Because rituals and feelings, prayers and magic spells, blessings, curses, have been detached from life, they have become abstract and 'inner', to use the terminology of self-justification. Convictions have become weaker, sacrifices shallower, less intense. People cope – badly – with a smaller outlay. Pleasures have become weaker and weaker. The only thing that has not diminished is the old disquiet, that feeling of weakness, that foreboding. But what was formerly a sense of disquiet has become worry, anguish. Religion, ethics, metaphysics – these are merely the 'spiritual' and 'inner' festivals of human anguish, ways of channelling the black waters of anxiety – and towards what abyss?

And if beauty has disappeared from everyday life, what of its great *mystical* heroes? No, the mystic hero is virtually extinct. Everything is calculated on a cut-price basis. A penny for heaven. A little bit more (but as little as possible!) to pacify the 'poor', whose real power is visibly on the increase ...

And yet, the more meaningless gestures become, the more solemn they are; and the more solemn they are, the more ludicrous, sparking off life's revenges: laughter and parody ...

And now let us go for a moment into the little village church, surrounded by its graveyard.

I hesitate on its humble, unadorned threshold, held back by a kind of apprehension. I know what I shall find: an empty, echoing space, with hidden recesses crammed with hundreds of objects, each uttering the silent cry that makes it a sign. What a strange power! I know that I cannot fail to understand their 'meanings', because they were explained to me years ago. It is impossible to close your eyes and your ears to these symbols: they occupy you, they preoccupy you immediately, insistent, insidious – and the more so for their simplicity. Already a feeling of disquiet, suppressed anger, mingled with the reluctant but tenacious memories of a childhood and adolescence shaped by Christianity ... And I know that this suppressed anger is another aspect of the power, the nascent fascination of the 'sacred' object. It is impossible to free myself from it. For me this space can never be just like any other space. But precisely because I feel this obscure emotion I can begin to understand its obscure causes. So I must not despair, the fight goes on ...

The country church is small and dark, despite its whitewashed walls. A sickly light filters through the grimy little panes of its narrow windows. Small, dark, mysterious, a bit like a cave. An ambiguous perfume – its familiar side: damp; its strange side: incense – hits the nostrils. The mystical, far-away splendour of the incense penetrates the ordinary smell of must and mould. Already I am inhaling the perfume of the Orient, I want to inhale it despite myself, to identify it. Unalloyed it would be overpowering, but here its mystical appeal is tainted with something mundane.

And now I can begin to make out the coloured or gilded objects and signs which surround the faithful and impose their presence upon them.

Around the vault, above the choir, a clumsy but inspired artist has painted a border festooned with stars (in silver and gold) on a blue background. This humble decoration on the vault is the church's way of offering undisputable proof that it sums up the cosmic order that the god who made the heavens is housed within it, but now time has almost erased it. (I forgot to check whether it is turned eastward towards Jerusalem and the sunrise.) And this lamp, shining dimly on the end of a wire hanging from the centre of the building's vaguely cross-shaped structure, what does it signify? Is it the light of the sun or the eternal light of the Spirit? Is it the mind of man which must remain ever-wakeful until the tragic final curtain?

Ah! Now here's something better, or more precise. In a relatively wide, deep recess (a chapel) two painted wooden statuettes face to face: St Blasius and St Roch. The region we are in has a long pastoral tradition. St Blasius and St Roch are the little patron saints of cattle and sheep. The inhabitants of P ... have been crafty enough to obtain the protection of both saints simultaneously. At the back of the recess a rather sketchy painting (a fresco or a painting on wood? impossible to tell in the half-light) portrays the two saints in shepherd's smocks, their dogs at their feet, and carrying crooks which are drawn to look vaguely like bishop's crosiers. The damp has obliterated patches of sky, bits of meadow. Around the chapel, a low railing. Beyond the railing, coins, roughly-folded notes. Offerings, sacrifices. On their name days, the peasants burn a few bristles from the tails of diseased cows under their patron saints' noses.

In another, smaller recess, on a plinth, the statuette of a little patron saint of the family: St Anthony, who helps to find lost property. At his feet, a simple collection box. The saint's right toe is discoloured and worn down by the kisses of his supplicants.

But here, sovereign and placatory, on the right of the high altar, here is the Great Mother, who distanced herself from the Earth in the celestial mystery of a virginity made fruitful by God alone, the Father of all things. Eternal Virgin, yet at the same time the divine Mother of all men – and also known by such attractive names as The Gates of Heaven, The Morning Star, the Ivory Tower and the Consolation of the Afflicted. God is remote and terrible is the Father. The Virgin Mother is near. Absolute mother, absolute virgin, she conjures up mysteriously and poetically the feminine totality. Mother, she receives her children. Virgin, she reassures, for a virginity which has not been surrendered to anyone belongs to everyone. Great goddess in the process of formation (or revival), but reduced by a prudent theology to the rank of mediator, it is she who attracts the most wishes, the most support, the most prayers.

On the other side of the altar, Joseph holding a golden lily.

The lowly church presents the absolute, human Family, lit by the stars and the cosmos above and flanked by the two guardians of the regularity and the fertility of herds and flocks: the Mother whose infinite purity renders her universal – the earthly, fictitious husband, naïve and hesitant – the real, heavenly husband, the fearsome creative power that leads the drama – and her divine Son.

The heavenly family is visited by earthly families, who offer it their good luck and their misfortunes in homage. It gives them a magnified image of themselves. The heavenly and the earthly are joined: the human is still mingled with the heavenly.

And in the tabernacle, Power united with Goodness, fearsome despite the abstraction in which He has draped Himself (a circle of something white, light and dry, without taste or perfume): God, in a threatening offering! Should a sacrilege be committed (ah! the stories they tell in their pious conversations and their parish newspapers, of the host bleeding and speaking, of sudden deaths and unexpected conversions ...), should a sacrilege be committed, the world might collapse into nothingness! The firmament, that solid vault which supports the stars, might crumble. Fearful angels would trump forth the end of Time. For if God does not accomplish all that He is perfectly capable of as cosmic Father, vain, vindictive Creator, Lord of heaven, Master of good and evil, Throne of glory built upon azure, gold and banknotes, it is because He is also the Son, controlling Himself, checking His Justice and His Wrath, and showing Himself to be equally and at one and the same time very good, very mild, very brotherly towards the little human families which crawl along in this vale of tears.

If this church offers us the world and the human drama in résumé, it also gives us history. I can see Joan of Arc in her suit of armour; the Tricolour spreads its folds around her painted plaster breastplate; a plaque carries the names of the dead of the last war (the Great War, as the old men have long called it ...).

O Church, O Holy Church, when I finally managed to escape from your control I asked myself where your power came from. Now I can see through your sordid secrets, all the more obvious here for being without the beguiling adornments of art. How naïve people were to believe that they could get rid of you with a few sacrilegious protests. How holy men must have laughed at the 'freethinkers' (while pretending to be deeply shocked and making sure to retaliate at the earliest opportunity). Now I can see the fearful depths, the fearful reality of human alienation! O Holy Church, for centuries you have tapped and accumulated every illusion, every fiction, every vain hope, every frustration. You have garnered them in your houses like some precious harvest, and each generation, each era, each age of man adds something new to them. And now before my very eyes I see the terrors of human childhood, the worries of adolescence, the hopes and misgivings which greet adulthood, even the terrors and despair of old age, for it costs you nothing to say that the evening of the world is nigh and that Man is already old and will perish without realizing his potential! There are men who withdraw slightly from life so as to control it, using skills amassed by over more than twenty centuries of experience. And precisely because they have sacrificed themselves to the utmost, these men appear to be sacred; many of them believe they are sacred, and perhaps in a sense some of them are indeed sacred ... From the newborn babe's first breath to the dying man's last sigh they are there, ministering to questioning children, frightened virgins and tormented adolescents, to the anxieties of the destitute and even to the sufferings of the powerful; whenever man experiences a moment of weakness, there they are. For their old, ever-more-skilful tactics, for the 'spiritual' body of the Church, everything is grist to the mill – including doubts and heresies, and even attacks. The Church is nothing more and nothing less than the unlimited ability to absorb and accumulate the inhuman. Recently they have made their position more 'flexible', but I know that this is merely an attempt to absorb the enemy. Having condemned 'modernism' a dozen times, the Church now wants to be 'modern'. Her craftiest followers will say (they are already saying it) that she embodies man's progress towards the Divine, his centuries-old effort to transcend himself, and gradual divine revelation. But no – you are nothing more than man's alienation, the self torn asunder, a magic spell. I can read the message unadorned on the walls of this country church. They sum up your history, which is the history of human poverty! All your strategies are here in miniature, all the skills with which you have controlled and preserved the massive dehumanization which weighs men down, growing larger and larger like some living monster! You have served Roman emperors, feudal lords, absolute monarchs, a triumphant bourgeoisie. You were always on the side of the strongest (not without some craftily reticent manoeuvres to prove how independent and superior you were), but by appearing to stand up for the weak you ended up being the strongest of all. And now you have the gall to take up the cause of Man, promising to turn yesterday's slave into tomorrow's master! No. The trick is too obvious, and above all the task is too great. Until now the Holy Church has always been able to digest everything, but for the first time her mighty stomach may prove not strong enough. And she knows it. And she is afraid. And she wants to be everywhere, double-dealing, treble-dealing, winning on all the tables. But people can see it, and people know it. So what is to become of this accumulation of every conceivable myth and empty abstraction, of this extraordinary apparatus which combines the flaws of every State that ever was without even the virtue of some connection to the life of any one people or any one nation?

Sunday morning!

The bell has already rung twice, the first time slow and inoffensive, the second hurried, threatening, domineering. Away in the distant meadows, its reverberations have a melancholy sound; closer at hand, in the narrow streets of the apparently deserted village, it is something else again: it is the voice of the eternal father thundering down from the top of the belfry onto a barnyard of squat houses, scouring them, encircling every corner, every head, catching everyone by the ears, vibrating inside their skulls and their very bones. Come on, you childish, decrepit lot, get a move on!

The murmur of a threshing machine can be heard getting slowly louder, suddenly cutting out and then starting again. The godless are working on this holy day.

Through the open door and the clear window panes a soft, tawny sunlight redolent of October and the grape harvest floods the still-empty church; its beams dispel the Christian mystery which must have half-light; I can hear cockerels crowing, and the sound is astonishing.

Across the cold paving glides a black shape, the folds in its dress completely immobile. A widow! It's a widow! everything about her signals it. An unspeakably insipid, unspeakably dreary placidity fills her chubby face, settles at the bottom of her faded cheeks. Fat and stiff, she glides noiselessly. Surely nothing has ever disturbed this stagnating placidity. Surely she was born a widow. They say she is very good to the church; she comes to sweep it, tending to the decorations, replacing the dying flowers with armfuls of fresh ones; she is intoxicated with her own humility and self-effacement; she picks up the rubbish with her bare hands; she is the handmaiden of this holy house – but under her falsely pious modesty what pride lies hidden!

A sudden flight of sparrows and pigeons, a loud scuffling of chairs and benches; the clatter of clogs on the stone floor. Hands are dipped into the font and chests are hurriedly crossed. 'Religion' is about to attempt to 're-link' all this disparate human material into a community: old women enveloped in the black shroud of their *capulet*,[5] sly, impatient urchins, shopkeepers' daughters who have come to show off their Sunday dresses, one or two men. On one side, the guild of women. On the other, farther back, nearer the door, the men. They are the last to come and the first to leave. But nevertheless they come, they are there, holding their berets rolled up in their hands.

How many people here are genuine believers, not satisfied with gestures but ardently grasping their faith as an *object*? This young girl, perhaps, her whole body tensed and bent forward on her chair, gazing spellbound on the great Christ, his pink body stained with the blood of his wounds? There is something distraught about her eyes which contrasts with the peacefulness, the already unutterably bored peacefulness, of her face. Someone else cut out to be a widow, or an eternal virgin? With what sacrifices is she purchasing this peace of the true believer, innocently confident in an earthly and heavenly future, a little soul in the arms of the Father, a little lamb beneath the shepherd's crook? Contemptible, unfought-for peace; whatever deprivations and conflicts may exist, they are placidly ignored, disdained; childishness is prolonged, cultivated even – a premature annihilation; I recognize you, despicable peace of my childhood! But what torments it takes just to be free, just to destroy these ashes! They say that the true believer must always experience conflict, that faith is born of anguish. But what anguish? Yes, maybe the anguish which lies bogged down and rotting in its own peacefulness, where the deepest 'deprivations' are indistinguishable from mystical certainties! And yet surely they know that when it becomes clear that faith does not even exist, that it is an illusion, that there is nothing to have faith in, that there is only nothingness, then anguish is born in its place; and that once faith is gone it leaves the blood contaminated with nothingness. Then anyone who has been alienated and dehumanized by his childhood faith will begin a desperate quest for a pathway, a link with life; but his lost illusions still obsess him; his need for faith fills him with anguish, and he tries in vain to keep on believing. What a pack of lies: it is faith which produces anguish, like a painful scar, nothingness activated ...

Mass begins, mundane, reduced to its bare essentials, with no grand organ, canon's kiss or plumed verger.

Basically, this Catholic Mass revives the oldest form of dramatic art, tragedy: an audience which participates in the action, a choir which responds to the protagonist, who conjures up the founder of the community, his life, his destiny and the inevitable catastrophe, the sacrifice and death of the hero. In the ceremony, the hero comes back to life and the participants identify with him; through him they can re-form a community which is both cosmic and human.

In a sense the Catholic model turns out to be richer, more complex than tragedy. What a poetic drama, where anyone watching who is not insensitive or immune is challenged, gripped if only by the style and flow of imagery – forced to participate, drawn on by the senses even into the realm of theological meanings! And here in this country church there is not even music, nor the magnificence and mystique of stained glass and sumptuous ceremony. What a combination – the art of fascination and the art of control! And until now there has been nothing to compare with its versatility. Mass for marriage, Mass for the dead, Mass for soldiers and Mass to bless the coming battle, High Mass in cathedrals (and one day I will describe a cathedral, in minute detail ...), Low Mass in suburban and village churches ... Yes, wherever something of man is born or dies, wherever there is something vulnerable, like a child, like love, or something threatened, like a soldier, like a peasant, there will the divine tragedy be acted out. A bench and an upturned crate make as good a stage as the most extravagant marble altar.

On the other hand, the pathos is less than in high tragedy, and less perceptible. Despite the scope of the subject, the drama is far from perfect. Too many abstractions have had to be included, too many symbols piled one upon the other, too many gestures for their own sake. The fall in quality is inevitable! In the first place the foreign language,[6] while helping to reinforce the mystery, limits the number of dramatic effects available (it is true that the sermon in French comes just at the right time to compensate for this). The rhythm is slow. The audience is bored to tears by the respectful abstraction of it all. Religion will end in boredom; and to offer boredom to the Lord is hardly a living sacrifice. (Yet as I write these lines, I wonder if I'm not making a crude mistake. Magic has always gone hand in hand with emotion, hope and terror, and still does. But are there such things as religious 'emotions'? Probably no more so than there is a 'psychological state' – consciousness or thought without an object – that could be called 'faith'. These are ideological fictions. Surely religion, like theology, metaphysics, ceremonies, academic literature and official poets, has always been boring. This has never been a hindrance, because one of the aims of 'spiritual' discipline and asceticism has always been precisely to disguise and to transfigure this living boredom ...)

The divine tragedy is overladen with riches. The journey the solemn words and gestures of the protagonist take us on is too long. Here too, as in the church itself, the listener, his suspicions aroused, discovers the secretions, the accumulated sediments of centuries. In a minute we shall be in a market stall in Alexandria, where some wily cabbalists are discussing mystical names and entities with a bearded Jew who has just arrived from Athens: *In initio erat Verbum* ...[7] For the moment we are in the age of kings and princes. Armed with their pikes and with a great roar the infantry are setting off in a cloud of dust behind the war chariots, wheels bristling with sharp blades. And the High Priest invokes the divine Names: '*Deus, deus, Sabaoth* ... Lord of Hosts! ...' Did Judith murmur these words as she carried away Holofernes's head in her bag, his eyes closed in the voluptuousness of death? Yes, God was always on the side of the strongest, since victory proved whose side God was on, and defeat was explained as the wages of His Wrath. How childish, simple and profound divine mystification is! Lord of Hosts, Lord of Armies! But what armies, and armed with what arms? ... But hush! We mustn't be flippant. Pay attention.

Introibo ad altare Dei, qui laetificat juventutem meam. What magnificent poetry. 'The God who makes my youth rejoice.' Really moving, really splendid, isn't it, this marriage of youth and eternity! Doesn't anyone here think about the young people who have been burdened, sickened, poisoned, by the philtre of the absolute, the venom of sin and the yearning for the dreary peace of innocence? What can these words mean to these people? Have they discovered how to avoid mental torture? Can I have been the last of the faithful?

I mustn't get annoyed. I merely want to understand 'their' secrets. *Et Verbum Caro factum est.* More abstractions, more symbols, but this time with the fascinating information that they are now merged with life. The Word, the mysterious, holy, magic Word of Words, is made flesh! Does that mean that speech takes the form of a tongue, or a mouth?

Maybe.

And now the priest turns towards the audience and begins making grander gestures. He is ageless, young rather than old; the son of a peasant, one can tell from his face; a slight figure in a tight black robe, but amplified by the alb and surplice; a long, pale countenance, bony and bluish with beard; a shy man, with little authority in the village. They say he has a weak chest, and that he's under his sister's thumb. But here he is another man; he becomes assured, imposing. Almost too much so: some of his gestures seem to be lifting some enormous but meaningless weight up towards heaven, and it's rather comical.

Now the moment for the holy meal has come. Time once more for the most venerable of these rituals. Will the bread and wine reanimate the faithful once again, restoring their oneness with nature and humanity? But how cold it all is, and how dried up! Where's the joy? Where are the overflowing cups and the huge, consecrated loaves of bread? Only the priest gets to eat and drink, consuming the principles of life in the form of the two basics, bread and wine. Then, to a couple of old women in black and the mystical young girl, he will hand out an insipid symbol of infinity ...

So this is what the holy meal has been reduced to: torn away from community to be accomplished by those who mediate between us and the absolute – torn away from the life of the senses and from real festivity to become symbolic, abstract, distant. Transferred entirely to another plane – a spiritual and 'interior' plane, apparently. But where is the human community for these people in black I see filing back to their seats, their eyes half-closed, their hands clasped piously together, absorbed in the dreariness of what their mouths and their souls have just tasted? A caricature of a community! Profound? Inner? No! These dehumanized beings are self-absorbed from the moment they are born to the moment they die, and the only community they know is fictitious and abstract.

I remember a time when I hated them because I still loved them. My adolescence was drawing to a close – an adolescence which had lived through more than one season in hell. Hatching fiendish plans of revenge, I continued going to church and mixing with priests. Even the most terrible acts of violence seemed too tame, too simple. My friends made do with various small sacrilegious gestures which to me seemed meaningless (it was the time when Breton tied a crucifix to the lavatory chain in his toilet and thought he was exterminating Christianity). I thought about vaster – but no less naïve – ventures. I studied the history of the Church in the hope of ferreting out a vintage heresy I could resurrect, an indestructible, indigestible heresy with which to torpedo the Church. Jansen's? Too dry, too terribly eighteenth-century petty bourgeois, and as far as boredom goes, his *Augustinus* beats even the *Summa Theologiae*.[8] Only one heresy appealed to me. Everyone can see for themselves how far the Holy Ghost is absent from the Church; it appears only in the dubious shape of a pigeon, or as an excellent teacher of modern languages. So I started planning a revival of the cult of the Holy Ghost, making it as much a living presence as the other personalities in the Holy Trinity. I wanted to show that the incarnation of the Son was not enough to save the world (which is obvious), and to proclaim the imminent arrival and incarnation of the Holy Ghost. As a prophet of the Holy Ghost, I would have carried my ardent prediction into the very bosom of the Church, in the name of a neglected dogma. I would have paid anything – made any 'sacrifice' – in order to spread this heresy, and the best of it was that I didn't even believe in it! I wanted revenge so much, I would even have been willing to become a martyr.

One fine day, in an effort to think clearly which from this distance may seem facile, even comical, I understood that my whole satanic venture was just another way of *perpetuating mystical themes*; that by going in that direction I was simply a future prodigal son – a man in despair – one of the last believers – that I hadn't realized just how extraordinarily naïve the whole plan was (it wasn't as though the Church had never been attacked before!) ... and just how *clerical* my fiendish scheme really was!

So for a little while I adopted one of Nietzsche's great visionary theories. Dionysius – the living cosmos – is born and dies in order to be reborn. The Eternal Recurrence, the Great Year, the periodic Return of things, which so many wise men and philosophers have sensed are not and cannot be simply a dry, frigid theory. The universe, the Whole, is a god who becomes and accedes to consciousness within man; he is a Whole, but dismembered into fragments which also like him know suffering and joy. Through the torments of his cosmic journey, through the tortures of human consciousness, his eternal destiny moves on with each new cycle towards the joy of supreme consciousness, and at the same time towards the tragic catastrophe, the death of the planets and the stars, the new ice age or the gigantic atomic cataclysm. The god's destiny is accomplished; and because the god – creative energy – cannot end, he is reborn; he starts again. Spring of springtimes and everlasting joy. Sunrise, immense procession of resurrections, ascension of life, and also pain, immortal death of all forms and all past moments, winters and old age, cataclysms and massacres, a billion tragedies in the cosmic Tragedy ...

Since the sufferings of Dionysius could be identified with Christ on the cross, since all the symbols of art and religion must take on a new meaning in Dionysius, I dreamt of a total celebration, a Mass and a tragedy, intense and absolute, extraordinarily poetic and powerfully dramatic, which would rejoice in the tragic destiny of Nature, finite and infinite, divine and human, joyful and harrowing! ... Zarathustra would have been merely the prophet and the herald of this super-human Celebration, this offering and supreme sacrifice of man to the absolute! ...

Such are the difficulties we face when we try to liberate ourselves from mystiques, from our predilection for illusory greatness, for self-effacement, for the sacrifice of man ... The cruellest and most rigorous of self-examinations will always unearth some hidden radicle of alienation, of the perverse pleasure alienation of the self affords! ...

To conclude these notes, I would like to sum up briefly what dialectical method can bring to such chaos:

(a) *It allows us to* re-establish *order and reason in ideas*

Using Marxist method, every cultivated and truly 'modern' man will soon be able to look at the irksome and incomprehensible mumbo-jumbo of our towns and villages, our churches and our works of art, and read them out loud, like an open book.

(b) *Marxist method enables us to understand the 'secrets', the obscure aspects of the 'social mystery' and of history*

Thus Catholicism appears in its historical truth as a 'movement' rather than a doctrine, a vast movement, thoroughly skilled in the art of assimilation, which never creates anything new but in which nothing is ever lost, particularly the oldest and most tenacious myths, which for various reasons go on being accepted or being seen as acceptable by the vast majority (agrarian myths).

224

The mystifying skill of this 'movement' can be measured by the fact that it has been able to disguise itself as a rigid dogmatism. In fact it is exactly the opposite (like a crafty child who slides along while insisting he is sitting still). And this disguise is a cover for its press-gang tactics. Anyone who criticizes 'Catholic dogmatism' in the name of free-thinking and independent individuality is being ridiculously naïve.

This movement taps human weakness and helplessness; to be absolutely exact, it 'capitalizes' on them. Where does it get its univer-sality from? From its ability to live with all the myths and rituals it has taken from the various social formations, to superimpose them and overdetermine them, and to churn them back in the guise of doctrinal 'rigour'.

This unstructured syncretism has been working unceasingly since the death of Christ up until the present day, and it is obviously the Church, in its role as a social and *political* organism, which props it up.

(c) *The problem of the Human cannot be resolved by inventing new rituals, be they spiritual or material, mystical or aesthetic, public or private*

That path (which is the one nearly all our philosophers and men of letters have followed) is the path of 'alienation'.

The Church has tapped and accumulated all human (or rather 'inhuman') alienation.

Its power comes from the fact that *it penetrates everyday life*. On the one hand it has created a dehumanized ceremonial, an official magnificence, an extra-national State, an abstract theory; on the other, it has produced an extremely subtle and precise psychological and moral technique.

In every act of one's immediate life, no matter how insignificant, religion can be present: in the 'internalized' form of a ritual or in the external form of the priest who listens, understands, advises, repri-mands or 'pardons'.

Past religion and past moral doctrines (which deep down are always religious) tell us *what we must do* (according to them) in an everyday life which seems all the more derelict, uncertain and humiliated for the fact that the life of the mind, of knowledge, of art, of the State, is getting more and more vast, more 'elevated' and more ritualized.

We spend each day of our lives crawling along at ground level, while the 'superior' moments fly away into the far reaches of the stratosphere. Religion 'snowballs' as a result of all the practical helplessness of human beings, constituting an immense obstacle; it is there in life's most infinitesimal detail, knowing the weaknesses and provoking them, breathing in the positive substance of everyday life and *concentrating its negative aspects*. At each everyday event, at each emotive, disturbing moment when something begins or when something ends, religion will raise its head; it reassures, consoles, and above all supplies an attitude, a way to behave. It tells us what we must do (in its view – but until now no one has offered an alternative) when faced with death or birth. It provides a ceremonial; it relieves people not only of the embarrassment of not knowing what to do and what to say, but also of the fear and remorse their embarrassment produces (as though all misfortunes, past, present or future, were in any way their fault). It gives everyone the impression of doing something. The ritual gesture when a funeral procession goes by, words of insult, an 'A-Dieu' when we part, a wish, a propitious phrase of greeting or thanks – all such everyday attitudes still come down to us from magic and religion; they are really religious, or potentially so. And that is where in the end the secret of religion's strength lies.

In this way the illusion by which religion deceives us (that vain and ever-broken promise of community, of the power to act) tends to be born again with every action in our everyday lives. Exactly as, on another level, economic fetishism is reanimated every single time an individual, unaware of the social structure, uses a coin or a note to buy the product of human labour, transformed into a commodity.

(d) *The problem posed by Marxism is thus revealed in all its breadth*

We now know that Marxism wants to transform the 'world' (and no longer just to interpret it). But we need to understand fully what we mean by the term 'world'. It is not simply a matter of intensifying production, of cultivating new spaces, of industrializing agriculture, of building giant factories, of changing the State and then finishing once and for all with that monster, 'of all cold monsters the coldest'. These are merely means to an end.

And what is that end? It is the transformation of life in its smallest, most everyday detail. The world is man's future because man is the creator of his 'world'. And the problem is not simply to change the idea of man, to found the idea of the *total* man – nature and consciousness, instinct and lucidity, power over things and over his own products – and to place it at the apex of culture. The problem is not simply to achieve a dialectical unity of knowledge, to bring together the results of all the sciences in an organized and rational encyclopedic system. It is not simply to form a new type of men or to establish new general relations between men.

Those are still only means. The end, the aim, is to make thought – the power of man, the participation in and the consciousness of that power – intervene in life in its humblest detail.

More ambitious, more difficult, more remote than the means, the aim is to change life, lucidly to recreate everyday life. This is the exact opposite of the aim and the essence of religion.

By revealing its positive and negative duality, the critique of everyday life will help to pose and resolve the problem of life itself.

Human culture and consciousness incorporate every conquest, every past moment of history. In contrast, religion *accumulates* all man's helplessness. It offers a critique of life; it is itself that critique: a reactionary, destructive critique. Marxism, the consciousness of the new man and the new consciousness of the world, offers an effective, constructive critique of life. And Marxism alone! ...

227

6

What Is Possible

When the world the sun shines on is always new, how could everyday life be forever unchangeable, unchangeable in its boredom, its greyness, its repetition of the same actions?

Many who have lost faith in the human, and who get hypocritically emotional about the 'immemorial gestures' of peasants, mothers, or housewives, think it is ...

Everyday life is not unchangeable; it can decline, therefore it changes. And moreover the only genuine, profound human changes are those which cut into this substance and make their mark upon it.

It is fairly easy to demonstrate decline using one simple, important example, life in the country, because in many ways the traces of 'another life', a community life, are still more perceptible there than elsewhere.

A later instalment of the present study will endeavour to describe the decline of everyday life, on industrial housing estates, in so-called 'modern' everyday activity.

But for the moment we have to consider another factor, one which will make our investigation yet more complicated. Just as this decline proceeds to its ultimate consequences, *possibilities* become more apparent, more immediately perceptible, in this sphere than elsewhere.

Human life can decline and it can progress. Up until now it has followed this dual movement: on the one hand, and in one direction, decline; on the other hand, and in another direction, progress.

Life has 'got better', and we cannot entirely disagree with those optimists who insist obstinately that, favoured by some unspecified theological or metaphysical Providence, the human species is slowly advancing like a well-drilled army along a pre-ordained path from barbarism to civilization. They are not entirely wrong; and likewise the theory of 'decadence' is just as metaphysical – and just as dubious – as the optimism of the partisans of Progress, which it opposes. The abstract idea of 'decadence' in general conceals a very real decadence, present in the world today, albeit only momentarily: the decadence of the bourgeoisie.

And yet the optimistic idea of 'Progress' lacks flexibility and dialectical understanding. It fails to grasp the different aspects of human becoming. *Up until now* progress has carried within itself certain elements of regression. Spontaneous, objective, like a process of nature, this 'progress' has not been guided by a Reason. Thought has realized this at a very late stage; and it is only now that efficient Reason is making an attempt to penetrate it actively, to understand its laws and to transform it into a rational progress without negative repercussions.

Human life has progressed: material progress, 'moral' progress – but that is only part of the truth. The deprivation, the alienation of life is its other aspect.

In reply to the naïve theoreticians of complete, continuous progress we must demonstrate in particular the decline of everyday life since the community of Antiquity, and man's growing alienation. We must present a firm answer to the Robinson Crusoe-esque idyllists who denigrate the present and theorize the 'good old days', by demonstrating the progress that has been accomplished: in knowledge and in consciousness, in power over nature. Above all we must demonstrate the breadth and magnificence of the *possibilities* which are opening out for man; and which are so really possible, so near, so rationally achievable (once the *political* obstacles are shattered) that this proximity of what is possible can be taken for *one of the meanings* (painfully and frighteningly unconscious) of the famous 'modern disquiet', the anguish caused by 'existence' as it still is! ...

Now the simplest, most mundane events can show how economic and technical 'progress' has worked.

Several years ago a world-wide firm which was trying to extend the market and put a rival firm out of business decided to distribute paraffin lamps to Chinese peasants free of charge, while its rivals, less 'generous' or less shrewd, went on selling them. And now in several million poverty-stricken Chinese households artificial light (an

immense progress) shines down on muddy floors and rotten matting –
because even peasants who cannot afford to buy a lamp can afford to
buy paraffin ... The 'progress' capitalism brings, like its 'generosity', is
just a means to an end: profit.

To take an example from much nearer home: in France, in the
Pyrenees, just a stone's throw from dams and powerful ultra-modern
hydro-electric installations, there are many hamlets, thousands of
houses where peasants live almost as 'primitive' a life as the Chinese.
They have no electric light either. Elsewhere, more or less everywhere,
in town and country alike, electric light illuminates the peeling plaster
of slums and the sordid walls of hovels. (Although even in Paris there
are still houses and flats without modern lighting.)

Mundane, without literary interest, and picked at random from an
infinity of possible equally significant examples, these facts show that
up until now 'progress' has affected existing social realities only
secondarily, modifying them as little as possible, according to the strict
dictates of capitalist profitability. The important thing is that human
beings be profitable, not that their lives be changed. As far as is
possible, capitalism respects the pre-existing shape and contours of
people's lives. Only grudgingly, so to speak, does it bring about any
change. Criticism of capitalism as a contradictory 'mode of production'
which is dying as a result of its contradictions is strengthened by
criticism of capitalism as the distributor of the wealth and 'progress' it
has produced.

And so, constantly staring us in the face, mundane and therefore
generally unnoticed – whereas in the future it will be seen as a
characteristic and scandalous trait of our era, the era of the decadent
bourgeoisie – is this fact: that *life is lagging behind what is possible*, that it
is retarded. What incredible backwardness. This has up until now been
constantly increasing; it parallels the growing disparity between the
knowledge of the contemporary physicist and that of the 'average' man,
or between that of the Marxist sociologist and that of the bourgeois
politician.

Once pointed out, the contrast becomes staggeringly obvious,
blinding; it is to be found everywhere, whichever way we turn, and
never ceases to amaze.

Compare an 'average' house in one of our towns, not with an
ostentatious and absurd palace, nor with some characteristically

grotesque dwelling of the haute bourgeoisie, but rather with a 'modern' industrial installation – a power station, for example. Here we find hyper-precise technology, light, and a dazzling cleanliness; power methodically condensed into strictly contoured appliances. These machines are so amazing in the way they conceal their strength beneath an apparent immobility that more than one writer has used them to resuscitate the feeling of sanctity, of awe in the face of 'powerful', motionless fetishes. On the other hand, in the house where decent, 'average' people live out their everyday lives, all is petty, disorganized; dusty nooks and crannies; mean, pretentious furniture; petty-bourgeois knick-knacks; the strictly useless is accompanied by the absence of anything useful – and yet the cult of utility reigns; dark rooms; feather dusters, brooms, carpets which are shaken out of the window ...

Which is to say nothing of workers' lodgings and peasants' houses where the doorstep is a pool of liquid manure!

The power acquired thanks to technology and thought thus remains outside of life, above it, far away. And, if asked, very few of those affected by these simple facts would be able to account for them or for their consequences.

Likewise, compare an ordinary street, with its little shops, its rows of windows stretching drearily along like gravestones in a cemetery, with any monument screaming power and arrogance ...

In this country there is a striking, strident contrast between the appearance of things and the symbols of power.

In this quiet little town, there is nothing to make us think of war, of the tragic feeling of life, of the will to power.

Between the houses of the bourgeoisie, heavy, angular, with their ornamental structure, the breeze is heavy with a disturbing scent of lindens. In the nearby canal, thousands of frogs can be heard croaking interminably. Priests stroll by, little girls, prisoners, basset hounds. In a belfry daubed with green and gold, the bells are ringing. There must be a mistake somewhere in this picture ...

And at a bend in the road, that mistake becomes clear: a monument to some victory or other: a conglomeration of steel and stone, of predatory eagles and sharp swords, of taut muscles and stubborn faces ...[1]

That was how Pierre Courtade saw Germany just after the war. But the mistake in question was not specifically German. It was universal. A mistake that allowed human power to become the will of a few men to hold power. That allowed power to be placed outside of life, to be transposed to the level of State control – in a word, to be *alienated*. And it is not only in Germany that the contrast is so blatantly obvious between the painful or ridiculous situation of 'private' life (even among privileged people) and a power which only becomes 'public' in absurdly externalized forms and manifestations. Factories that are technological marvels (and 'private' properties!) are paralleled by monuments which *magically* concentrate not only the prestige of the State and the power of the rulers but also all the artificiality of empty celebrations, ceremonies and rituals – not to mention a host of mystical ideas, grandiose theories and 'official' abstractions; their only real purpose, however, is to proclaim, to express – and indeed to betray – the 'will to power'. The will to power? It is real power, stolen from the community (itself smashed and atomized into 'private' individuals) and turned into power over men, set up brutally above men, instead of being power over things. And it is precisely into things that it wishes to transform human beings, 'depriving' them of any real consciousness, and turning them into economic and political tools. As life drags on in all its weakness and humiliation, the will to power expresses itself in these cancerous monstrosities; to admire one of them is not only stupid and tasteless, it also amounts to acquiescence in a potential holocaust.

Everything great and splendid is founded on power and wealth. They are the basis of beauty. This is why the rebel and the anarchic protester who decries all of history and all the works of past centuries because he sees in them only the skills and the threat of domination is making a mistake. He sees alienated forms, but not the greatness within. The rebel can only see to the end of his own 'private' consciousness, which he levels against *everything* human, confusing the oppressors with the oppressed masses, who were nevertheless the basis and the meaning of history and past works. Castles, palaces, cathedrals, fortresses, all speak in their various ways of the greatness and the strength of the people who built them and against whom they were built. This real greatness shines through the fake grandeur of rulers and endows these buildings with a lasting 'beauty'. The bourgeoisie is alone in having given its buildings a single, over-obvious meaning, impoverished, deprived of reality: that meaning is abstract wealth and brutal domination; that is why it has succeeded in producing perfect ugliness and perfect vulgarity. The man who denigrates the past, and who nearly always denigrates the present and the possible as well, cannot understand this dialectic of art, this dual character of works and of history. He does not even sense it. Protesting against bourgeois stupidity and oppression, the anarchic individualist is enclosed in 'private' consciousness, itself a product of the bourgeois era, and no longer understands human power and the community upon which that power is founded. The historical forms of this community, from the village to the nation, escape him. He is, and only wants to be, a human atom (in the scientifically archaic sense of the word, where 'atom' meant the lowest isolatable reality). By following alienation to its very extremes he is merely playing into the hands of the bourgeoisie. Embryonic or unconscious, this kind of anarchism is very widespread. There is a kind of revolt, a kind of criticism of life, that implies and results in the acceptance of this life *as the only one possible*. As a direct consequence this attitude precludes any understanding of *what is humanly possible*.

Our towns may be read like a book (the comparison is not completely exact: a book signifies, whereas towns and rural areas 'are' what they signify). Towns show us the history of power and of human possibilities which, while becoming increasingly broad, have at the same time been increasingly taken over and controlled, until that point of total control, set up entirely above life and community, which is bourgeois control.

Rural areas tell us above all of the dislocation of primitive community, of poor technical progress, of the decline of a way of life which is much less different from that of ancient times than is generally believed. Towns tell us of the almost total decomposition of community, of the atomization of society into 'private' individuals as a result of the activities and way of life of a bourgeoisie which still dares claim that it represents 'the general interest'.

On the other hand, provided our purpose in deciphering them is neither the search for the superficially picturesque (after the fashion of a Jules Romains),[2] nor the search for would-be modern myths, then our towns will show us something quite different: the rebirth and reforming of community in factories and working-class neighbourhoods. There, other modes of everyday living, other needs, other requirements, are entering into conflict with the modalities of everyday life as imposed by the capitalist structure of society and life, and tending to re-establish a solidarity, an effective alliance between individuals and groups. How does this conflict manifest itself? Constantly beaten down, constantly born again, how is this solidarity expressed? How does it translate in concrete terms? This is exactly what the positive side of the *Critique of Everyday Life* should discover and describe.

It is not the academic literary hacks from the smart side of town, nor the 'populists' in search of ever-more-picturesque poverty to stimulate their descriptive whimsy, who can understand industrial housing estates and working-class neighbourhoods. Nor is it those false dreamers 'who leisurely imagine sublime anguishes, revel in lunacies, abysses and other evasions, while harsh reality is imprisoning the bodies, minds, days and nights of millions of men and women ...'.[3] Among the rare valid expressions of this reality are the *Poems by American Workers* translated in 1930 by Norbert Guterman and Pierre Morhange.[4] Listen to Martin Russak, a silk weaver:

> And so I was born, how strange, how strange,
> In the city of many tongues
> And came when a baby in arms and remain
> Rootless and restless in the city of silk ...[5]

> O Paterson, my home, my town, Paterson,
> With your church-spires and chimneys racing for heaven,
> With your statue of justice on your court-house dome
> Who has lost her sword and her scales and stands
> Blindfold and helpless in the smoky air, –
> When I lie on the cliffs at Garret Rock
> Eating a bag of lunch at noon,
> And considering you spread out below
> I could weep for myself and you, if only
> I did not know how to curse ...[6]

But Miriam Allen adds a moving message of combat to this curse:

> When you hear a bird singing, remember Sacco and Vanzetti
> When you see a wild flower growing, remember Sacco and Vanzetti ...[7]

and Ralph Cheyney adds a message of hope:

These little fingers soft as the fronds of a fern
must grow hard to grab an axe, pick, spade ...
In your dimpled hands and those of millions of other
working-class babies – white, black, yellow –
the future of the world rests.
Open your little mouth and bawl!
Clench those rosebud fists!
Suck hard so they'll grow strong
to smash the old world in which you were born ...[8]

Since these *Poems by American Workers* were published, American novelists have shown us the contradictions of that illustrious America and the poverty and slavery her real greatness implies.

While our own literature remained academic, abstract, psychological, *outside of everyday life* (to such a point that our most intelligent critics and novelists only noticed Faulkner and Dos Passos for their technical innovations!), American writers were accomplishing something we had not even been able to begin: the trial of so-called 'modern' life, the analysis of its contradictory aspects, poverty and wealth, weakness and power, blindness and lucidity, individuality and massiveness ...

A curious situation. In America, a country where the general crisis of capitalism has scarcely begun, and where imperialism is alive and well, writers have been able to open their eyes to what is nearest to them – everyday life – and to find themes in it which amaze us by their violence and originality. But in France, where the economic crisis has already turned into a political crisis, a crisis of the social structure and of culture, a crisis of life (it is becoming impossible for the French to go on living as before, or to even want to, although there are plenty who try to turn the clock back at every possible opportunity ...), writers are seeking the themes and the content of their books *far away*, in the unreal, the surreal, in abstraction, in pure technical virtuosity.

Instead of looking lucidly around them, they lose themselves in a distant vision (and it is taken as read that every young poet must live 'in ecstasy', 'out of his mind', intoxicated if only with words). In our country, with its tradition of struggle, there is not a single book to compare with Steinbeck's *In Dubious Battle*.

Considered as a symptom, what does the situation of French literature tell us? Could it be a proof of decadence or creative impotence? Or does it indicate that for a people like us with an old culture everyday life has lost that spontaneity, that violence, that tangible, dramatic side which American writers have been able to uncover and make conscious?

Impotence? To a degree, yes. The comparison between American books and French books which have been inspired by them, is instructive. Monsieur Sartre's *Roads to Freedom* reveals an indisputable literary talent and above all a rather remarkable gift of *workmanship*; the content has not determined the form; the first wish of this over-intellectual, over-abstract novelist has been to master technique; his starting point is a formula, a procedure, and he even calls upon an entire metaphysics to help him out. Just as reading Faulkner forcefully engages our interest, awakening a thousand undefined emotions swarming beneath the everyday surface – cruelty, sexuality, surprise, worry, etc. – so reading Sartre is an increasingly cold, dry experience, overladen with falsely concrete details (noted down deliberately and consciously in order to be concrete!), without passion, without interest in life, without youth and without maturity, and quite simply boring.

Yes, a certain impotence. And above all a lack of vitality, an abstract attitude, a lack of direct and immediate interest in human beings and in the violence and drama of their lives. For in France, in spite of our relatively relaxed social mores, the lower classes – workers or peasants – would appear to enjoy their fair share of dramas, spontaneity, passions, elemental violence and humanity. Be that as it may, we do not know how to see them or to understand them. And it is the dreary, rigidly codified lives of the petty bourgeoisie and the middle classes which have imposed their style upon nearly all our literature. Class divisions, which are much more accentuated here than in America, stop our writers from watching the people live and from knowing how to watch them. For many years the rigid parameters and false freedom of petty-bourgeois life were thought to express eternal Reason, and to prove its validity. And when these parameters are threatened, petty-bourgeois anguish takes on metaphysical proportions for one and all. Only a few writers (Gide, Valéry Larbaud, Cocteau) have brought another element to our literature: facility, a free and easy air, cynicism, refined sophistication, the exquisite taste of the cultivated haute bourgeoisie; but no new way of looking at the world – Monsieur Gide's ridiculous claims notwithstanding.[9]

Petty-bourgeois individualism has reached the extreme limit of exhaustion, and that goes for the intellectual as well as the writer. In the 'human sand', each grain, which is so dreadfully similar to all the others (unless we look at it through a psychological microscope) thinks it is frightfully original, and even unique! *Individualism ends up as the impersonality of the individual.* It is the dialectical result of the 'private' consciousness and of its internal contradiction: the separation of the human being from the human. Nothing is easier to express literally than the abstract 'psychology' of this individuality, devoid of any content which might be difficult to express. Only a little knowledge of grammar is necessary. And there is plenty of that around! But unfortunately the tone of all these confidences and all these descriptions happens to be that of *impersonality*; therefore of boredom. The accusation that the Marxist dialectician levels at modern French literature as a whole is not that it expresses individuality, but rather that it expresses only false individuality, *a façade of individuality*, and abstraction. Nor is it by working in an element of 'anguish' that a young writer can give his descriptions or his story the direct, visual, physical, moving style, so much more individualized and varied, that one finds in Faulkner's characters and novels!

To see things properly, it is not enough simply to look. People who look at life – purely as witnesses, spectators – are not rare; and one of the strangest lessons to be learnt from our literature is that professional spectators, judges by vocation and witnesses by predestination, contemplate life with less understanding and grasp of its rich content than anyone else. There really is no substitute for participation!

And it is not that there is any shortage of subjects to write about. For example: in France the mixture of moral doctrines and politics has produced a species composed of some very varied types: the worthy-father type, the sexton type, the Pharisee type sweating with fear and guilty conscience, etc. Shared characteristics: immensely serious, generous or morally scrupulous to a fault, the kind of loyalty that fully expects its reward (in honours and influence, not to mention money), a few moral ideals linked to a very limited sense of immediate realities, and above all an excessive sensitivity (any attack on their ideals is taken as a personal affront!). Meeting places and social habitat of the species in question: certain political parties, which shall remain nameless.

This human species, so characteristic of our times, has not yet appeared in literature. And yet how picturesque, how comic it is! (There is nothing like the sight of an old lag from the dungeons of political idealism haranguing a critic (actually quite moderate), beating his breast with a combination of self-pity, terror at such sacrilege, and disappointment for not yet having received the honours and the positions his long martyrdom deserve, shouting: 'You young wretch, you are insulting an old Republican!' ...)

Why this silence? Could it not be that a large proportion of our witnesses and judges – of our writers – are recruited from these same Pharisees of idealism?

And is this not the reason why our era has allowed itself to be literally dominated by Gidean cynicism – in spite of everything that might be said, and indeed has been said, against Gide?

Abstract culture places an almost opaque screen (if it were completely opaque the situation would be simpler) between the cultivated man and everyday life.

Abstract culture not only supplies him with words and ideas, but also with an attitude which forces him to seek the 'meaning' of his life and his consciousness outside of himself and his real relations with the world.

The exact nature of 'deprivation' and the relation between the 'private' consciousness and the 'public' consciousness changes as a function of social level. For the 'cultivated' man (one who has received what is traditionally called 'culture'), this relation undergoes a curious inversion. For him 'his' thought, 'his' culture, are a part of his most intimate self. He carries them with him in the silence of his office, in the even-more barren silence of his 'inner life'. He tends to forget that thought is human and not 'private'. He will readily talk about his 'social life' when he means his relations with family, friends and business partners, i.e. his 'private' life. This inversion of consciousness does not constitute an absolute error, for there is no such thing as an absolute error. In the course of his historical development, the individual has to take thought 'upon himself'. This is one of the meanings of the Cartesian 'Cogito'. In the context of individualism, of a highly fragmented division of labour, and of the division of society into classes, this absolutely necessary action, this 'assumption' of human thought, finds expression in an inversion of consciousness – a relative error, but one which has serious consequences. The 'cultivated' man forgets the social foundations of 'his' thought. When he looks for the secret of his behaviour and his situation in words and ideas that he has received from without, he imagines that he is looking 'deep into himself'. And at the very moment when he thinks the search for his own self is over, he is actually leaving himself, taking the path of alienation. Consequently his practical, everyday life, his *real* relations, he sees as external to him. The structure of his consciousness tends to annihilate any genuine consciousness of 'his' life. In individual life this error of structural origin is expressed by conflicts, by specific 'psychological' errors, by a shift of consciousness (so exacerbating what has up to now been the natural and inevitable tendency of consciousness to lag behind). Without resorting to any kind of psychoanalysis, we can use this error, to which all 'cultivated' consciousnesses within an individualist structure are prone, to explain a number of barely 'a-social' minor neuroses, accepted if not encouraged, which have until now been considered the bailiwick of psychoanalysis.

To attain a consciousness of life *in its movement* (its reality and its unfulfilled possibilities), but without losing anything of culture, our first task must be to break the limiting, narrow, erroneous form of this culture.

Intellectuals, 'cultivated' men, are convinced in advance (why?) that everyday life has only triviality to offer. In fact this belief plays an important role in so-called 'existential' philosophy, which condemns all non-metaphysical life to triviality and inauthenticity.

The study of everyday life shows clearly that people with secrets, with inner lives, with mysteries, lead mundane everyday lives.

Thus 'mysterious' young girls and women are mainly passive, with little reality; they hide behind the feminine mystery, which offers them a glamour and a means of control which they cannot find elsewhere. In literature, the case of Kierkegaard, who invented the 'category of the secret', is equally very significant (and not without its link with the myth of the 'mysterious' woman).

The myth of the triviality of everyday life is dispelled whenever *what seems to be mysterious turns out to be really trivial, and what seems exceptional is exposed as manifestly banal.*

It would be possible to interpret the works of Faulkner and above all of Kafka along these lines. But there is another, more moving question to be asked: what about urban life, the life of the people, the life on industrial housing estates? Where, how and in what experiences can its essence be discovered?

When the first documents about the concentration camps in Germany arrived, they showed a horrible brutality: crematoria, living skeletons with crazy eyes, mass graves, corpses in gigantic heaps. News coverage, photos, then films, all the 'objective' accounts – but from outside the world of the concentration camps – stressed this first impression: they seemed to be revealing atrocities outside our experience, outside Western civilization and outside civilization itself.

Since then, the survivors have returned. And some of them have made the effort to speak of what they saw and endured. Even the most lucid of them have realized how extremely difficult it is to organize their recollections, to discover a guiding thread, to give their experience a measure of unity. Exhaustion has affected their memories; their sufferings have dulled their sensibilities; they are accustomed to horror, habit has trivialized it. But it is not simply that. Bit by bit, in the most interesting of these accounts, a conviction develops: the 'objective' reports have not fully explored the horror of the concentration camps; this horror is now an accepted fact that nobody can dare contradict; but it has a 'meaning'. Clear-minded observers ask the question: 'Why?' and fail to come up with a satisfactory answer. Were the concentration camps extermination camps? It would have been easier to shoot the detainees en masse. Were they work camps? The amount of work produced was insignificant. And so it seems that this unique 'experience', the strangest, the most immense experience of the war (between twenty and thirty million human beings were deported to the camps), has still not revealed its meaning.

The question 'Why?' was already being asked while the experience was being lived out, in the very heart of the world of the concentration camps. 'What characterizes German cruelty is a certain systematization of the absurd, a certain technique for driving men mad ...'[10] The universe of the absurd! As early as April 1945, a talented journalist offered the following striking vision of this universe:

It was always the same. Nothing corresponded to anything. One of the characteristics of Hitlerian sadism is to rob things of their meaning, to plunge its victims live into a disorientating world ... From that point of view, the journey to the deportation camp was a masterpiece: an interminable roll call which lasted an entire day, carefully packaged bundles which would never be sent on, disconcertingly polite SS officers who became increasingly harsh and brutal as the frontier approached ... Food distributed, but nothing to drink. They had been told to dress up warm, but at Neubourg they were stripped, completely in some carriages, partially in others ...[11]

Then, on arrival at the camp (Buchenwald), frozen with cold, exhausted with thirst, these naked men are ushered into a huge, well-heated hall. Many of them begin to feel more hopeful. Now they are moved to another hall festooned with electric shears; they are shaved by assistants in white coats, and taken to the showers. A veritable resurrection: hot showers, clean towels. Then, suddenly, they are beaten with sticks. Then something makes them laugh, uncontrollably; they are in fits of laughter:

> Behind a counter there were several men who handed us shirts, trousers, hats. They were clothes taken from blokes who had been arrested all over Europe. What a scream ... Cossack trousers, Czech embroidered shirts, hats with feathers ... all of it too small or too big, creased, faded, stretched. When we saw each other we started laughing, and we couldn't stop ...[12]

Clean, disinfected, showered, these men are taken to filthy huts piled high with bunk beds, their restless, emaciated occupants crawling with vermin. The torture begins.

In a recent book, Pelagia Lewinska explains how she had to break with the *moral* way of thinking she had been used to until that point:

> When they arrive the detainees are packed into a bare hall ... A young woman goes into labour. All her friends become concerned, they lay her out on the floor, a woman doctor – also a deportee – tries to take care of her ... But the expected stretcher fails to materialize; the women are surprised, but nevertheless find reasons from 'the other world' for the delay: shortage of staff, poor organization ... And yet someone has the bright idea of asking one of the detainees who was already there. Her answer stuns everyone: 'It's irrelevant ...'[13]

And according to Pelagia Lewinska, everyone began concentrating on one, dreadful question: 'What is Auschwitz?'

And Pelagia Lewinska is still asking herself the question: 'What is Auschwitz?'

The full meaning goes beyond the brute, objective facts. People who were there feel this. Their accounts are clearly marked by the effort to go back in time, back to the numbness, the suffering which killed their feelings and their power to remember, in order to recapture the things 'objective' reports have been unable to grasp. David Rousset has tried to define what he calls 'the universe of the concentration camp'.

> The camps are Ubuesque. Life at Buchenwald is lived under the sign of an outrageous humour, a tragic buffoonery ... [The universe of the concentration camp is] another world, a monstrous universe where human thought falters and ends up lost; a nightmarish Kafka-esque world where everything seems organized according to some implacable, rigid, rational mind; but which one? since everything here is unnatural, dehumanized, mad, manic ...[14]

Madame Lewinska has also evoked this contrast between an obvious absurdity and the hidden and yet rigid rationality which rules overall:

> The idea which governed the way the camp was organized had been well and consciously thought out ... They wanted to debase and humiliate the human dignity within us, to eradicate every trace of humanity from us, to make us feel horrified and disgusted with ourselves ... That was the aim, that was the idea ...[15] What at first seemed carelessness was in fact perversity. What had given the impression of disorder was premeditated, what appeared to be ignorance was subtlety. In organizing a concentration camp they had called upon all the German talent for meticulousness, all the absolute brutality of Hitlerism ...[16]

And as David Rousset writes:

> It is dark. Around five, the men start assembling. There is snow everywhere. The searchlights on the main gate are yelling through the storm like powerful, barbaric horns. 45,000 detainees move towards the parade ground. Every evening, without fail. The sick, the living, the dead. Curses are bitten back and silenced before the gods of the main gate. An emaciated people drag their feet in time to the music of an incongruous, ludicrous band. It is a universe apart. This intense life of the camps has its

laws and its raisons d'être. This people of concentrationists has motivations of its own which have little in common with the existence of a man in Paris or Toulouse, New York or Tbilisi. But the fact that this universe of the concentration camp exists is not unimportant for the meaning of the universe of ordinary people.[17]

A very striking assertion. But if the writer senses a link, he seems to find it rather difficult to define what it is. If the camps formed a universe completely apart, if the 'depths of the camps' afforded an absolutely unique experience, what can they reveal about the meaning of the human universe? He senses a link and cannot discover what it is because he believes (or so it seems) in the rather literary and idealized notion of distinct 'universes'.

The absurd and the rational coexist; absurdity of detail, of appearance, conceals and reveals an overall rationality. This rationality is rigid, cruel, inhuman. It is *scientific barbarity*! ... The 'why' is a torture, which only stops when habit finally kills rationality off (for it is still rationality which asks the questions and which affords the feeling of absurdity!).

These feelings may be pushed to crisis point in the 'universe of the concentration camp', but are they unknown to us men of Paris or Toulouse, New York or Tbilisi? Are they not precisely the most constant of all the feelings underlying everyday life, its very bedrock?

At every moment of lucidity we experience the torture of 'why'. It is the 'normal' state of childhood, which poetry and metaphysics prolong (and we know how much our poets rely on childhood!).

In moments of lucidity we sense the social mystery – all around us, in our most 'modern' towns. Why this? Why that? Habit and familiarity gradually dull our curiosity and bring, not peace, but a comforting indifference. And yet, how many times do we feel ourselves carried away by some enormous power, absurd and yet fearfully rational? In factories, government offices, courts of law, barracks, or simply in cities, an implacable mechanism is at work. And human Reason appears only as a terrifying, distant, dehumanized reason: scientific barbarity. If we are not so stupid as to believe that we have a hold over Reason simply because we utter the word, or that it can be invoked like some cheap goddess, then the only time we are aware of Reason within ourselves is when it raises its head to provoke a feeling of absurdity and to pose the generally unanswerable question: 'Why?' Hidden beneath what appears to be human reason lies an irrational reality; but lying even more deeply hidden beneath what appears to be absurd is a dehumanized Rationality. Where? All around us – though not so much in rural areas as in our 'modern' towns.

All or nearly all accounts of the 'universe of the concentration camp' are reminiscent of the strange universe of Kafka. It is an enlightening reference. Kafka's 'universe' is not and is not intended to be extraordinary, nor does it aspire to be a universe; it is everyday life – or Kafka's view of it – meticulously described and captured in its essence. How should we interpret *The Castle*? Is the hidden, malicious, punctilious, tedious power which drives K ... towards his fate in the village dominated by the Castle the power of bureaucracy? Of Reason? Of Providence or Divine Grace? How easy it is to pass from the social mystery to the theological one! It matters little whether it is the one or the other. The essential thing is that the everyday life of the 'modern' man in modern towns and on industrial housing estates (and above all the life of the ordinary man, the poor man, the worker like K ... in *The Castle*) is *tragically* controlled by unresolved contradictions and by the most painful contradiction of all: that between absurdity and Reason, both equally inhuman, both indivisibly united.

And if we are to understand the *everyday* universe of the modern man, surely we must abandon the illusions created by moral doctrines, together with the illusions – which form such a thick screen between consciousness and the real – of a beneficial Reason and a fully realized individuality. It seems that Madame Lewinska left her illusions behind without falling into another illusion, that of 'another world':

I can only admire the skill with which the Germans had introduced the modern science of man into the way they organized life in the camp. Not only had they applied a system of conditions which killed people, but also, with great precision, they had used the science of psychology in order to disorganize the human soul, to destroy the human being morally ... Who were the women detained in Auschwitz? A motley crew, with every nationality, every faith, every social class, every kind of delinquent. Alongside a handful of political detainees, there were people arrested in street raids, in cafés, in trains, people dealing on the black market or haunting brothels ...[18]

Had this mass of detainees been swept together by chance? Nothing was left to chance at Auschwitz. The Germans made sure that no community could be formed in the camp ... They consciously created a jungle where brutal egoism, trickery, the lack of all deference towards anyone physically weaker, stifled any sense of human solidarity ...[19]

And here is probably the true vision of the concentration camp, the one which sums the experience up:

In this jungle which represented a condensed social image of the Third Reich, humanitarian scruples and thoughtfulness became a ridiculous weakness, while the bestial struggle to go on living was intended to produce a camp 'elite' in the image of the one that governed Germany. Men with a developed social sense, people with a certain cultural or ideological standard, had to perish crushed beneath a blind and primitive animality, paying the price for having subtler minds, for a generosity of spirit which in Hitler's book meant nothing but weakness and inferiority ...[20]

As if in a small State, a social organization was created which was based, and not at all fortuitously, on the Hitlerian theory of the people, the masters and the State.

At the base, a large grey mass of slaves working hard. At the apex the ruling class: white-collar women detainees, all-powerful, with the power of life and death over the majority; well-fed, well-housed, enjoying even the right to love (with the SS and the male detainees).[21]

And here is Auschwitz, *capitalist housing estate*:

If the material conditions of the camp improved it was the upper strata which benefited: the women who had all the wealth – what they had plundered from the slaves. The workers and agricultural labourers went on sleeping in the same huts, went on toiling, being beaten, and dying.[22]

That the concentration camps had other meanings – that they satisfied Hitlerian sadism, that they collected millions of potential hostages, etc. – is doubtless true. But the dominant, essential meaning seems to be this: if Fascism represents the most extreme form of capitalism, the concentration camp is the most extreme and paroxysmal form of a modern housing estate, or of an industrial town.

There are many intermediary stages between our towns and the concentration camps: miners' villages, temporary housing on construction sites, villages for immigrant workers ... Nevertheless, the link is clear.

And it is in the experience of the darkest tragedy – in the seemingly exceptional, at the pinnacle of absurdity, in the pathetic antagonism between man and a still-inhuman Reason – that the very essence of *our* everyday lives, of the most mundane of everyday lives, stands revealed. Will they understand, those who have never been able to see what is all around them? Will the cruel light of the concentration camps at last enable them to understand what towns and 'modern' life really are? And will they be able to understand that the *possibilities* of man and Reason can be transformed into the most monstrous of realities? ...

Up until now human possibilities have only been made available in a limited way, even though it is the 'masses' – the human community – who by their labour supply those possibilities with their material basis.

Through a lack of imagination derived from a lack of (dialectical) reason, most people (among the 'masses' themselves) do not think that things can ever really change. They are quite ready to believe that there will always be the same little shop – or a shop like it – in the same place; or that the same house, the same field, will remain where they are forever.

There are writers who have allowed their imagination to be stimulated by what is possible. They have dreamed; they have 'looked into the future'. And what have they seen? Fabulous palaces, buildings, entire cities devoted to pleasure, cosmic excursions. How many of them have tried to picture what would be in store for everyday life, if bit by bit it were to be raised to the level of what modern technology and science allows? If wealth and power were no longer outside of the community; if those cancerous monstrosities, art for art's sake, thought for thought's sake, power for the sake of power over men, were to disappear?

But should we in turn wish to 'look into the future' and form an image of what it will be, there is one childish error we must avoid: to base the man of the future on what we are now, simply granting him a greater quantity of mechanical means and appliances.

Also (and this is much more difficult and complex), we should acquire a sense of *qualitative* changes, of modifications in the quality of life – and above all of *another attitude of the human being towards himself.*

Our civilization, like every reality, has progressed in an uneven, spasmodic manner, complete with deviations, winding paths and sudden changes of direction.

The natural sciences were the first to progress. For a wide variety of reasons, certain sectors of knowledge and life lagged behind. The sciences of human reality (medicine, physiology and psychology – history – political economy and its applications, etc.) are still behind the natural sciences. As for practical, everyday life – a fundamental sector nevertheless – it is so backward that it can often appear unchanged or merely down-graded.

At certain privileged moments of lucidity or action, an increasingly large number of individuals are able to partake of science, of (technical) power over nature, of political power (organization, State, political life). Rarely, these individuals may succeed in thinking on the level of the Total Man – the level of the Possible. But aside from such privileged moments, even these individuals live almost every instant at a vastly inferior level. The contrast between the possible and the real, which is historical and social in character, is thus shifted (within) the most gifted individuals; it becomes the more-or-less conscious conflict between theory and practice, dream and reality; and this conflict results in disquiet and anguish, like any contradiction which remains unresolved or appears unresolvable.

As far as the majority of human beings are concerned, they only accede to the real and the possible by means of fragmented, monotonous labour, and no one individual can really grasp what the overall meaning and consequences of his labour might be. New forms of community appear tentatively – in action, in politics – but in our country, France, they have not yet been consolidated or made to enter into life, except in the case of the most advanced and lucid 'militants'. In their work as in their 'private' life and leisure activities, most people remain imprisoned within narrow, out-of-date frames of reference. Even if they are worried or discontented, even if they want to smash these social limits, they have no clear idea of the possibilities. They only enjoy derisory scraps and fragments of the power and the splendour they have themselves brought into being. This contradiction is an intolerable one, though it is familiar, and disguised, smothered beneath mountains of ideologies.

In terms of himself, and putting to one side the varieties of

247

community which appear and disappear according to political circumstances, modern man finds himself ever more on his own and defence-
less (by the expression 'modern man', we also mean today's children,
today's adolescents). Moralists call this situation 'moral crisis',
although it definitely concerns something other than moral issues.
Deprived of the wisdom of Antiquity, which no longer has any
meaning in a life so distanced from nature, modern man has not yet
discovered a new wisdom, founded on power over nature (and over his
own nature). Nobody has devised subtler techniques for him which
would allow him to understand himself, to direct his passions, to
control his life. The point has been made many times: we know more
about what goes on in atoms or in the stars than in our own bodies and
'souls'. Everyday life thus still belongs to what Marxist theoreticians
call the 'uncontrolled sector'. And this is what gives a final, sad
meaning to the term 'private life'. The modern individual is 'deprived'
not only of social reality and truth, but of power over himself.

So progress in the way life is organized cannot be limited to
technical progress in external equipment, cannot be confined to an
increase in the quantity of tools.

It will also be a qualitative progress: the individual will stop being a
fiction, a myth of the bourgeois democracies – an empty, negative form
– a pleasant illusion for each human grain of sand. He will cease being
'private' by becoming at the same time more social, more human –
and more individual. We have shown how the forward march of
human reality was progressing according to a dialectical process:
greater *objectification* (the human being becoming more social, and
realizing himself in a world of social, material and human objects) and
deeper *subjectivization* (a more highly developed consciousness,
reflecting on and conscious of power over all reality).

This dialectical progress supposes that the human individual will
become the object (will take himself as the object) of certain infinitely
delicate but efficacious techniques which will give him active power
over himself qua content (and not simply as the empty form of
individuality). Our pedagogy, our psychology, are but tentative
sketches for these future techniques, which will make the subject into
an object for itself (and therefore more real) and the social and
biological object into a subject (consciousness, freedom, active power).

Although they are still very inadequate, and contaminated by the myth of the individual as *already-realized* – a given, a fact like any other biological or social fact – our developing pedagogy and psychology are already showing us that this power over our nature is possible. Here again, the way the real is lagging behind what is possible (not the fictions or the illusions, but what is really possible) is peculiarly characteristic of our times.

So it really is a question of man establishing a new attitude towards man, of a *qualitative* modification in life and culture. We already have the means to demonstrate that this fundamental modification is *possible*. We cannot begin even to imagine its inexhaustible consequences.

All we know is that the gigantic, shapeless movement, with its incoherent and complicated strategies and groundplans, that we have called 'human alienation', must eventually come to an end.

Alienation has stripped life of everything which blessed its primitive frailty with joy and wisdom. Science and power have been acquired, but at the cost of many sacrifices (so much so that the very idea of human sacrifice was an 'essential' stage in man's progress!). The human, stripped bare and projected outside of itself, was and remains at the mercy of forces which in fact come from the human and are nothing but human – but torn apart and dehumanized. This alienation was *economic* (the division of labour; 'private' property; the formation of economic fetishes: money, commodities, capital); *social* (the formation of classes); *political* (the formation of the State); *ideological* (religions, metaphysics, moral doctrines). It was also *philosophical*: primitive man, simple, living on the same level as nature, became divided up into subject and object, form and content, nature and power, reality and possibility, truth and illusion, community and individuality, body and consciousness ('soul', 'mind'). Via these ideological illusions, philosophy has given confused expression to this situation of man: division and supersession, dialectical process, subjectivity and objectivity progressively attained. With its speculative (metaphysical) vocabulary, philosophy is itself part of human alienation. But man has developed only through alienation: the history of truth cannot be separated from the history of errors. So it is that, in so far as it can be separated from an extra-human metaphysics, philosophy must not be condemned in toto, since now it has begun 'superseding' itself and is providing the means to denounce alienation and to indict dehumanization. With its help the problem can be formulated in all its scope: *it poses the question of the total man in its totality*, taking into account the entire range of our knowledge (physics, biology, economy, history . . .). It asserts that the total problem of man (the problem of the total man) is posed and is resolved on the level of everyday life – by a new consciousness of that life, by the transformation of that life. And so philosophy is evolving into a new whole: the theory of knowledge, logic and methodology, social criticism of ideas, criticism of life. Philosophy is no longer speculative, separated from action and life, abstract, contemplative. And yet it is still philosophy: the search for, the discovery of a 'conception of the world', of a *living totality*. By superseding itself, philosophy has achieved a widening, a deepening of philosophy.

But henceforth neither philosophy nor the philosopher can be satisfied with themselves alone, closing their horizons and considering their work done.

Thought, even at its most genuine, is still no more than an exceptional moment. The mass of everyday moments (for the 'philosopher' and the 'scientist', as for everyone else) are only indirectly involved in these flashes of inspiration, these total visions. The metaphor which links thought to mountain tops and clouds is not a completely empty one. We may take it as proven that this metaphor does not express an eternal truth. But the problem remains: how can the 'masses' – whether masses of moments or masses of human beings – 'participate' in a total vision?

Mystics and metaphysicians used to acknowledge that everything in life revolved around exceptional moments. In their view, life found expression and was concentrated in them. These moments were festivals: festivals of the mind or the heart, public or intimate festivals. In order to attack and mortally wound mysticism, it was necessary to show that in fact festivals had lost their meaning, the power they had in the days when all their magnificence came from life, and when life drew its magnificence from festivals. Up until now the principle of Festival has stood for a divorce from life. Whether a festival for the inner or for the outer man, it has involved an increasing proportion of play-acting. Is this life's fate? And are we – the human masses, a mere accumulation of moments in time, fog-bound marshy plains, 'enormous, stupid' crowds – are we fated to contemplate and adore the pinnacles above us, raising ourselves to their level occasionally, only to find ourselves subsequently cast down from the highest points to the lowest depths?

Dialectical materialism negates this destiny, as it negates every 'destiny' which weighs down upon action from without. It negates it –and demonstrates this negation. On this precise point, from this point of view, we are witnessing the 'essence' of Marxism – one of its essential aspects.

Dialectical method applies its criticism to its own efforts as well. The 'vision' of the world it strives for, a vision it first glimpses at certain 'moments' of thought – the total conception of the world, the possiblility of the *total man* – will only make sense once it stops being a 'vision' and a 'conception': once it penetrates life and transforms it. This 'philosophy' wants to be serious without taking itself seriously.

The truly human man will not be a man of a few dazzling moments, a drunken man, a man who feeds upon himself. There have been and will always be visionaries, geniuses or heroes who have their 'moments', moments which may be extraordinarily important and effective. But man will appropriate nature, and will make the world 'the joy man gives himself',[23] for the days, for the centuries yet to come.

The programme we have sketched for a critique of everyday life can be summed up as follows:

(a) It will involve a methodical confrontation of so-called 'modern' life on the one hand, with the past, and on the other – and above all – with *the possible*, so that the points or sectors where a 'decadence' or a withdrawal from life have occurred – the points of backwardness in terms of what is possible – the points where new forms are appearing, rich in possibilities – can be determined.

(b) Studied from this point of view, human reality appears as an opposition and 'contrast' between a certain number of terms: everyday life and festival – mass moments and exceptional moments – triviality and splendour – seriousness and play – reality and dreams, etc.

The critique of everyday life involves an investigation of the exact relations between these terms. It implies criticism of the trivial by the exceptional – *but at the same time* criticism of the exceptional by the trivial, of the 'elite' by the mass – of festival, dreams, art and poetry, by reality.

(c) Equally, the critique of everyday life implies a confrontation of effective human reality with its 'expressions': moral doctrines, psychology, philosophy, religion, literature.

From this point of view, religion is nothing but a direct, immediate, negative, destructive, incessant and skilful criticism of life – skilful enough even to give itself the appearance of not being what it really is.

Philosophy was an *indirect* criticism of life by an external (metaphysical) 'truth'. It is now appropriate to examine the philosophy of the past from this perspective – and that is the task facing 'today's' philosopher. To study philosophy as an indirect criticism of life is to perceive (everyday) life as a direct critique of philosophy.

(d) The relations between groups and individuals in everyday life interact in a manner which in part escapes the specialized sciences. By a process of abstraction these sciences infer certain relations, certain essential aspects, from the extraordinary complexities of human reality. But have they completed this task? It seems that once the relations identified by history, political economy or biology have been extracted from human reality, a kind of enormous, shapeless, ill-defined mass remains. This is the murky background from which known relations and superior activities (scientific, political, aesthetic) are picked out.

It is this 'human raw material' that the study of everyday life takes as its proper object. It studies it both in itself and in its relation with the differentiated, superior forms that it underpins. In this way it will help to grasp the 'total content' of consciousness; this will be its contribution towards the attempt to achieve unity, totality – the realization of the total man.

Going beyond the emotional attempts by philanthropists and sentimental (petty-bourgeois) humanists to 'magnify' humble gestures, and beyond that allegedly superior irony which has systematically devalued life, seeing it merely as back-stage activity or comic relief in a tragedy, the critique of everyday life – critical and positive – must clear the way for a genuine humanism, for a humanism which believes in the human because it knows it.

Toulouse, August–December 1945

Notes

Preface

1. Jean Kanapa, 'Henri Lefebvre ou la philosophie vivante', *La Pensée*, no. 15, November–December 1947.

2. 'Introduction à l'esthétique', *Arts de France*, nos. 19–20 and 21–2, 1947. Detailed bibliography in Rémi Hess, *Henri Lefebvre et l'aventure du siècle*, A.M. Métaillé, Paris 1988.

3. Jean Beaufret, 'A propos de l'existentialisme' (six articles), *Confluences*, 1945; Jean-Paul Sartre, 'A propos de l'existentialisme, mise au point', *Action*, no. 17, 29 December 1944; Henri Lefebvre, 'Existentialisme et marxisme: réponse à une mise au point', *Action*, no. 40, 8 June 1945. On this debate, see Mark Poster, *Existentialist Marxism in Postwar France*, Princeton University Press, Princeton, NJ, 1975.

4. *La Pensée*, no. 15, November–December 1947, p. 2.

5. Unpublished letter to Norbert Guterman, 4 September 1947 (Guterman Papers, Butler Library, Columbia University, New York). See also Hess, *Henri Lefebvre*, pp. 115–20.

6. Jean Bothorel, *Bernard Grasset. Vie et passions d'un editeur*, Grasset, Paris 1989, p. 409.

7. The most detailed account of the 'Nizan affair' is in Pascal Ory, *Nizan. Destin d'un révolté*, Ramsay, Paris 1980, pp. 237–60.

8. Pierre Hervé, *Lettre à Sartre et à quelques autres par la même occasion*, Table Ronde, Paris 1956, p. 124. Henri Lefebvre, 'Autocritique. Contribution à l'effort d'éclaircissement idéologique', *La Nouvelle Critique*, no. 4, March 1949, pp. 41–57; see also his 'Lettre sur Hegel', ibid., no. 22, January 1951.

9. Henri Lefebvre describes these episodes in *La Somme et le reste*, La Nef, Paris 1959, pp. 535–42 and pp. 555–8. I have a copy of *Méthodologie des sciences*.

10. (*Trans.*) 'Art is the highest joy that man can give himself'. See below p. 269, n. 33.

11. Michel Trebitsch, 'Philosophie et marxisme dans les années trente: le marxisme critique d'Henri Lefebvre', *Actes du colloque L'engagement des intellectuels dans la France des années trente*, CERAT, University of Quebec, Montreal 1990.

12. See below p. 270, n. 2.

13. Norbert Guterman and Henri Lefebvre, *La Conscience mystifiée*, Gallimard, Coll. 'Les Essais', Paris 1936. The 'Cinq essais de philosophie matérialiste' listed on the front page are respectively: *La Conscience mystifiée, La Conscience privée, Critique de la vie quotidienne, La Science des idéologies, Matérialisme et culture.*

14. Michel Trebitsch, 'Henri Lefebvre et la revue *Avant-Poste*: une analyse marxiste marginale du fascisme', *Lendemains*, no. 57, 1990.

15. *Avant-Poste*, no. 1, June 1933, pp. 1–9, and no. 2, August 1933, pp. 91–107.

16. *La Conscience mystifiée*, pp. 69–70.

17. Marx, *Early Writings*, trans. R. Livingstone and G. Benton, Penguin, Harmondsworth 1975, p. 379.

18. Guterman Papers, letter dated 17 February 1936.

19. Cf. Agnes Heller, *Everyday Life*, trans. G.L. Campbell, Routledge Chapman and Hall, London 1984.

20. Lukács, *History and Class Consciousness: Studies in Marxist Dialectics*, trans. R. Livingstone, Merlin Press, London 1971.

21. Adorno, *Negative Dialectics*, Seabury Press, New York 1973.

22. Henri Lefebvre, *De la modernité au modernisme (Pour une métaphilosophie du quotidien)*, l'Arche, Paris 1981, pp. 23–5. See also Henri Lefebvre, *Lukàcs 1955*, Aubier, Paris 1986.

23. Heidegger, *Being and Time*, Harper and Row, New York 1962.

24. (*Trans.*) The German *Man* can be rendered in English as 'they' or 'one'. For the problems of translating Heidegger's terminology into English, see George Steiner, *Heidegger*, Harvest Press 1978, pp. 25–71.

25. Lucien Goldmann, *Lukács and Heidegger*, Routledge and Kegan Paul, London 1977.

26. Lukács, *Introduction to Metaphysics*, Yale University Press, New Haven, Conn., 1959.

27. For the broader issues of this debate, see Perry Anderson, *Considerations on Western Marxism*, Verso, London 1976, and Martin Jay, *Marxism and Totality*, University of California Press, Berkeley and Los Angeles 1984.

28. Henri Lefebvre, *La Somme et le reste*, pp. 408–9.

29. Idem, 'Du culte de "l'esprit" au matérialisme dialectique', in Denis de Rougement, 'Cahiers de revendications. Onze témoignages', *Nouvelle Revue Française*, no. 232, 1 December 1932.

30. (*Trans.*) See below p. 127, in fact, the concluding pages of the first chapter.

31. Michel Trebitsch, 'Les mésaventures du groupe *Philosophies* (1924–1933)', *La Revue des revues*, no. 3, Spring 1987; and 'Le groupe *Philosophies* et les Surréalistes (1924–1925)', *Mélusine*, no. XI, 1990. See also the thesis by Bud Burkhard, 'Priests and Jesters: The Philosophies Circle and French Marxism between the Wars', PhD Georgetown University, Washington 1986, typescript.

32. See below p. 123.

33. *L'Esprit*, no. 2, 1927. Published in 1930, *Le Malheur de la conscience dans la philosophie de Hegel* was followed by *Vers le concret* (1932) and *Etudes kierkegaardiennes* (1938).

34. Michel Trebitsch, 'Le renouveau philosophique avorté des années trente. Entretien avec Henri Lefebvre', *Europe*, no. 683, March 1986. On the *Revue marxiste* 'affair', see *La Somme et le reste*, pp. 429–35.

35. In particular in *Philosophies* Henri Lefebvre published 'Fragments d'une philosophie de la conscience' (no. 4, 1924), 'Positions d'attaque et de défense du

nouveau mysticisme' (nos. 5–6, 1925); and in *L'Esprit*: 'La pensée et l'esprit' (no. 1, 1926), 'Reconnaissance de l'unique' and 'Notes pour le procès de la chrétienté' (no. 2, 1927).

36. 'Le même et l'autre' is the title of the introduction he wrote for the 1926 French translation of Schelling's *Of Human Freedom* (Open Court, Chicago 1936).

37. See below p. 216.

38. Ibid., p. 207.

39. Ibid., p. 132.

40. Cf. *La Somme et le reste*, pp. 251–66, and the analysis by Kurt Meyer, *Henri Lefebvre: ein romantischer Revolutionär*, Europa Verlag, Vienna 1973.

41. Hess, *Henri Lefebvre*, p. 114 and pp. 165–8. Cf. Henri Lefebvre, *La vallée de Campan. Etude de sociologie rurale*, PUF, Paris 1963.

42. See below p. 133.

43. In 1946: Georges Friedmann, *Problèmes humains du machinisme industriel*; in 1948: André Varagnac, *Civilisation traditionnelle et genre de vie* and Philippe Ariès, *Histoire des populations françaises et leurs attitudes devant la vie depuis le XVIIIe siècle*; and in 1949 alone: Georges Bataille, *La Part maudite*, Jean Fourastié, *Le Grand espoir de XXe siècle*, Georges Dumézil, *L'Héritage indo-européen à Rome*, Mircéa Eliade, *Le Mythe de d'éternel retour*, Fernand Braudel, *The Mediterranean*, Claude Lévi-Strauss, *The Elementary Structures of Kinship*.

44. Marcel Gauchet, 'Changement de paradigme dans les sciences sociales', in *Les idées en France, 1945–1988, une chronologie*, Gallimard, Paris 1989. On Lefebvre's attacks on 'bourgeois sociology', see his report for the Cercle de Sociologues, at the Journées nationales d'études des intellectuels communistes in *La Nouvelle Critique*, no. 45, April–May 1953.

45. Henri Lefebvre, *Everyday Life in the Modern World*, trans. S. Rabinowitch, Allen Lane, The Penguin Press, London 1971, p. 25.

46. Ibid., p. 24.

47. Henri Lefebvre, *La Proclamation de la Commune*, Gallimard, Paris 1965. See also: Richard Gombin, *Les origines du gauchisme*, Seuil, Paris 1971; *Internationale situationniste, 1958–1969*, facsimile reprint, Champ libre, Paris 1975. The influence on Jean Baudrillard, who was Lefebvre's assistant at Nanterre, is also undeniable (*La société de consommation*, Gallimard, Paris 1970).

48. See above all Thomas Kleinspehn, *Der Verdrängte Alltag: Henri Lefebvres marxistische Kritik des Alltagslebens*, Focus Verlag, Glessen 1975.

Foreword

1. Written in 1945, published by Editions Grasset, Paris 1947. The text is reissued here in its entirety, including certain passages which the author now considers out-of-date.

2. Lenin, 'What the Friends of the People Are', in *Collected Works*, vol. 1, Progress Publishers, Moscow 1963, p. 141.

3. Lenin, 'On the Question of Dialectics', in *Collected Works*, vol. 38, p. 360. Since the Twentieth Congress of the Soviet Communist Party it has become fashionable

among Marxists to make fun of quotations: 'the shortest way from one idea to another'. The men who started this fashion are precisely the ones who were unable to write a single line or say a single sentence without quoting Stalin. Nowadays they have found other ways of disguising their ignorance and the emptiness of their minds.

4. (*Trans.*) Not only were the ideas not 'ripe', but the Stalinist dogmatism of the French Communist Party had been and was a formidable obstacle to their development. Lefebvre felt this keenly, and during the decade between the two editions of the *Introduction* he was regarded with increasing suspicion by the Party directorate. The development of his critique of everyday life must be seen in the context of his growing malaise with the prevailing ideologies within the PCF. The Khrushchev report of 1956 was instrumental in permitting the open criticisms of Stalinism which appear in this Foreword, but in any event Lefebvre was disciplined and excluded from the Party shortly after its publication, making it one of the last things he wrote before his independence, which he inaugurated in 1959 with his remarkable autobiography *La Somme et le reste*.

5. (*Trans.*) Lefebvre's translations of the *1844 Manuscripts* were the first to appear in France (in the review *Avant-Poste*, 1933, and in *Morceaux choisis de Marx*, 1934, both in collaboration with Norbert Guterman), and the theory of alienation they propose was to afford one of the linchpins of his critique of everyday life. Marx uses various words to express the concept – *Entfremdung, Verfremdung, Entwirklichung, Verselbständigung, Entaüsserung, Vergängliching* – but it is Lefebvre's practice to translate them all by the single word 'alienation'. His particular contribution is to extend it from the domain of work into everyday life in general, and specifically – in this Foreword – into the realm of leisure activities. For problems relating to the translation of these terms from German into English, see the Glossary of Key Terms in Marx's *Early Writings*, Penguin, Harmondsworth 1975.

6. This argument was developed in my *Pour comprendre la pensée de Marx*, Bordas, Paris 1947. It is of course well known that various interpretations of Marx's early writings have been proposed by Gurvitch, Merleau-Ponty and Sartre. Some important recent works have helped to pose the question more clearly, notably Pierre Bigo's *Marxisme et humanisme*, PUF, Paris 1953, and Jean-Yves Calvez's *La Pensée de Karl Marx*, Seuil, Paris 1956.

7. Presented in the Preface to *Capital* as well as in Lenin's 'What the Friends of the People Are', something that Henri Chambre appears to neglect in his *Le Marxisme en Union Soviétique*, Seuil, Paris 1955, cf. pp. 48, 505, etc.

8. (*Trans.*) Léon Brunschvicg was a leading figure of the French philosophical establishment, and Lefebvre studied under him at the Sorbonne in 1920. In response to Brunschvicg's scientific culture and mathematical intellectualism, Lefebvre began for the first time to develop the desire for a concrete, total reality which was to lead him to Marx and to the critique of everyday life.

9. (*Trans.*) The group which was associated with A. Kojève just after the war, and which included Maurice Merleau-Ponty, Jean-Paul Sartre, Jean Hyppolite, le Père Fessard, etc.

10. It would be unfair, however, not to recall that Emmanuel Mounier and Georges Gurvitch indicated their approval.

11. (*Trans.*) Husserl's 'phenomenological reduction', namely the 'bracketing' or suspension of belief in objects.

12. Cf. for example Jacques Soustelle's book on *La Vie quotidienne des Aztèques*, Hachette, Paris 1955. (*Trans.*: A similar series of books was published in England and

the United States during the 1960s by Batsford and Putnam respectively.)

13. Cf. Lévi-Strauss, 'Diogène caché', *Les Temps Modernes*, no. 110, p. 203. Is Lévi-Strauss not going too far in this direction? Is this perhaps his way of compensating for the extreme intellectuality of his position?

14. *L'Express*, no. 5, March 1955. Unsigned.

15. Ermilov, *Dramaturgie de Tcheckhov*, Moscow 1948 (quoted in the French edition of Chekhov's plays, translated by Elsa Triolet, Editeurs français réunis, Paris 1954, p. 17).

16. Which cannot be separated from the extraordinary success of the 'Salon des Arts Ménagers' (*trans.*: Ideal Home Exhibition).

17. Cf. the sociological studies of Chombart de Lauwe, Andrée Michel, Lucien Brams, etc. There is a complex of economic phenomena, social facts and 'crises' of various kinds from which the housing crisis cannot be separated.

18. A distinction must be made between the deterioration of everyday life and impoverishment. They are related but different phenomena, and up to a point one can exist without the other.

19. Jean Duvignaud, 'Le mythe Chaplin', *Critique*, May 1954 (a survey of recent works on Chaplin). But Duvignaud lays too much emphasis on the defeated, tragic, 'down-and-out' aspect of Charlie Chaplin. In this connection it is worth noting a curious mythology that has developed in recent years, one which treats failure as an index of authenticity. This is a form (or ethic) worked up on the basis of a fact of everyday life, namely disappointment, to which has been added an important ideological dimension, namely the proof of authenticity. We shall need to come back later to the nature of this disappointment, its content and meaning. Embracing such a mythology could make Stalinists out of people with not the slightest inclination in that direction. For when history judges him, Stalin's one and only justification will be that he was victorious. Moreover, it is certain that if a new optimism is to be founded and if humanism is to be renewed, at least one victory without lies and violence must be demonstrated, at least one victory which is not smeared with blood and mire . . .

20. The theory of the *reverse image* differs considerably from the magical theory of the *double* on which Edgar Morin bases his analysis of the cinema (cf. *Le Cinéma ou l'homme imaginaire*, Editions de Minuit, Paris 1956, notably pp. 31ff.). In the romantic press we find the *reverse image* of the everyday life of women, of their aspirations and their profound needs in contemporary society. But a book like Hemingway's *The Old Man and the Sea* also contains a reverse image – that of the toil, the illusions and the failures of individual and 'private' everyday life. He presents these in all their profound drama, while placing them in the very setting that they lack: the luminosity of the sea, the immensity of the horizon . . .

21. (*Trans.*) Directed in 1953 by Herbert J. Biberman, and sponsored by the International Union of Mine, Mill and Smelter Workers, this film used Mexican-American miners to reconstruct a strike which had actually taken place. Many of the people involved in the production were persecuted by the Unamerican Activities Committee.

22. Too often 'realist' writers, authors or film directors do the opposite. Instead of extracting *the extraordinary from the ordinary*, they take the ordinary as it stands (the average actions of a man like any other man, the average events in a day like any other day) and are at great pains to make them interesting by putting them under a microscope like 'specimens', and insisting how very interesting they are. When in fact they have merely painted the grey in proletarian, peasant or petty-bourgeois life with

false colours. As Brecht said, such 'realists' merely repeat the obvious ad nauseam.

23. Brecht, 'The Street Scene', in *Brecht on Theatre*, ed. J. Willett, Methuen, London 1978, p. 126.

24. Brecht, 'The Life of Galileo', in *Plays*, vol. 1, trans. J. Willett, Methuen, London 1960, p. 231.

25. (*Trans.*) A reference to Sartre's *Being and Nothingness* (trans. H. Barnes, Methuen, London 1957, pp. 59ff.).

26. The chapter 'Having, Doing and Being' in Sartre's *Being and Nothingness* offers an indirect critique of everyday life, carried out in a speculative manner and aimed at solving the problem that 'there is nothing in consciousness which is not consciousness of being ... Nothing comes to me that I have not chosen.' This way of posing the question completely avoids the problem of concrete alienation. Cf. ibid., pp. 525ff. for the difficulties Sartre encounters when he tries to show that alienation is (after all) desired as such. (*Trans.*: In French the word 'privé' and its derivatives mean both 'private' and 'deprived', and Lefebvre ironizes on this throughout in a way which is inevitably blunted in translation.)

27. The 'ego', with its (apparently) well-defined outlines, is a fact of history. It appears in the eighteenth century (although of course its seeds were sown earlier, it was prefigured in various ways, etc.). It has a practical foundation in the internal contradiction of bourgeois life, where relations become more numerous while the individual himself becomes more isolated. Concomitant with it are ideologies and ethical attitudes. The impression of well-defined outlines comes from the influence of individual attitudes and ideologies upon lived experience. And yet, beyond these outlines (and the people concerned admit it themselves) there persists a zone of obscurity which is only gradually being explored.

28. Cf. *In Camera* (Sartre) or *Waiting for Godot* (Beckett), or the plays of Ionesco, Adamov, etc.

29. (*Trans.*) In French the word 'jeu' and its derivatives mean 'play', 'gambling' and 'acting', which permit ambiguities which are difficult to render in translation.

30. We are even sometimes unsure on the political level, despite the fact that – in principle – it is a level on which the element of chance is reduced to a minimum; and on the strategic level, where the aim is always to determine an outcome.

31. Here specialists will recognize analyses borrowed from operational logic (considered as a reflection of everyday life *as well*) and from decision theory. This theory takes an aspect of what seems to be the domain of the irrational (pure will, etc.) and makes it rational.

32. Action based on knowledge transforms necessity into freedom, certainly. But knowledge – even when directed towards an 'essence' – can only ever be approximate. That is why decisions always involve risk, while at the same time partaking of the absolute; and why they often imply a gamble or wager. Do they also perhaps involve art? For the classic Marxist theorists, politics becomes a science, but insurrection remains an *art*. (Cf. in particular Lenin and his commentary on Marx in 'Advice of an Onlooker', in *Selected Works*, Progress Publishers, Moscow 1967, pp. 426–7).

33. (*Trans.*) Transliteration of the Greek *koivov*, meaning 'common to all the people'.

34. Brecht, *Brecht on Theatre*, p. 37.

35. In the book referred to above, Edgar Morin studies some bad films (considered in the same way as 'good' films, as sociological data) and concludes that aesthetic emotions are of a magical nature. Here he is following Jean-Paul Sartre's analyses of the

imagination, and this leads him to make some superficial evaluations (cf. *Le Cinéma du l'homme imaginaire*, note, p. 160).

36. As Geneviève Serreau has pointed out in *Brecht*, Editions de l'Arche, Paris 1955, pp. 44, 82, etc.

37. (*Trans.*) In English in the original.

38. Cf. René Wintzen, *Introduction aux poèmes de Brecht*, Seghers, Paris 1954, p. 139.

39. Georg Buchner, *Danton's Death*, trans. J. Maxwell, Methuen, London 1968, p. 38.

40. (*Trans.*) Vailland was a personal friend of Lefebvre's, and a PCF member until the Khrushchev report and the invasion of Hungary led him to resign. His novel *The Law* (1957) was a great international success.

41. In his book *L'Expérience du drame*, Corréa, Paris 1953.

42. Club du Livre du Mois, Paris 1956.

43. (*Trans.*) The *pays du Tendre* was the allegorical region of amorous feelings invented in the seventeenth century by Mme de Scudéry.

44. *Beau Masque*, Gallimard, Paris 1954, p. 153.

45. 'Nothing is more graceful than a woman occupied in the small tasks of the kitchen', ibid., p. 148.

46. Irwin Shaw. *The Troubled Air* (1951), Hodder and Stoughton, London 1988, p. 75.

47. Ibid., p. 299. (*Trans.*: Set during the period of the Unamerican Activities Committee, Shaw's book gives a gripping account of the destructive effect of dogmatism on the left as well as the right, and one can understand Lefebvre's interest in it in 1958.)

48. Virginia Woolf, *A Room of One's Own*, Hogarth Press, London 1935, p. 131.

49. Autocritique: in the text below, first published in 1947, the reader will find a partially unjust assessment of Surrealism. The author was carried away by his polemic, and consequently his point of view was one-sided. The errors of Surrealism as a doctrine (pseudo-philosophical, with a pseudo-dialectic of the real and the dream, the physical and the image, the everyday and the marvellous) notwithstanding, it did express some of the aspirations of its time. As a doctrine, Surrealism ended up with some particular forms of alienation: with the *image-thing*, magic and the occult, semi-morbid states of mind. However, its scorn for the prosaic bourgeois world, its radical rebellion, did mean something. And the hypothesis that only the *excessive* image can come to grips with the profundity of the real world – a hypothesis which one can identify just as much with Picasso, Eluard and Tzara as with André Breton – needs to be taken seriously.

50. (*Trans.*) Made in 1931, Nikolai Ekk's celebrated film was about the rehabilitation of a group of juvenile delinquents in Russia.

51. Reserving the term *individuality* stricto sensu for forms of consciousness and activity which emerged in the eighteenth century.

52. Definition of leisure given by Joffre Dumazedier: 'An occupation to which the worker can devote himself of his own free will, outside of professional, familial and social needs and obligations, in order to relax, to be entertained or to become more cultivated' (Symposium on Leisure at the Centre d'études sociologiques, 10.1.54). Cf. also the article by the same author in the *Encyclopédie française* on 'la Civilisation quotidienne'.

53. Such exploitation was examined during a study week at Marly, from 28 March 1955 to 3 April 1955 (Publications du centre d'Education populaire de Marly [roneo]). (*Trans.*: This study week dealt specifically with the problems of youth activities with

special concern for leisure and cultural activities. Lefebvre's own contribution was a paper on the women's press. His interest in this area in the 1950s is touched upon in this Foreword, but left undeveloped. The paper itself, though short, is much more explicit, and presents a model and a method for cultural analysis which seems well ahead of its time.)

54. Replies to various surveys, notably those carried out by Joffre Dumazedier and his team.

55. Psycho-physiologically the sexual image abruptly 'refreshes' the unconditioned stimulus which is already linked to a number of conditional stimuli and inserted in 'stereotypes'. It links it to a new signal (for example the trademark on a poster). That these images are effective presupposes both conditioning (triviality) and the inadequacy of this conditioning, the absence of social fixation and human determination by 'instinct'. It presupposes the hidden demands imposed by the shift from habitual but unstable and uncontrolled conditioning to a new type of conditioning: i.e. dis-satisfaction.

56. Genuine strangeness (a *valid* aesthetic category) can be seen in Melville, Gogol or Kafka. It must be properly distinguished from a strange (and mystifying) *tone* used to speak about trivial things in a trivial way. The reverse image can also produce valid literary procedures (*In Camera*, a dark, brilliant, *definitive* little play, and Jean-Paul Sartre's best). The case of the children's press is different from the 'case' of the romantic press and crime fiction. They have a common element: the break with – and transport out of – normality. However, the children's press and children's literature have their own set of themes. Less structured than, and differently structured to, the world of the adult, the child's world does not require the same kind of reverse image. In fact there is no world of the child. The child lives in society, and in his eyes the adult world is what is strange and marvellous – or odious. *Simply being a child makes him already a critic of adult everyday life*, but it is in this everyday life that he must search for his future and disentangle his own potential. In the works which are most successful from this point of view, a familiar animal (a dog, a duck, a mouse) supports a reverse image in which the trivial changes into fantasy and the fantastic, with an element of explicit criticism.

57. (*Trans.*) 'Sportsmen' and 'supporters' are in English in the original.

58. (*Trans.*) An independent Marxist sociologist who specialized in the world of work and leisure. Lefebvre and he were fellow students at the Sorbonne, but after Friedmann left the PCF in 1939, their relationship became increasingly acrimonious.

59. Georges Friedmann, *Où va le travail humain*, Gallimard, Paris 1950, p. 22.

60. Ibid., p. 242.

61. Ibid., p. 244.

62. Ibid., pp. 336–64.

63. Ibid., p. 268.

64. Ibid., p. 370.

65. Lenin, 'The Highest Stage of Capitalism', in *Selected Works*, vol. 1, Progress Publishers, Moscow 1967, p. 776.

66. Marx, *Capital*, vol. 3, trans. D. Fernbach, Penguin, Harmondsworth 1981, p. 959.

67. (*Trans.*) In English in the original.

68. Jean-Marie Domenach, 'La Yougoslavie et la relance du socialisme, *Esprit*, December 1956, pp. 812–13.

69. Unfortunately materialism is presented in far too many publications as the most depressing of platitudes. In fact it appears to reach the heights of platitude (so to

speak). If it were a completed system, or simply a weapon for the working-class struggle, why indeed would it have to be *interesting*? After all, when philosophy lost metaphysics, it might also be said to have lost its picturesqueness! ...

70. Let us reiterate that the *everyday* struggle in Russia to achieve properly observed labour norms and increased yield and productivity in factories and collective farms can also express itself in an *epic* style. This alone does not suffice as a definition of socialism. The Stalinist definition: 'to maintain the maximum satisfaction of material and cultural needs ...' does not get very far. For what is required is to show *what needs* are specific to socialist society, what needs characterize it, are born in it and from it. Khrushchev has already gone beyond this in his Report at the Twentieth Congress in his demand for an improvement in 'the qualitative structure of consumption'.

71. (*Trans.*) *Critique de la vie quotidienne 2: fondements d'une sociologie de la quotidienneté*, L'Arche, Paris 1961.

72. Let us be clear about this. Stalin was a Marxist; and even a great one, according to Khrushchev (on 1 January 1957). And yet it is impossible not to talk about a Stalinist *interpretation* of Marxism (or even of Leninism).

73. Lenin, 'Plan of Hegel's Dialectics', in *Collected Works*, vol. 38, p. 320.

74. Cf. *Introduction à la critique de l'économie politique* in Laura Lafargue's translation, Edition Giard, p. 342, and *La Pensée*, Colloque du 19 mai 1955, no. 66, p. 35, and also Emile Bottigelli, 'Faits et lois dans les sciences sociales', *La Nouvelle Critique*, January 1956.

75. It is easy to see how this interpretation differs from class and party subjectivism. Marx discovered the working class, its alienation, its 'negativity', its struggles, its historic mission, *and he took its side*, analysing bourgeois society, starting from all existing knowledge, *gaining knowledge* of it in its *totality*, with all its becoming, its aspects, its limits.

76. Marx, 'Economic and Philosophical Manuscripts', in *Early Writings*, Penguin, Harmondsworth 1975, pp. 322–30.

77. Ibid., p. 360.

78. Ibid., p. 369.

79. Ibid., p. 349.

80. Ibid., p. 358.

81. Ibid., p. 366.

82. Which is what some otherwise highly informed exponents or critics of Marxism appear to believe (cf. for example Calvez, *La Pensée de Karl Marx*, pp. 626ff.).

83. (*Trans.*) László Rajk was a minister in the Hungarian government from 1943 until 1949, when he was arrested as part of the Stalinist purges. He was executed after a 'show trial' which aroused an international outcry, and was posthumously rehabilitated in 1956. The Khrushchev report to the Twentieth Congress of the Soviet Communist Party has been called 'one of the most important documents of our century'. It caused disarray in the PCF, where it was denounced as a forgery. In *La Somme et le reste* (1959) Lefebvre describes how his friends in the Party were 'traumatized, morally and physically sickened' by it, while he himself remained unmoved. Obviously, the crimes of Stalinism came as no surprise to him.

84. Marx, 'Economic and Philosophical Manuscripts', p. 351.

85. (*Trans.*) The pages which follow draw extensively upon Hegel cf. note 86 below).

86. Cf. Norbert Guterman and Henri Lefebvre, *Morceaux choisis de Hegel*, Gallimard, Paris 1939, notably pp. 144ff.; also Jean Hyppolite, *Logique et existence*, PUF,

Paris 1953, notably pp. 91ff., and idem, *Etudes sur Marx et Hegel*, Rivière, Paris 1955, which poses several problems remarkably well, but which draws conclusions which we would disagree with. (*Trans*. Lefebvre's Introduction to the *Morceaux choisis* attempted to rehabilitate Hegel's reputation in France, arguing that the opposition between Fascism and Marxism rendered his work of great contemporary importance, since both had their roots in Hegel's philosophy.)

87. This is something Jean Wahl has seen perfectly in his *La Conscience malheureuse chez Hegel*, Reider, 1926. Cf. also Benjamin Fondane, *La Conscience malheureuse*, Denoël et Steele, Paris 1936, Georg Lukàcs, *Die Zeistörung der Vernunft* (The Destruction of Reason), Berlin 1954, and Löwith, *Von Hegel bis Nietzsche*, Europa Verlag, Zurich 1947.

88. This is what J.-Y. Calvez seems to be saying in *La Pensée de Karl Marx*, particularly in the section where he argues against Marx's analysis of the formation of capitalism at the heart of the feudal mode of production (pp. 610ff). It is an argument which paves the way not for mysticism but for a reinstatement of traditional theology.

89. Here we are faced once more with the difficulty of terminology pointed out above (cf. note 51). The individual *stricto sensu* did not appear before the eighteenth century, with the growing complexity of social relations.

90. In everyday life, *ready-made expressions*, frequently taken from eras long past and remote activities, play an important role (as 'throw down the gauntlet', 'fire a Parthian shaft', and so on). Such commonplaces are in fact strange places, where analysis discovers both archaic modes of behaviour and superseded models. The same remarks apply to the thousands of superstitions (touching wood, throwing spilt salt over one's shoulder), to interjections, whose magical character is often quite clear, to the rituals of politeness and etiquette, etc. In this sense, the collecting of archaisms and the study of their uses is a task for anthropology and sociology.

91. Any professional philosopher who reads this will recognize a variety of contemporary doctrines, despite the brevity and the particular slant they are given here. We are happy to leave the task of naming them and analysing them to him. It's a philosophical guessing game.

92. (*Trans.*) A reference to Rimbaud's 'Letter to Paul Demeny', *Collected Poems*, Penguin, Harmondsworth 1960, p. 10.

93. Cf. Descartes: 'I will always be more indebted to those to whose favour I owe the ability to enjoy my leisure without restriction, than to those who might offer me the most honourable employment on earth.'

94. (*Trans.*) Cf. above, n. 11.

95. In this sense and from this point of view phenomenology and existentialism can be defined as philosophies which have fallen to the level of the everyday (a symptom of the crisis of 'pure' philosophy), but which have retained the negative characteristics of traditional philosophy: devaluation of the everyday (of the factitious, of the instrumental, etc.) in favour of pure or tragic moments – criticism of life through anguish or death – artificial criteria of authenticity, etc.

96. (*Trans.*) Lefebvre's translation has 'philosophical' here instead of 'German'.

97. Marx, 'A Contribution to the Critique of Hegel's Philosophy of Right. Introduction', in *Early Writings*, p. 250.

98. Marx, 'On the Jewish Question', ibid., p. 234.

99. Ibid., p. 220.

100. Ibid., p. 233.

101. Cf. Stalin, *Anarchism and Socialism*.

102. In the capitalist economy, commodities exchanged must be consumed. It is a

matter of indifference to the capitalist whether the commodity produced corresponds to a genuine need or not, or whether it is effectively consumed, as long as it is paid for and the profit (surplus-value) is realized as money. It is even possible to stimulate false needs. The theory of a capitalist production determined by needs is therefore a mystification; however, like all mystifications, it contains an element of truth, without which it would be meaningless. Sooner or later need intervenes; and the commodity which does not correspond to a need disappears from the market.

103. Including the disappearance (loss? theft?) of several notebooks containing the draft of the second volume.

104. (*Trans.*) Inevitably the second volume differs in many respects from this proposed plan.

Chapter I

1. (*Trans.*) Thinly veiled references to Gide's *Fruits of the Earth* (1897) and *The Immoralist* (1902).

2. (*Trans.*) In his translation of Baudelaire's *Intimate Journals*, Christopher Isherwood renders this as 'Squibs and Crackers'.

3. I shall deal with failure, defeat and the duality of the individual in *La Conscience privée*, where I shall study the history and structure of individuality. (*Trans.*: The book never appeared.)

4. (*Trans.*) Notably in *Le Génie du Christianisme* (1802), which contributed to the revival of religion in France in the aftermath of the Revolution.

5. (*Trans.*) Set in Scotland, 'L'Aigle du Casque' (*La Légende des siècles* 1, 1859) tells of the pursuit and slaughter of the youth Angus by the evil Tiphaine. The eagle in question comes to life from Tiphaine's helmet and exacts a bloody retribution. *La Légende des siècles* itself was written between 1859 and 1883, and is composed of a series of epic poems which set out to portray the history of humanity. As the title suggests, Hugo envisages history as legend or myth.

6. Baudelaire, 'The Painter of Modern Life', in *Selected Writings on Art and Artists*, trans. P.E. Charvet, Cambridge University Press, Cambridge 1981, p. 329. (*Trans.*: The essay examines the paintings and sketches of Constantin Guys.)

7. Ibid.

8. Ibid., p. 398.

9. Baudelaire, *Intimate Journals*, trans. Christopher Isherwood, Blackamore Press, London 1930, p. 36.

10. Ibid., p. 39.

11. Baudelaire possessed specific information about this dialectic, although it is difficult to say how he obtained it. Who is he referring to in the following lines: 'Portrait of the literary rabble. Doctor Estaminetus Crapulosus Pedantissimus ... His Hegelism'? (Ibid., p. 74.) He himself (Baudelaire) could write in the purest Hegelian spirit: 'What is the Fall? If it is unity become duality, it is God who has fallen. In other words, would not creation be the fall of God?' (Ibid., p. 75.) And a little further on: 'two contradictory ideas ... are identical ... this identity has always existed. This identity is history.' (Ibid., p. 98.)

12. Ibid., p. 49.
13. Ibid., p. 69.
14. Ibid., p. 99.
15. Ibid., p. 91.
16. Ibid., p. 42.
17. Ibid., p. 37.

18. Here it is appropriate to distinguish between the case made with such obstinate ill-humour by Julien Benda and our own. Benda proclaimed himself the censor of his age in the name of classical, eternal, unchanging Reason. His bill of indictment was based precariously on a misunderstanding: as Gaëtan Picon properly points out in *Confluences*, no. 6, the target for his attacks shifted back and forth between what may be called anti-intellectualism and what may be called anti-rationalism. He failed to understand fully the philosophical distinction between intelligence (the faculty for understanding and analysis) and reason (the faculty for unity and synthesis). Instead of carefully defining his terms, he relied on the common-sense and accepted opinions of 'the man in the street' for the meaning of the words he used. But, 'if we ask the man in the street what his views are on Proust, Valéry and Gide, he will reply that they are too intellectual' (Auguste Anglès, *Action*, 28 September 1945).

One can accuse all 'modernity' of not respecting the canon of traditional reason, but not of being anti-intellectual, quite the reverse.

And in any case, if traditional reason, embodied in Julien Benda, complains that it is being abandoned, then surely there is something complacent about its claim to be eternal. And should not traditional reason itself accept some responsibility? What we went in search of, however, was a new Reason capable of organizing the human world, of acting within time rather than claiming to be beyond it. And we found a new Reason, effective and concrete. As the reader will have realized, we are referring to Dialectical Reason.

We do not put 'modernity' in the dock on the grounds that it is irrational, but more generally because it is an attack on mankind in its very life and totality – an attack which, seen in another light, has helped to define the problem, to sharpen the sense that it is serious, and even to contribute some elements towards its solution. (*Trans.*: Benda was an ardent critic of most forms of modernism, and considered that it was the duty of the intellectual (the 'clerc') to defend against the erosion of universal values by the introduction of transitory concerns (such as politics) into literature. His most famous book was *La Trahison des clercs*, but Lefebvre himself was particularly influenced in his youth by *Belphégor* (1918). Writing about this in *La Somme et le reste*, he says: 'I could have become a Surrealist ... if it had not been for André Breton's insufferable personality – and for Julien Benda ... His very existence proves that the thesis of the "destruction of reason" is not valid for France, and that Lukács is exaggerating when he suggests that this destruction is characteristic of the philosophical history of capitalism, imperialism and the bourgeoisie. Moreover, Benda's dogmatism paved the way rather well for Marxist dogmatism ... Influenced by Benda, I began deliberately to do the things I didn't enjoy – like abandoning my first love, Schumann, and adopting his polar opposite, Bach ...')

19. Rimbaud, 'The Drunken Boat', in *Collected Poems*, Penguin, Harmondsworth 1960, p. 167.
20. 'Letter to Paul Demeny', ibid., p. 10.
21. 'Letter to Georges Izambard', ibid., p. 6.
22. Ibid.

23. (*Trans.*) Coined by Franz Roh in 1925 to qualify an aspect of German art, the term has of course been used subsequently for a wide range of authors.

24. André Breton, *Manifestos of Surrealism*, University of Michigan Press, Ann Arbor, 1977, p. 123. (*Trans.*: This use of the title 'Monsieur' is particularly contemptuous – a tonal device adopted by Lefebvre elsewhere in this book – and reveals the personal antipathy he felt for Breton. However, his relations with the Surrealist group as a whole had always been difficult. The Surrealists had been perceived as rivals by the *Philosophies* group which Lefebvre led between 1921 and 1929. An attempt to merge the two groups in 1925 was unsuccessful (ironically Lefebvre was instructed by his colleagues to tell the Surrealists that the *philosophes* would not be prepared to relinquish their belief in 'the Eternal'), and subsequent relations between them were acrimonious. In *La Somme et le reste* Lefebvre admits that under different circumstances he could have been a Surrealist, and in the Foreword to this *Introduction to the Critique of Everyday Life* he qualifies his antagonism. Cf. above, Foreword, n. 49. Nevertheless, Lefebvre continued to consider Surrealism as an extreme form of aesthetic individualism.)

25. Antonin Artaud, *Oeuvres complètes*, vol. 6, Gallimard, Paris 1966, p. 16.

26. Cf. Maurice Nadeau, *The History of Surrealism*, trans. R. Howard, Penguin, Harmondsworth 1978.

27. Ibid., p. 85.

28. André Breton, *Les pas perdus*, NRF, Paris 1924, p. 110.

29. On the subject of this *Pedantissimus*, his literary career and the principles of government he employed, we may relish *A Corpse* by Jacques Prévert, and reprinted in Nadeau's *History of Surrealism*, p. 301: 'When he was alive, he wrote to shorten his time, he said, to find men, and when he happened to find them, he was mortally afraid, and pretending an overpowering affection, lay in wait for the moment when he could cover them with filth.'

30. Breton, *Manifestos of Surrealism*, p. 26.

31. Ibid.

32. Ibid., p. 14.

33. Louis Aragon, *Paris Peasant*, trans. Simon Watson Taylor, Cape, London 1971, p. 24.

34. Ibid., p. 27.

35. Ibid., p. 28.

36. (*Trans.*) A reference to Eugène Sue's novel of criminality in nineteenth-century Paris (*Mysteries of Paris*, Dedalus, Sawtry, UK 1988). Marx examines it at length in *The Holy Family*.

37. Salvador Dali, quoted in *The History of Surrealism*, p. 200.

38. Ibid., p. 204. (*Trans.*: The object described is Giacometti's sculpture *L'Heure des traces.*)

39. Ibid., pp. 204–5.

40. André Breton, *Mad Love*, trans. Mary Ann Caws, University of Nebraska, Lincoln and London, 1987, pp. 15–16.

41. This law, the first of the laws which the critique of everyday life will formulate, has already been hinted at by some sociologists, but on the whole it has been disregarded. Thus Roger Caillois, for whom the 'sacred' is an external category of feeling, has simply failed to understand its fate.

Jean Effel's charming drawings of angels, saints and holy fathers in comic postures are much more 'profound' in this connection than much of what the professional sociologists have produced.

42. (*Trans.*) A reference to Apollinaire's poem 'L'Enchanteur pourrissant'.

43. *Intimate Journals*, p. 92.

44. (*Trans.*) Baudelaire's most famous presentation of this idea is in the sonnet 'Correspondences', in *Selected Poems*, trans. and introd. Joanna Richardson, Penguin, Harmondsworth 1975, p. 43.

45. M. Chestov, *Pouvoirs des clefs*, Pléiade, Paris 1928, p. 382.

46. Benjamin Fondane, *La Conscience malheureuse*, Denoël et Steele, Paris 1936, pp. 270–71.

47. (*Trans.*) Between 1945 and 1950 the PCF attempted to put on a united front to condemn Sartre's existentialism, which was perceived as being idealist, individualistic and anti-Communist, and as the Party's leading intellectual Lefebvre directed the attack, notably in *L'existentialisme* (1946). Some of the acrimony of this classic 'argument', which is well-documented in Mark Poster's *Existentialist Marxism in Postwar France*, is apparent in the references made to Sartre throughout the *Introduction*.

48. (*Trans.*) Garcin in *In Camera*.

49. (*Trans.*) Brilliant for the power and inventiveness of his novels (the most famous being *Journey to the End of the Night*), despicable – presumably – on account of his anti-semitism and his defection to the Nazis in 1944.

50. Jean Cassou, *Le Centre du monde*, Sagittaire, Paris 1945, p. 199.

51. Ibid., p. 238.

52. It is rather significant that Aragon's great novel *Aurélien* should also be a novel of defeat (the failure of a man and a woman, the failure of a love). Why failure? Through duality. Bérénice is in love with Aurélien, and her love is 'absolute': Aurélien is in love with Bérénice. As both of them are indecisive, idle beings, as 'relative' as it is possible to be, and led on by circumstances over which they have no control, they are unable either to fulfil or even to recognize their love. The most moving parts of the book are achieved through the intervention of a *magical* object: a strangely beautiful plaster mask ...

The author's social realism appears only marginally in the story. By an analogous contradiction, Marcenac's short story 'A Merveille' is a satire on the marvellous written in a wonder-struck manner.

Chapter 2

1. (*Trans.*) Charles Maurras and Maurice Barrès were both writers with nationalist right-wing credentials. Maurras was a founder member of Action française.

2. Marc Bloch, *Caractères originaux de l'histoire rurale française*, Colin, Paris 1956, pp. 64–5.

3. (*Trans.*) Pierre Emmanuel's poetry is a complex mixture of Catholicism, Freudianism and myth, and attempts to continue the tradition of French Symbolism.

4. Now and again, even in the time of sublime history, someone would let the cat out of the bag. For example the naïve historian of Gascony, abbé Monlezun, who around 1850 gave a learned account of how the Church had accumulated its wealth in the Middle Ages: lords and kings spent rashly and became impoverished; but the Church 'managed the assets' of the poor prudently; and in its blessed hands, those assets bore fruit.

Chapter 3

1. Kant, 'Preface to First Edition', in *Critique of Pure Reason*, trans. N.K. Smith, Macmillan, London 1973, p. 9.

2. (*Trans.*) All the preceding quotations have been from Kierkegaard's *Journal*, in my translation from Lefebvre's unspecified French version.

3. (*Trans.*) This seventeenth-century theologian is most famous for his funeral orations. His *Discourse* gives a theological interpretation of history.

4. (*Trans.*) Cf. Chapter 1, p. 117, where it is categorized as the law of the 'transformation' of the irrational.

5. Cf. Norbert Guterman and Henri Lefebvre, *La Conscience mystifiée*, Gallimard, Coll. 'Les Essais', Paris 1936.

6. (*Trans.*) Cf. Foreword, n. 26 on the word 'privé'.

7. (*Trans.*) The first section of *The Human Comedy* is in fact subtitled 'Scenes from Private Life'.

8. Cf. Norbert Guterman and Henri Lefebvre, 'Individu et classe', *Avant-Poste*, no. 1, Paris 1933; also *La Conscience privée*, sequel to *La Conscience mystifiée*, in preparation (*Trans.*: but never published).

9. (*Trans.*) Charles Péguy was a poet and essayist who transferred his allegiance from socialism to a kind of idiosyncratic Catholicism. He was an ardent nationalist, and was closely associated with the cult of Joan of Arc. He died in 1914.

10. Marx, 'The Holy Family', in *Collected Works*, vol. 4, Lawrence and Wishart, London 1975, p. 42.

11. Ibid.

12. Ibid., p. 43.

13. Cf. Léon Blum's speech at the 1945 Socialist Congress, etc.

14. (*Trans.*) Cf. Proudhon's *Théorie de la propriété*, vol. 4.

15. Marx, 'The Holy Family', p. 42.

16. Marx, 'Economic and Philosophical Manuscripts', in *Early Writings*, Penguin, Harmondsworth 1975, p. 361.

17. Ibid.

18. Ibid., p. 377.

19. Ibid., p. 358.

20. Ibid., p. 359.

21. Ibid.

22. Ibid.

23. Ibid., p. 352.

24. Marx, *Capital* Volume 1, Penguin, Harmondsworth 1976, p. 310.

25. Marx, 'Economic and Philosophical Manuscripts', p. 324.

26. Marx, *The German Ideology*, Progress Publishers, Moscow 1968, p. 45.

27. Marx, 'On the Jewish Question', *Early Writings*, p. 183.

28. Ibid.

29. Marx, *Capital*, vol. 3, p. 959.

30. Marx, 'Economic and Philosophical Manuscripts', p. 351.

31. Ibid.

32. Ibid.

33. (*Trans.*) This 'quotation' – 'l'art est la plus haute joie que l'homme se donne à lui-même' – is Lefebvre's own formula, although he used it later as a preface to his

Contribution à l'esthétique (1954), attributed to Marx. This 'forgery' was included among the reasons given for his suspension from the FCP in 1958.

34. Ibid., pp. 351–2.
35. Ibid., p. 352.
36. Marx, *Capital,* vol. 3, p. 959.
37. Ibid.
38. Ibid.

Chapter 4

1. (*Trans.*) This is a perennial problem for translators of Marx and Marxist literature, and is compounded when one is translating *from* a language other than German. I have used 'supersede' and its derivatives throughout. Cf. the Glossary in the Penguin edition of Marx's *Early Writings*.

2. The aim of several books which were written before this *Critique of Everyday Life* was to rediscover authentic Marxism, to bring these fundamental notions to light and readopt them. In our introduction to Marx, *Morceaux choisis*, Norbert Guterman and I drew attention to *economic fetishism* (a notion long neglected by Marxists) as well as to dialectical method. In *La Conscience mystifiée* we showed how the movement from appearance to reality (and vice versa) functions in the domain of ideas and represent-ations. We attempted to analyse this movement in our times, by showing how, on the basis of an existing 'mode of production', the bourgeoisie pushes towards mystification, while the proletariat and its representatives struggle towards demystification. In the second part of that book we presented the entire scope of the alienation of 'modern' man. Lastly, in *Dialectical Materialism*, I developed for the first time in modern philosophy the notion of the 'total man', linking it to the fundamental theses of Marxism, to dialectical logic and to the theories of alienation and of economic fetishism. Since these works are either out of print or were destroyed in 1940, it seemed worthwhile drawing attention here to the overall plan on which they were based. (*Trans. Dialectical Materialism* has been reprinted at least seven times, and has been translated into many languages. *La Conscience mystifiée* was reissued in 1979.)

3. (*Trans.*) Although Lefebvre has become better known as a theorist of urban space, his studies of rural communities were crucial to the development of his critique of everyday life. In 1948 he undertook research in rural sociology at the CNRS (Centre National de la Recherche Scientifique), and in 1954 he defended two doctoral theses on rural communities in the Pyrenees.

4. (*Trans.*) Lefebvre was to address this question in more detail fifteen years later in his *Introduction à la modernité* (1962).

5. Cf. an attempt to analyse this interaction in *La Conscience mystifiée*.

Psychoanalysts have attempted to examine this situation of the so-called 'modern' man. The higher mental agency they describe, though without understanding its social nature – censorship, superego, etc. – corresponds to the 'public' consciousness. But their realistic conception of the unconscious limits the value of their analysis considerably. What we must discover in this mystifying notion is precisely the real content of our consciousness, merged with deprivation and the growing awareness of it, and repressed by the 'public' consciousness.

Kafka's novels also try to describe the life of men who move forward blindly towards their 'fate'. And yet by overemphasizing the tone of anguish, he misses the worst deception of all: the moral or social euphoria in which public consciousness attempts to keep the 'private' individual (unless it casts him down brutally, and without transition, into so deep a despair that he no longer even attempts to realize his 'destiny').

6. In particular, the life of women and the way their tasks are organized, etc., constitutes one of these little-known sectors which are explained officially by a mystifying moral scheme (sacrifice or dedication as a 'vocation' – or else a lack of moral sense with prostitution as a 'vocation' – these alternatives are what the average public consciousness proposes as explanations for the lives of individual women) . . .

7. The study of everyday life can supply socio-economic science with some extremely important documentary material. For example, it confirms the following fact, or rather law, established by Marx: class implies not only a *quantitative* difference (in salaries, wages and income), but also a *qualitative* one (in the distribution and use of income). Thus in Paris (quoting the prices for 1938) the boundary between poor-quality, unsanitary accommodation and bigger, better-lit, better-situated and equipped housing clearly lay between 4,000 and 5,000 francs rent a year. With a relatively small amount of money extra – but too much for the proletarian to afford – one could move from working-class or very petty-bourgeois accommodation to a 'middle-class' flat. Other examples: normally or even under black market situations, a shoddy suit would cost *x* francs, while a high-quality one costing one and a half times more, apart from being nicer to wear, would last three times as long. Labour-saving devices in bourgeois flats (refrigerators, washing machines, etc.) were also much more economical. Proletarian life is not defined simply by lack of money, but also by pointless but unavoidable expenditure and waste.

A law can be formulated: the richer one is, the cheaper one's life will be (relatively).

During an 'abnormal' period of black market or underproduction, well-off families with a farm or a smallholding are able to lay their hands on foodstuffs which are of better quality and much cheaper than those 'poor people' have to buy.

The boundaries between classes may not be rigorously defined, but they exist none the less, and in every area of everyday life: accommodation (space, surface area, ventilation, sunlight), food, clothing, use of leisure time, etc.

The well-off classes generally spend their income more wisely than the working classes or the peasants, who are always short of something and who are thus unable to use their money *rationally*. A relatively small increase in income results in a move up from one category into another because of the things it makes possible.

8. (*Trans.*) Drieu la Rochelle was a novelist and right-wing ideologue. He edited the *Nouvelle Revue Française* during the Occupation. He committed suicide in 1945.

9. (*Trans.*) Cf. Chapter 3, n. 33.

Chapter 5

1. (*Trans.*) A reference to Baudelaire's sonnet 'Correspondences': 'In unity profound and recondite . . . Sounds, fragrances and colours correspond.' (*Selected Poems*, Penguin, Harmondsworth 1975, p. 43.)

2. Aeschylus, 'The Choephori', in *The Oresteian Trilogy*, trans. R. Fagels, Penguin, Harmondsworth, 1959.

3. In Romantic drama and in melodrama, great crimes, betrayals, parricides, all take place during violent storms (cf. the third act of *Trente ans ou la vie d'un joueur*). The next part of this work will include a sociological study of melodrama, its relation to life and the curious fact that at the beginning of the twentieth century a huge number of people stopped understanding melodrama; certain myths, certain moral postulates implied by melodrama and still 'lived out' during the Romantic era, suddenly disappeared from people's consciousness.

4. In a 'modern' ceremony which deserves a detailed ethnological analysis – the drawing of the *Loterie Nationale* – the mathematical chance by which fortunes are made used to be set off by children in care. (Did this practice become ritualized, and is it still maintained?) It exemplifies an 'apparent immorality' which conceals an underlying 'morality', and some characteristic myths. It seems that only the hands of children and paupers are 'pure' enough (pure in what way – unsullied by money?) to act as an instrument for the Goddess of Luck, to embody her momentarily, to observe the laws of absolute chance and to confer wealth unearned by labour without incurring some kind of divine wrath. In this ceremony dedicated to Money, poverty is there, not as a metaphor, but present in its cruellest form: poverty-stricken little orphans. Money, the capitalist Fetish, deigns to come down from its heavenly throne and move among those whom it has damned, and who are therefore in some sense dedicated to it. Apparently it was customary for the first-prize winners to donate part of their winnings to these children (the 'sacrifice'); thus the children's participation in the ceremony gave them a kind of 'right'. The winners, meanwhile, were in this way somehow excused for their excessive good luck, vouchsafed more luck for the future, and enabled to justify themselves vis-à-vis morality, the law and the last remnants of human community ... This remarkable form of festival, ceremony and sacrifice makes the 'modern' meaning of these fairly clear; it also helps to situate our 'civilization', with its metaphysical and moral fictions.

5. (*Trans.*) A Pyrenean woman's hood.

6. (*Trans.*) In 1945 Latin was still the liturgical language of the Catholic church.

7. (*Trans.*) 'In the beginning was the word.'

8. (*Trans.*) Jansen's *Augustinus* (1640) develops a doctrine of almost Calvinistic severity, which denies free will. In *La Somme et le reste*, Lefebvre talks of the narrow, 'almost Jansenist' faith of his mother. During his studies under Brunschvicg at the Sorbonne, Lefebvre's *diplôme d'études supérieures* was on Jansen and Pascal. The *Summa Theologiae* is by Thomas Aquinas.

Chapter 6

1. Pierre Courtade, *Action*, July 1945.

2. (*Trans.*) Jules Romains founded the Unanimist group (1908) which tried to replace fin de siècle individualism with a vague communal spirit. His most famous work is the sequence of novels *Les hommes de bonne volonté*.

3. Pierre Morhange. (*Trans.*: The exact source is unspecified.)

4. (*Trans.*) The poems collected here had originally been published in the American Communist revue *New Masses*.

5. Martin Russak, 'The Candle', *New Masses*, November 1928.

6. Martin Russak, 'Paterson', ibid., June 1928.

7. Miriam Allen deFord, 'August 22, 1927', ibid., February 1929.

8. Ralph Cheyney, 'Bawl, Kid', ibid., July 1929.

9. (*Trans.*) Lefebvre was always very scornful about Gide, who had been a significant influence on many of his generation, but whom he considered to be over-intellectual, and a crypto-puritan. In *La Somme et le reste* he says that 'I could well have become a follower of Gide, just as I could have been a Surrealist ... [but] he failed to reach me because – his homosexuality apart – I had already lived through most of the tribulations he describes, but much more violently.'

10. (*Trans.*) The source given by Lefebvre for this quotation is *Confluences*, no.5, but this appears to be incorrect.

11. Pierre Courtade, *Action*, 25 April 1945.

12. Henri Meggle, *Récit d'un rescapé*. (*Trans.*: I was unable to trace this text.)

13. Pelagia Lewinska, *Vingt mois à Auschwitz*, Paris 1945, pp. 40–41.

14. David Rousset, *Revue internationale*, no. 1.

15. Lewinska, *Vingt mois à Auschwitz*, p. 61.

16. Ibid., p. 70.

17. Rousset, *Revue internationale*, no. 1.

18. Lewinska, *Vingt mois à Auschwitz*, p. 126.

19. Ibid., p. 129.

20. Ibid., p. 130.

21. Ibid., p. 135.

22. Ibid.

23. (*Trans.*) Cf. Chapter 3, n. 33.

Index

freedom 38–9, 65, 78, 104, 144, 145, 156, 157, 170–75, 198
Friedmann, Georges xxv, xxvi, 36–7, 39, 262
funeral festivals 206–7
funfairs 41
'Fusées' (Baudelaire) 105

Galileo (Brecht) 14
Gide, André 159, 236, 238, 266, 273
Giono, Jean 193
Giraudoux, Jean 114
Gogol, Nikolai 262
Goldmann, Lucien xvii, xviii
Grand Meaulnes, Le (Alain-Fournier) 110
Grasset (publisher) xiii
Greece, ancient 191, 201–6
Gurvitch, Georges xxv, xxvi, 258
Guterman, Norbert xi–xiii, xv, xvii, xviii, xx, 234, 258, 270
Guys, Constantin 106

Habermas, Jürgen xxviii
Hegel, G.W.F.; Hegelianism xiv, xv, xvii, xviii, xxi, 4, 5, 15, 39, 56, 68–70, 74–8, 89–90, 113, 132, 150, 177, 265
Heidegger, Martin xviii–xi, xxiii–xxiv, 124
Heller, Agnes xvii
Hemingway, Ernest 259
Hervé, Pierre xi, xiii–xiv
History and Class Consciousness (Lukács) xvii, xviii
Hitler, Adolf 245
Homer 105–6
honnête homme 30
Hugo, Victor 106, 265
Human Comedy, The (Balzac) 149–50

'human nature' 62, 144, 147, 151, 159, 162, 174, 180, 181
'human raw material' 189–91, 252
humanism 156, 157, 177, 190, 252
Hyppolite, Jean 258, 263–4

Idea (Hegel) 68–9
'ideal home' 8–9
idealism 155–6, 162, 164, 180
ideology 54, 62, 73, 74, 76, 83–4, 87, 93–5, 97, 141, 145–8, 152–3, 167, 169, 174, 179, 187, 196, 209, 247, 249
images 33–5
Imperialism, The Highest Stage of Capitalism (Lenin) 66
impoverishment, Marx's theory of 58, 62–3, 259
In Camera (Sartre) 260, 262
In Dubious Battle (Steinbeck) 235
individual ('private') consciousness 15–16, 31, 32, 40, 69, 72–5, 78, 81, 89–94, 132–3, 139, 143–4, 146, 148–54, 164–5, 171, 183, 195, 198, 199, 233, 237–9, 248
individualism 233, 237
induction 179–81
Introduction to Metaphysics (Heidegger) xviii
Introduction à la modernité (Lefebvre) ix, xxvi, 270
irony 16, 64
'irrationality' 117, 188–9

Jansen, Cornelis 223
Joliot-Curie, Frédéric xi
Jouglet, René xiii
Journey to the End of the Night (Céline) 187
Joyce, James 27
'judgements' 19–21, 24

Plato 74
Plutarch 122
Poems by American Workers 234–5
political economy (economics) 52, 59,
    80, 92, 96, 97
political sphere 88–92, 247, 249
Politzer, Georges xx
Population (periodical) xxv
'populists' 234
'possession' 155–8
Poster, Mark xxviii
Pour connaître la pensée de Karl Marx
    (Lefebvre) x
poverty 44, 58, 62–3, 153–4
Prévert, Jacques 267
'private' life *see* individual
    consciousness
Proclamation de la commune, La
    (Lefebvre) xxviii
products 96, 97
'progress' 228–33, 247–9
proletariat 11, 12, 25–6, 142–8, 151,
    157, 160–62, 179, 263, 270, 271
See also alienation, of labour
Proudhon, Pierre-Joseph 155, 157

qualitative change 246, 248, 249
qualitative class differences 271

Rabelais, François xiv, 13, 30
Radio-Toulouse xii–xiii
Rajk, Lászlo 64
realism 14
realization/derealization 71–2, 78
reason 75–6, 132–3, 138, 141, 142,
    147, 188–9, 236, 243–4, 246, 266
'reflection' 92–5
reification x, xvii, xviii, xix
relative/absolute 67, 68
'relaxation' 34

religion 59, 73, 93–4, 138–41, 147,
    191, 208–26, 252
    See also Catholic Church
Renan, Ernest 134
'reverse image' 12, 35
revolution 48–50, 63, 65, 182
Révolution d'abord et toujours, La
    (manifesto) xx
Revue marxiste, La xxi
Rimbaud, Arthur, xx, xxi, 109–10,
    114, 120, 121, 141
Road to Life (film) 29
Roads to Freedom (Sartre) 187, 236
roles 15–17
Romains, Jules 233
Romanticism 25, 49, 105, 106, 117, 272
Room of One's Own, A (Woolf) 28
Rougemont, Denis de xix
Rousseau, Jean-Jacques 105
Rousset, David 242
rural community(ies) 201–22,
    228–33, 270
    in ancient world 201–6
Russak, Martin 234

'sacred, the' 117, 212, 214
'sacrifice' 212, 249
Salammbô (Flaubert) 109
Salt of the Earth (film) 14
Sartre, Jean-Paul xi–xii, 124, 125,
    187, 236, 258, 260–62, 268
Schumann, Robert 266
Shaw, Irwin 28
Schelling, F.W.J. xxi, xxii, xxiii
Sentimental Education (Flaubert) 105,
    109
sexuality 34–5, 155–6
Situationists xxvii–xxviii
Soboul, Albert xxv
social labour 58, 74–5, 78, 88, 134,
    165–6